Citizenship, Democracy and Belonging in Suburban Britain

Citizenship, Democracy and Belonging in Suburban Britain

Making the Local

David Jeevendrampillai

First published in 2021 by
UCL Press
University College London
Gower Street
London WC1E 6BT

Available to download free: www.uclpress.co.uk

Text © Author, 2021
Images © Author and copyright holders named in captions, 2021

The author has asserted his rights under the Copyright, Designs and Patents Act 1988 to be identified as the author of this work.

A CIP catalogue record for this book is available from the British Library.

Any third-party material in this book is not covered by the book's Creative Commons licence. Details of the copyright ownership and permitted use of third-party material is given in the image (or extract) credit lines. If you would like to reuse any third-party material not covered by the book's Creative Commons licence, you will need to obtain permission directly from the copyright owner.

This book is published under a Creative Commons Attribution-Non-Commercial 4.0 International licence (CC BY-NC 4.0), https://creativecommons.org/licenses/by-nc/4.0/. This licence allows you to share and adapt the work for non-commercial use provided attribution is made to the author and publisher (but not in any way that suggests that they endorse you or your use of the work) and any changes are indicated. Attribution should include the following information:

Jeevendrampillai, D. 2021. *Citizenship, Democracy and Belonging in Suburban Britain: Making the local*: UCL Press. https://doi.org/10.14324/111.9781800080539

Further details about Creative Commons licences are available at http://creativecommons.org/licenses/

ISBN: 978-1-80008-055-3 (Hbk.)
ISBN: 978-1-80008-054-6 (Pbk.)
ISBN: 978-1-80008-053-9 (PDF)
ISBN: 978-1-80008-056-0 (epub)
ISBN: 978-1-80008-057-7(mobi)
DOI: https://doi.org/10.14324/111.9781800080539

IWLWHW

Contents

List of figures		ix
Preface		xi
Acknowledgements		xvii
1	Introduction	1
2	The theoretical frames of the book	23
3	The making of an unused map: moments of incommensurability	48
4	How to make a suburb. Part 1: diagrams, expertise and cake	74
5	Being stupid in the suburbs: life in the state of Seething	102
6	How to make a suburb. Part 2: the research activities of the Free University of Seething	134
7	Citizenship in the suburbs: shit and the story of the filter beds	167
8	Conclusion	191
Afterword, by an anonymous interlocutor		200
Index		208

List of figures

1.1 The PPGIS 'Community Map' from the Adaptable Suburbs Project: http://www.mappingforchange.org.uk/services/community-maps/ (accessed 3 April 2013). 3

1.2 The Lefi Day Parade with a crafted giant Thamas Deeton. Author's own, 2013. 10

3.1 A map to show the stories of Seething (with cycle route). Thames Ditton Island is at the upper left of the image. Courtesy of Seethingers, 2014. 61

3.2 'I live in Seething. It's a state of mind' t-shirt featuring the Mount of Seething. Author's own, 2014. 62

4.1 Images of Surbiton analysed using axial, ITN and OSM lines at different scales. Blue lines indicate low movement and red high. Adapted from figures 7–21, Dhanani et al. (2012). © Adaptable Suburbs Project, UCL (EPSRC grant ref: EP/I001212/1), with permission. 83

4.2 Overlaid image of axial (blue), ITN (red) and OSM (green) network models adapted from figure 5, Dhanani et al. (2012). © Adaptable Suburbs Project, UCL (EPSRC grant ref: EP/I001212/1), with permission. 87

4.3 Built form and land uses in Surbiton in 1880, 1910, 1960 and 2013 (top left to bottom right), overlaid with segment angular integration 800 metres. © Crown Copyright/database right 2013. Map scale 1:1500. From Laura Vaughan, *Suburban Urbanities: Suburbs and the life of the High Street* (London: UCL Press, 2015). 93

5.1 The Lefi Day Parade on Surbiton High Street. Author's own, 2015. 109

5.2 Thamas the giant parades down a typical Surbiton street with Pooley houses. Author's own, 2015. 111

5.3 River road houses. Author's own, 2015. 111

5.4 Suburban skiing. Author's own, 2014. 116

5.5	Seethingers pulling 'Seething freshwater sardines' from the River Thames. Author's own, 2014.	118
5.6	The Seething Freshwater Sardine Parade. Author's own, 2014.	119
5.7	A reading of 'The tale of the last sardine'. Author's own, 2014.	119
6.1	The Free University of Seething crest replete with cheese and Lefi heads. Courtesy of the Free University of Seething, 2014.	135
6.2	Zara's 'map of Surbiton' drawn during a drawing interview, 2012.	138
6.3	Cuttings from the *Surrey Comet*: 25 March 1988, 'Kingston stunned by news it may vanish'; 5 July 2005, 'So are we in Surrey or not?' by Yvonne Gordon; 12 July 2005, 'Defiant council decides to fly the flag for Surrey' by Yvonne Gordon. With thanks to the Kingston Local Studies Archive.	150
6.4	Seethingers marking the boundaries of Surbiton. Photograph by Tangle photography, 2013.	151
6.5	Beating the boundary stone. Photograph by Tangle photography, 2013.	152
6.6	Seethingers about to beat the bounds. Photograph by Tangle photography, 2013.	153
6.7	Seethingers beating the bounds by the filter beds. Photograph by Tangle photography, 2013.	155
6.8	Free University of Seething graduation. Author's own, 2014.	156
7.1	The filter beds. Author's own, 2015.	168
7.2	Benton the Bat in the Lefi Parade. Author's own, 2014.	172

Preface

This book examines emergent subjectivities and citizenship in late liberalism. Over the course of the following chapters I will outline the sensibilities, experiences and effects of 'being local'. Late liberal democracies emphasise *participation*. This places the onus of responsibility for inclusion in social life on individuals and communities. The moral responsibility each citizen has for the articulation of their citizenship, alongside heightened individualism, constitutes the neoliberal social logic that informs the particular 'local' subjectivity I examine in this book. Whilst the book considers emerging notions of citizenship, dynamics of democracy and notions of belonging through a case study of community building in suburban London, the book's subtitle, 'making the local', is a phrase that deliberately refers to the processes of the making of a feeling of localness and citizenship within a person, alongside, and entwined with, the material production of local place in an age of socio-political localism. This being so, at times in the text I refer to the book via its shorter subtitle. Whilst its brevity makes its use practical, the subtitle also alludes to 'making the local' as a process in which notions of citizenship, democracy and belonging cannot be separated from emerging late liberal subjectivities and the politics of place which have seen heightened focus on the local. Further, it suggests the process of writing this book, which to some degree creates the 'local' through its analysis.

The book's evidence base emerges from long-term ethnographic fieldwork with two different social groups. The first is a group of community activists who aimed to make their home in Surbiton (a suburb in south-west London) 'better'. The second is the Adaptable Suburbs Project (henceforth ASP), an architectural research project based at UCL's Bartlett School of Architecture, which funded the PhD research on which this book is based. The two groups, and the interaction between them, broadly represent, respectively, the citizen and the state.

The ASP sought to understand the relationship between the built environment and the socio-economic life of the suburbs. Its research output was intended to guide urban planning policy. My role as part of this team was to work directly with community members in order to populate an online map with stories of the social life of Surbiton. However, things weren't quite that simple. The most active and certainly the most visible group of local enthusiasts I found in Surbiton were the 'Seething Villagers' (who also called themselves Seethingers or Villagers). This group used what they called 'stupid' events, based around myths of, for example, goat boys, giants and sardines, to build community. When they added these mythical stories to the online map, the ASP rejected them. In the moderation process, the ASP dismissed the data precisely because it was not 'historical fact'. I introduce this anecdote here to highlight how this book is concerned with the conflicts and gaps between groups, rather than concerned with any one discrete group. It is concerned with the governance of difference, the process and procedures of representation, and how the ethical and moral landscapes of democratic participation give rise to the particular (often competing) 'local' and 'expert' subjectivities, and to the particular relationships between state and citizen associated with late liberalism.

I use the term late liberalism throughout the book. It is a term employed in the work of Elizabeth Povinelli (2002, 2011, 2013a, 2013b, 2016) to indicate, as she puts it, 'a formation of power – the twined formations of neoliberalism and liberal cultural recognition – that emerged in the late 1960s as a method of solving the crisis of liberal economic and social legitimacy in the wake of economic stagflation and colonial and social revolutions' (2013a:30–1). Late liberalism refers specifically to the 'entwined but not determinate relations between a mode of governing difference and modes of governing markets' (2013b:237).

The book could well have been subtitled *The suburban citizen in neoliberalism*. The forms of governance and subjectivity and the modes of social life described in this book are profoundly neoliberal, in the sense that the subjectivities that emerge in this context are in the mould of what Wendy Brown (2015) would call *homo oeconomicus*. That is, they are of an age where 'All conduct is economic conduct; all spheres of existence are framed and measured by economic terms and metrics, even when those spheres are not directly monetized. ... [W]e are only and everywhere *homo oeconomicus*' (10). As I will outline, the suburb was seen as a place that could yield greater economic output (with the right expert knowledge and some well-informed urban planning). But the suburb also seemed to yield a kind of value that could not be measured economically. The suburb was cared for and nurtured by locals in a way that enacted a sense of community. This was understood to mitigate, or build 'resilience' to, the negative effects of neoliberalism, which overworked and dehumanised suburbanites, and undermined traditional community spirit. However, I argue that the labour associated with community building does not counter neoliberal social organisation, but, rather, supports it. That the burden of responsibility for the local environment lies with the community itself is consistent with neoliberal logic. Gershon et al. (2011) use the phrase 'neoliberal agency' to describe the shift of moral and ethical responsibility for governance from the state to the individual. Gershon et al. refer to job seekers (sculpting themselves and their attitude towards the job market), but we can apply it to the processes of community building. In both cases, ethical and moral responsibility has shifted away from the state and the free market and has become an issue of personal development and individual responsibility.

In my analysis of making the local I use the point of tension between the ASP and the Seethingers (the former refusing data offered by the latter) as a starting point to explore the (differing) logics and perspectives of these two social projects. Despite their differences they both aim to make places, such as Surbiton, 'better', and to do so in the rubric of late liberalism. The ideals of participation and inclusion are key characteristics of late liberal democracy. These ideals require different groups to communicate and to commensurate knowledge of their way of life, values and desires into a common matrix of understanding. Yet in this process some information, by necessity, must be excluded. This constitutes the later liberal governance of difference. My analysis is purposely attentive to moments of exclusion because it is here, I argue, that the local is made.

Whilst Povinelli and I use the term 'late liberalism' in reference to the governance of difference, it would be remiss to make an equivalence between our field sites. In fact, they could be considered polar opposites. Whereas the work of Povinelli considers worlds 'otherwise' – specifically the lives of her indigenous informants in Australia – the work presented here concerns the lives of largely white middle-class suburbanites on the outskirts of London. My interlocutors do not claim to have an ontological foundation to their existence which is radically different from that of figures of authority around the management of place, such as the ASP, the local council or the state. Indeed, one could say that my interlocutors are ideal neoliberal subjects. They are educated, and believe in democratic processes, inclusion, participation and local politics. My aim here is to show how, at the core of late liberal democracies, the issue of accounting for difference is fundamental to the ways in which a person lives a life. The struggles for and tensions about representation even at the heart of white liberal democratic communities inform daily activities, ethical outlooks and social relationships. They shape and inform subjectivities. The book outlines the ways in which 'the local' embodies a subjectivity that is always seeking a politically qualified life, one in which they are politically efficacious and agentive. This takes work, skills and commitment. And although my interlocutors were privileged in their skill base, time and relative affluence, this book demonstrates how this 'work' orientates one's reflections of one's self, one's values and one's relations to other people and place, and makes the local.

In the book's final ethnographic chapter (Chapter 7), I describe the conduct of community activists in a council meeting. Here they successfully object to a planning application. This success required time and effort; it required *work*. In this chapter, I show how such undertakings affect where citizens spend their time. If you are in meetings in pubs and school halls, you are not at home. It affects how you think of your responsibility to your kin, which may include locals, and indeed locals who have not yet been born (future generations who have not yet been able to enjoy the urban spaces, and the social relations they engender). It affects your health, who and how you trust, the friends you make and even the job you have. This book traces how being a good local, asserting one's citizenship, values and ways of life, informs the experience of a late liberal subjectivity. In this sense my work is similar to Povinelli's in its focus on power, agency, the body, governance and representation, but focuses on the heart of liberal democratic societies in communities of radical similarity rather than radical difference.

Whilst undertaking my research, I was always interested in the question 'Where are you from?' Perhaps I should say that I'm more interested in the answer. I have, in my life, been asked this question often, and have to guess if people are really asking why I am the colour I am. This is most clear when answers such as 'Manchester' don't satisfy, and people ask again 'No ... where are you really from?' How one answers this, and how others respond to that answer, tells of more than a geographical location. It tells of one's associations, one's history, one's kin, and of perceptions of race, of belonging, of community, and of one's ideas about one's future. Who gets to control the narrative of place, and the narrative of who has a right to that space, is also a question of who gets to control the sorts of people we think we are and can be. This book is a study of representation. It examines the ways in which being local, in a largely white middle-class suburb, requires labour. To be an effective citizen in late liberalism one must energetically articulate legitimate knowledge of place, and seize and then wield efficacious political power to affect the conditions of dwelling. I argue that this labour – which informs, sculpts and enacts late liberal subjectivity – is equally effective in places beyond Surbiton. It is clear that an emphasis on individual responsibility for managing place, characteristic of late liberalism, has given rise to new imperatives for community.

In addition to exploring the gaps between different social projects, the book explores the gaps between the academy and the field site and between legitimate and excluded knowledge. In doing so, it considers the position of the anthropologist. It explores how we write about others. It particularly asks how we choose what to write – that is to say, what gets said and what does not. The book reflects on the ways in which my interlocutors changed and informed my practice as the study progressed. Whilst the book thinks through different social projects and different ways of seeing the world, it is deeply invested in a material culture approach. It acknowledges that whilst there may be different, competing knowledges, which inform different ways of interacting with place, place can only take one material form. The singularity of material form belies the multiplicity of social worlds for which narratives of recognition often advocate. In practice, this means you can recognise rights to a place as much as you like, but either this building is demolished and that land developed, or they are not. Making the local is about contestation, commensuration, recognition, and the ethical and moral work of living with others in late liberalism, in dialogue with the limits of materiality.

References

Brown, Wendy. 2015. *Undoing the Demos: Neoliberalism's stealth revolution*. New York: Zone Books.

Gershon, Ilana. 2011. 'Neoliberal agency.' *Current Anthropology* 52, no. 4: 537–55. https://doi.org/10.1086/660866.

Povinelli, Elizabeth A. 2002. *The Cunning of Recognition: Indigenous alterities and the making of Australian multiculturalism*. Durham, NC: Duke University Press.

Povinelli, Elizabeth A. 2011. *Economies of Abandonment: Social belonging and endurance in late liberalism*. Durham, NC: Duke University Press,.

Povinelli, Elizabeth A. 2013a. 'Defining security in late liberalism: A comment on Pedersen and Holbraad.' In Martin Holbraad and Morten Axel Pedersen, eds, *Times of Security: Ethnographies of fear, protest and the future*, pp. 28–32. Abingdon: Routledge.

Povinelli, Elizabeth A. 2013b. 'The social projects of late liberalism.' *Dialogues in Human Geography* 3, no. 2: 236–9. https://doi.org/10.1177/2043820613495784.

Povinelli, Elizabeth A. 2016. *Geontologies: A requiem to late liberalism*. Durham, NC: Duke University Press.

Acknowledgements

With thanks to my interlocutors in Surbiton/Seething and in the Adaptable Suburbs Project. You gave generously, warmly and without reserve; it was beyond useful, it was inspiring. This work was funded by and contributes to the Adaptable Suburbs Project, UCL (EPSRC grant reference number: EP/I001212/1). It was enabled through the generous support of NTNU Anthropology, Trondheim, which gave me time and space to write; particular thanks to Professor Lorenzo Cañás Bottos, Tone Sommerfelt and Professor Jan Ketil Simonsen. Thank you to Professor Victor Buchli for his enduring support. Many thanks to Morten Nielsen and Professor Penny Harvey for their early and thought-provoking guidance on this text. I am indebted to 'the Council of Noor'. Thanks are extended to Aaron Parkhurst, Timothy Carroll, Delphine Mercier and Nikki Lan Xiao, as well as to the Trondheim International Writing Collective, especially Martin Loeng, Agata Kochaniewicz, Erik Lønne, Sophia Efstathiou, Grace Caray and the others (you know who you are). On a personal level I would like to thank my mother, always there, supporting. Thank you, Rebecca Williams, for putting up with me, Tuuli Malla, Adam Valance and Paul Carter-Bowman. I would like to thank Glynis Baguley, Jaimee Biggins and Chris Penfold at UCL Press as well as the anonymous reviewers for their advice and suggestions on how to improve this work. Thank you to Tangle Photography and Liron Gilenberg for the cover photograph and design respectively. A very special thanks to David Edger whose advice on this manuscript was invaluable. Extra-special thanks to the anonymous Seethinger who penned the valuable afterword to this text. Names of informants have been changed and identities have been aggregated in this work to protect anonymity. All mistakes, omissions and controversies remain my own.

1
Introduction

On a dark, wintry Thursday night, in the cold wind and rain of Surbiton, a south-western suburb of London, a large group of 'locals' shuffled themselves from the decadent surrounds of the bustling town hall council room to a nearby bar. They had just spent the previous three hours or so rammed into the splendidly officious chambers of the local government town planning committee in order to hear if their efforts to save a disused water filtration site, which they considered to have great historical and ecological importance, had been successful. The site was under threat from a proposal to develop luxury apartments, and the decision to save it rested with the council planning committee.

These locals had spent many months organising, campaigning and convincing people that the site should be saved. Some had an opportunity to speak at the meeting and, after a nervous few hours of deliberation, the council announced that the proposed development would not be permitted.

As I walked into the bar people were already busy popping champagne corks, cheering, and topping up each other's glasses. I had not yet taken off my coat when Steve thrust a glass into my hand and started pouring champagne before I could refuse. Steve was well known in the local community, had long been involved in community activity, and had played a key role in bringing people together to support the campaign. As soon as he had filled the glass, he looked me dead in the eye and said, 'What you have seen tonight, Jeeva, is a community that works.' I understand this statement in a double sense. The community was successful, but it was successful because it laboured. The act of making place is also an act of making people. 'Making the local' is not simply a description of how changes to the urban built environment come about, it is also a description of how particular ethical, moral and social subjectivities come about.

Taking from Sherry Ortner's work on the anthropology of subjectivity (Ortner 1995, 2005). I use the term 'subjectivity' to refer to 'the ensemble of modes of perception, affect, thought, desire, fear, and so forth that animate acting subjects', but also to 'the cultural and social formations that shape, organize, and provoke those modes of affect, thought and so on' (2005: 31). Ortner believes the study of subjectivity must 'move back and forth' between the examination of cultural, historical formations and the inner states of being, taking emotion, affect and psychology into account. For Ortner subjectivity is 'the basis of "agency"' and a 'necessary part of understanding how people ... act on the world even as they are acted upon' (2005: 34). In this book I outline the wider historical and political contexts of late liberal subjectivities, but I do so in order to outline not only how they penetrate the perception, affect, thoughts and desires of my local interlocutors, but also how being local affects the forms and experience of subjectivity at the level of the body.

My interlocutors are very reflexive about their citizenship: they consciously work to sculpt themselves into good locals. This book considers what Michel Foucault (1985) would call the 'ethical substance' of citizenship in late liberal democracies. This is what my interlocutors sculpt. Ethical substance is that which constitutes the prime material of ethical conduct, that is, the aspect of the self that is held to be morally problematic and taken as the object of one's ethical reflections and that motivates one's imperatives to act so as to fulfil one's practice of being human in a socially legitimate way. As James Faubion writes, Foucauldian ethical substance can be a range of 'stuff' – 'cognitive, emotional, physical, or what-not'. Whatever form it comes in, it is 'the object at once of conscious consideration and of those labors required to realize a systematic ethical end, which is to say the being of a subject of a certain qualitative kind' (2012:72). This book can be considered as a record of the labour required to be a 'subject of a certain qualitative kind', in this specific case, the labour required to be 'a good local citizen'.

The analysis presented here pivots around a moment when two groups of people meet. One of these two groups is associated with the academic project that funded and guided my research – the Adaptable Suburbs Project (ASP). The other group is constituted by the people whom I researched, the community enthusiasts of Surbiton. This group has various names throughout the book which reflect its members' various social positions within community activism. Firstly, the 'Seething Villagers' (or Seethingers or Villagers) applies to a group of local enthusiasts who put on the events, which they themselves describe as 'stupid', based on Seething myths and tales. This group claim that these events are about building community. With this object in mind, these events aim to include everyone and to exclude local politics and potentially divisive issues. Secondly there are 'local activists', who are people in the area who are distinctly political, particularly in reference to the campaign to save the water filtration site; for them, local politics is front and centre. This distinction between apolitical Seethingers and campaigning local activists is made by my interlocutors. Whilst each group largely involves the same people, they differ in their explicit political positions, organisation, aims and intentions.

The ASP aimed to 'uncover' the social value of the urban built environment, particularly suburban high streets, by gathering 'social data' on how people used and related to the area. This data was to be gathered by asking people to add text, photos and videos to an online mapping platform (see Figure 1.1). A couple of local Seethingers from Surbiton added such 'data points' to the map, as I had asked them to do during a workshop. However, this data did not pass the moderation standards of the ASP, because the ASP did not consider the data added, which concerned stories of goat boys and giants, to be 'historical fact'.

The ASP required these maps to be relatable and clear to people outside the community, whilst the Seething Villagers, as I will outline below, required their stories to be slightly mystifying and, in their word, 'stupid'.

I focus on this moment as it illuminated to me, as an ethnographer, the ways in which these two groups were trying to make places such as Surbiton 'better' in very different ways. Their differences were not rooted simply in epistemological difference. They were informed by the everyday

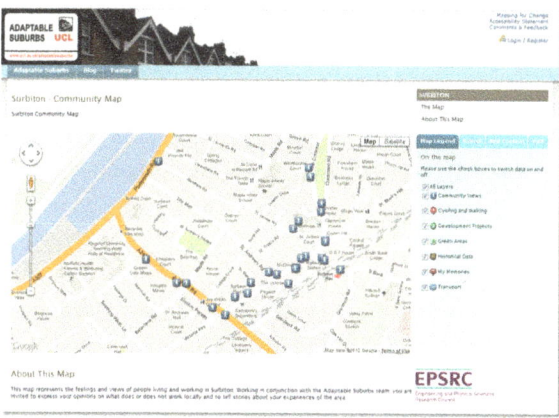

Figure 1.1 The PPGIS 'Community Map' from the Adaptable Suburbs Project: http://www.mappingforchange.org.uk/services/community-maps/ (accessed 3 April 2013).

ethical, moral and social positions they embodied, enacted and wished to see. The two groups were not in direct conflict as such. In fact, they barely noticed each other. By the end of my fieldwork period the map was still largely unused and neither group seemed concerned about it, if they mentioned it at all. However, this moment of mapping serves to guide the reader through the story of how these two social projects relate to each other and how they symbolise the tensions through which late liberal subjectivities emerge. Following Foucault (1985), I understand subjectification to involve the ways in which the individual establishes its relation to a moral code, and recognises itself as bound to act, and sculpt its ethical substance, according to that code. In Surbiton, as in all other late liberal contexts, subject positions are generated within (and by means of) the interplay of different social forces – socio-economic ideologies and other 'social projects' that seek to establish the morally correct way to be.

I understand the ASP and the Seethingers/locals as 'social projects'. This is a term I use throughout the book. It is borrowed from Elizabeth Povinelli, as elucidated in her 2011 book *Economies of Abandonment*. Povinelli herself borrows the term from the philosopher Bernard Williams, who used 'social project' to refer to moral projects and their associated actions. These projects are the 'thick subjective background effects of a life as it has been lived', which 'provide the context of moral and political calculation' (Povinelli 2011:6). However, a social project is not simply a reflection of ideology; rather, it is a particular manifestation of action that is motivated and shaped by an underlying ideology. Povinelli states:

> Social projects are not things – although they may appear to us as if they were. Social projects are instead activities of fixing and co-substantiating phenomena, aggregating and assembling disparate elements into a common form and purpose. The word 'project' means to convey the constant nature of such building as well as the constant tinkering with plan, draft, and scheme as the building is being made, maintained, and remade out of disparate materials.
> (Povinelli 2013:238)

Whilst the ASP and the community activists both live and work within the same late liberal ideological mode, they go about it in different ways. Consequently they work as two distinct social projects. Whilst the locals were largely able to ignore the ASP's map, their community was deeply entwined with the ASP's social project in less obvious ways. The ASP aimed to develop academic insights into the value of the suburban built environment that would inform urban planning policy. This meant that the local community indirectly encountered the ASP's social project via the bureaucratic and legal process of objecting to a planning application in the area. This book traces these kinds of interactions, as it explores the production of value in late liberal democracies. By 'value', I mean any action that adds to the building of a social project. For the ASP, value lay in understanding underlying structures and relations of a built environment and encouraging policies that produce healthy socio-economic spaces. For Seethingers, play was valuable, as was helping others, since they helped generate a healthy sense of community and personal connections. Value may also be assigned to anything that aids the successful production of an ideal subject position. Where the Seethingers were aiming to cultivate themselves as good locals through their actions, the ASP members sought to cultivate themselves as experts. Both projects work at different levels, dealing with everything from local matters to issues of national policy. Both projects are concerned with consensus-based politics and individual responsibility, and believe in the active role of people in the management of place and community. Whilst the projects are different in important ways, their share key similarities; they both believe in late liberal ideals, such as the cultivation of the self towards an ideal, individual responsibility, and active citizenship.

As already indicated, being a good local citizen requires *work*. Amongst my interlocutors, this labour was seen as necessary, but they recognised that it generated a range of effects in addition to concrete political goals. It determines where, how and with whom one spends one's time, where one places one's time and energy. It affects the body and the mind in inseparable ways, it affects one's sense of self and sense of relation to others, it affects one's very subjectivity. This labour not only serves an agenda within a specific urban planning context, but also relates to a wider historical moment of state–citizen relations. People must enact particular modes of local citizenship in order to maintain an active, politically qualified life within democracy. The modes of citizenship enacted in Surbiton were based on the logics of late liberalism. That is, late liberalism, as the default ideological background of reasoning, informs and motivates how moral personhood is sculpted. Late liberalism gives prominence to the ideals of inclusion, representation and democracy; I trace how these values inform modes of citizenship in Surbiton, enacted through everyday life.

Whilst I ostensibly focus on a community group in Surbiton called 'the Seething Villagers', I consider how their work comes about in relation to other social projects, particularly the ASP. That is to say, this text focuses its analysis not so much on the Seething Villagers, but rather on the edge of their social project, where they meet other groups or forces that seek to make 'better places'. Not only does a commitment to a social project result in the enactment of a desirable mode of subjectivity, it also forecloses the socially inconceivable by defining socially illegitimate action as it strives to reach a form of universality. Commitment to a social project also defines, shapes and responds to the material world, from bodies to buildings, as it orientates how the material world is understood as valuable and useful in relation to that social project.

Through their labour, my interlocutors in Surbiton cultivate a particular 'local' subjectivity, which orientates their relations to others, to kin, to themselves and to the daily practices that comprise an ethical life. In this book, late liberalism is deployed to describe prevailing ideals of individual and economic freedom, democracy and inclusion within the UK. These ideals are held, unconsciously, as supposed universal values of social life and underpin the thinking of the ASP, the Seethingers and local and national government. The book is written at a time when devolution of power and the idea of increased democracy are seen as vital processes to ensure the continued functioning of late liberalism.

The context of the study

The ideology underpinning the UK state's formulation of the idea and role of the citizen has shifted over the past 50 years. In the 1960s and 1970s, government ideology and policy strategy could be characterised by the prominent role of the state in the lives of its citizens, via housing, welfare and urban planning. By the 1980s and early 1990s the emphasis had shifted towards a free market ideology, characterised by reduction of the state and promotion of market forces as the drivers of socio-economic life. In the mid- to late 1990s the New Labour government sought a 'third way' politics (Kearns 2003); through a series of reforms the government sought to fundamentally alter the relationship between people and the state again. The Localism Act 2011 (Department for Communities and Local Government 2010) aimed to devolve power and decision making to local communities. David Cameron's Conservative government introduced the 'Big Society' as a flagship policy of its 2010 election manifesto.[1] The policy has been described as a political ideology foregrounding the integration of the free market with a theory of social solidarity based on hierarchy and voluntarism (see Scott 2011; Walker & Corbett 2013). It had a stated aim of creating a climate that empowered local people and communities, redistributing power away from politicians.

However, political theorists such as Wendy Brown (2015) have asserted that such policies have produced a devolution of responsibility, but not of real power. Thus, these policies reflect an emergent neoliberal 'normative order of reason' (9). Neoliberalism, argues Brown, 'aims simultaneously at deregulation and control. It carries purpose and has its own futurology (and futures markets), while eschewing planning. It seeks to privatize every public enterprise, yet valorizes public-private partnerships that imbue the market with ethical potential and social responsibility and the public realm with market metrics' (49). For Brown, new habits of citizenship and democratic imaginaries emerge when key ideals (such as freedom, sovereignty and democracy) shift from a political register to an economic one. These new habits and imaginaries emerge as the market logics of winners and losers are normalised. Such logic makes it possible to talk about a community that 'works' (and, conversely, those that do not). This is why 'NGOs, nonprofits, schools, neighborhood organizations, and even social movements that understand themselves as opposing neoliberal economic policies may nonetheless be organized by neoliberal rationality' (2015:202). Neoliberalism promises the separation of the citizen from the state yet simultaneously valorises the virtuous citizen (2015:212). Brown argues that the citizen, who takes on the responsibility of self-betterment, has no real power, whilst political democracy becomes occluded through devolution and empowerment rhetoric. Brown asserts that neoliberalism 'integrates both state and citizenship into serving the economy and morally fuses hyperbolic self-reliance with readiness to be sacrificed' (2015:212). Later in this book we see how Surbiton locals sacrifice their time, energy and more in order to create a community, and to build what they call 'resilience' to the pressures of modern socio-economic life.

This book is an ethnography of that process. It is an ethnography of how processes associated with 'making the local' are typical of the subject-ification associated with late liberalism. More specifically, it examines how particular modes of being human (local and community-orientated) are crafted as my interlocutors seek to be 'a subject of a certain qualitative kind' in late liberalism. It looks at how people acquire legitimacy through their subject position as 'local' or 'expert' and with it the power to affect the shape and meaning of the world (from bodies to buildings) which they inhabit.

The Adaptable Suburbs Project was funded by the Engineering and Physical Sciences Research Council and was the second major study by this group of academics. In both studies they were interested in the role that 'small settlements' within cities, namely suburbs, played within a wider socio-economic range of activity. They argued that suburbs had fallen 'beneath the policy radar'[2] and that detailed study was needed. They were particularly interested in how suburban infrastructure was adaptable to change. For this they used detailed mapping procedures in which the predicted movement of people was layered over types of building use. These dynamics were studied over a long time period using historical records (see Chapter 4).

By the time I began working with the ASP, it already had a significant amount of architectural data relating to Surbiton. It had sought to appoint an anthropologist to gather information about how Surbiton people felt about their urban environment. The ASP provided a tool to support this research. It had, in conjunction with UCL departments outside of architecture, including geography and engineering, designed a virtual platform to which locals could submit information about Surbiton in the form of an online map. The ASP envisaged that, via this map, a 'social layer' of data could be added to the existing architectural data, providing deeper insights into the nature of Surbiton, and help the ASP develop better policy advice relating to urban development in the area. It was envisaged that similar mapping platforms could be rolled out and used by local authorities for various projects wherever local knowledge, in the form of geographically pinned data, was required. Such projects were designed and promoted with the ideals of increased participation in local government and urban planning in mind.

My first task was to find people who had an active engagement with their local area. I spent time at the local studies archive and with groups for amateur historians, and went to local business meetings. Early on, a lot of people directed me to one particular group, who, indeed, by virtue of their flyers, posters and social media activity, seemed unavoidable in the area. They were the aforementioned Seething Villagers. I noted that their posters (in pubs, in libraries, on lampposts and in local shops), advertised an event they were organising called the 'Lefi Day Parade'. After emailing the address on one of the flyers, explaining that I hoped to conduct an ethnography with them, and getting no response, I decided to invite myself along to one of the public 'craft days' in preparation for the big parade.

The craft day was held on a sunny but chilly Sunday afternoon in mid-February. I walked into a nearly empty pub and looked around. 'You here for the Seething stuff?' asked the barman before directing me to the garden at the back of the pub. I walked out into a hive of people building, gluing and crafting giant wicker sculptures of lamps, giants, cheese and fish, amongst other things. I stood there confused for what seemed like a good 10 minutes (but was really a couple of seconds) before Steve saw me.

He headed straight towards me, weaving his way through the various wicker effigies that were coming into being. 'Hello buddy! Are you here for the Seething craft day?' 'Yes,' I responded, before rather awkwardly explaining that I had emailed and that I was 'an anthropologist from UCL'. 'Oh yeah, I saw that, I was hoping you would come down,' said Steve. He then introduced me to a few people and explained who was building what, leaving just enough mystery to maintain my intrigue. 'This is Wendy, she's making a giant's head, obviously; this is Andy, he's halfway through a cheese there, always with the cheese, Andy, and this is Imran, he's making a massive mining lamp.' I spent the rest of the afternoon making a giant wicker lamp and learning about the community of Seething.

The 'ancient Village of Seething' is an imagined community that holds mythical status in the Surbiton area. The stories of Seething – its imagined history – initially emerged, I was told, from a group of people who had made efforts to save an old public house from permanent closure. After it was indeed saved, the pub became a meeting point for like-minded people who wanted to develop a sense of community in the area. Over a series of 'cheese club' meetings the group developed, or 'discovered', the 'legends of Seething'. At first these stories were told as fun ways to think about the local area and aspects of its history and geography, but they were also an excuse to get together and celebrate living in the local area. They resolved to organise events, open to everyone, in order to create a sense of community. The stories about Seething were communally owned: anyone could add, embellish or create a Seething legend. The story of Lefi Ganderson is one of the earliest and arguably the most central Seething tale. It is certainly the best known. It is celebrated at the end of each February, with the Lefi Day Parade (see Figure 1.2), which I was helping to prepare on that February afternoon. This is the first major Seething event of the year and the story of Lefi outlines the basic moral and ethical position of the locals towards making community.

Central to the story are the ideals of welcoming all, not judging others and celebrating each other. These values are cultivated through Seething events. The degree to which a legend is revered and remembered amongst the Seethingers depends on how often the story is repeated. Over time new stories emerge but they always follow some basic rules (see Chapter 3).

Most importantly, the stories must be 'stupid'. I use this as an emic term, used by my interlocutors. The stories always play with the boundaries between fact and fiction. They are what Carrie Lambert-Beatty (2009) calls parafiction; that is to say, the narratives are partly real, and are used to show how other ways of being might be possible.

Figure 1.2 The Lefi Day Parade with a crafted giant Thamas Deeton. Author's own, 2013.

Box 1.1   The story of Lefi Ganderson

The ancient village of Seething was surrounded by wonderful forests, had a sparkling river and was overshadowed by a huge mountain, Mount Seething. At the base of the mountain there was a cave which was the home of little Lefi Ganderson. The Seething Villagers did not like or trust Lefi because, being half boy and half goat, he looked very different to them. However, the children of Seething, being of good heart and not yet having learnt to judge Lefi as the grown-ups had, brought him scraps of food from the village and played with him. Lefi taught the children how to make clothes and toys from all the things the Villagers threw away as rubbish.

On top of the mountain lived Thamas Deeton, the giant of Seething. Thamas, being a giant, spent most of his time visiting relatives, but would return to the top of Mount Seething every four years, upon a leap year, to terrorise the villagers. The villagers lived in constant fear of Thamas and stayed away from the mountain.

This continued for many years until one year Lefi decided to do something about it. Lefi plucked up the courage to challenge Thamas. Brave little Lefi held up a small gold ring and shouted to the giant, 'If I can live for one year on the food that can pass through the middle of this tiny ring then you must leave.'

Thamas looked at the tiny ring, and then looked at Lefi and thought how much food one would need to eat. He bellowed, 'I accept your challenge, as no one but a magician could live on such little food. I think you will die trying and the mountain will be mine once again.' Lefi and Thamas agreed that if Lefi managed it Thamas would have to leave Mount Seething and go far away, leaving the villagers alone for ever. Thinking the task was impossible, Thamas looked forward to seeing Lefi suffer the hunger he was sure to endure. The children of Seething took Lefi milk from the village. Then Lefi did something wonderful. He passed the milk through the ring again and again into small bowls. He did this so many times that he made 29 rounds of cheese. After a year, Lefi had survived on the 'cheesy goodness' he had made from that milk. Thamas, true to his word, left Mount Seething, but in one last fit of rage he stamped and thumped and smashed Mount Seething into many pieces before turning and stomping away. Rocks flew through the air in all directions. The villagers panicked and ran for cover. As Thamas was leaving, one of the stray rocks flew and hit him right on the back of the head. Thamas fell into the river and his body can still be seen today at what locals call Thamas Deeton Isle.[3]

Eventually the villagers emerged from their hiding places. Amidst the rocks they could not, for all their looking, find Lefi. Where his cave once was there was now only a hollow in the ground which had a small gold ring right there in the middle. As the villagers stared at the ring the leader of the village spoke and said:

> Villagers of Seething, we must learn from today and never behave like this again. Seething must become a village that is open to all. It should not matter what you look like, where you come from or who you are – you will be welcome here and Lefi has shown us the way. … Let us not forget what Lefi did. We shall hold a festival every year to celebrate him driving the giant away.
> (Hutchinson 2010)

And so, today, the Villagers of Seething, in modern-day Surbiton, remember Lefi each year at the weekend closest to the end of February. The date gets its name from the 'twenty-nine [cheeses] that fed you and me' and 29 February is an extra-special day known as Lefi Day, when people remember to be extra kind to each other.

Whereas Lambert-Beatty describes parafiction in the context of politically charged satire and art performance, Seething uses parafictional stupid stories to generate fun, stimulate play, and create idealised communities. At one Seething event I asked one of my regular interlocutors what he thought was happening. His response was, 'It is just an excuse to get together and be stupid.' This was a common explanation. The Seethingers emphasised the importance of play as a mechanism through which people could get together, hang out, and get to know each other. Play was a vital part of building familiarity and trust amongst members of the community. The Seethingers aimed to build 'community resilience'[4] with their events. They understood that action was needed to build community. They sought to enhance community feeling in response to the widely perceived increasing sense of isolation in everyday life, the threat of the suburb becoming a commuter town, and the threat of unchecked urban development. A strong community of people who know each other, who can say hello upon recognising each other when walking to the shops, was considered a vitally important thing to cultivate. It was needed to halt the coming about of the imagined suburban dystopia: a landscape of isolated individuals without meaning in their lives. They needed to develop and cultivate 'resilience' to counter the inevitable threat of the increased isolation, selfishness and greed they associated with neoliberalism or what they would call 'modern life'. Resilience here is an emic term. It is used by my interlocutors on the website of their community activities and manifests itself in the rhetoric of their activities. This is particularly evident when they talk of wanting to build community in order to deal with the threats of such things as the loss of local shops, becoming a commuter suburb dominated by alienated workers, and the loss of community. The notion of resilience underpins the community work of my interlocutors as they labour to build a social world that is able to withstand the pressures they see around them.

In order to welcome everyone, organisers sought to make the events 'non-political', and avoided discussing divisive issues, such as campaigns against a particular urban development. When attending local political gatherings, such as urban planning meetings, they did so independently, not as Seethingers. In effect, they occupied different identities at will, wearing different hats at different times. For this reason, when discussing my interlocutors in relation to Seething events, I will call them Seethingers, but I refer to them as 'locals' when discussing them as politically active, opinionated citizens (see Chapter 7).

Being stupid – having stories that play with local history and names, using humour and silliness – is a strategy to enhance inclusivity. The Seethingers aim to include everyone, but the majority of the group are white, middle-class professionals. This is in part because of the demographic make-up of the suburb itself, but it is also a reflection of the modes of socialising at work here. Meetings are in pubs; they require a degree of free time. I don't have the space here to analyse why the social make-up of the group is as it is, nor do I wish to offer strategies for inclusion. However, it is useful to note that my interlocutors are aware of their limited demographic. There is a wide range of ages, and the group conduct 'community surveys' to find gaps in who attends the events and extend outreach. Through stupidity, anyone can partake in storytelling, without an imposed hierarchy of who has lived there the longest or who knows the most about the history of the local area or the 'real story'. Seethingers encourage people to familiarise themselves with this Seething mode; anyone who can get the knack of it can take part. When faced with a Seething 'fact' as it is known – such as the story that the area once had a sardine cannery because of the prevalence of sardines in the river – one has a choice. If you are a relative newcomer to the group you may be told this 'fact' by a Seethinger who, most likely, will try to maintain a straight face. You may then consider the fact that you don't get sardines in fresh water, or that the tale of the sardines may or may not be related to the use of three fish by the local council as the official symbol of the area. At this point you can contest the story or play along. If you play along you are working to build community, you are being a Seethinger. This style of storytelling ensures that no one person can become the expert. Whilst I focus on Surbiton, it's worth noting that its use of playful storytelling is not an isolated instance. I encountered it within a community group in South Norwood, where I was sent to gather data for a smaller study linked to the ASP. Here the self-declared South Norwood Tourist Board would hold parties for tunnels, celebrate locally famous dogs, and assert absurd claims to fame such as having more lakes than that well-known tourist hotspot, the Lake District in northern England. Community groups in South Norwood and Surbiton both revelled in stupidity and invited anyone to play with them in order to establish an inclusive, ground-up authority for narrating place. In both locations, play was a mechanism for building community and asserting local citizenship. Surbiton and South Norwood shared not only this playful mode; in both contexts, volunteerism and the use of people's skills (such as building a website, writing applications for arts and community grants, or wiring a stage) are vital. Taking this into account, it is clear that relatively wealthy areas that have populations with high levels of free time and a rich pool of transferable professional skills are particularly suited to forming the kinds of community groups we can see in Surbiton and South Norwood. There are clear issues of class and accessibility at work here which a comparative study might be able to examine in more detail, but in this work I want to examine the precise workings of this Surbiton-based group in order to focus attention on the logics of late liberal citizenship.

The social rules of community building in Surbiton posed a challenge to my work. The Seethingers didn't answer my email, I later discovered, because they didn't want to engage with me in a formal academic sense. They wanted me to come and meet them face to face; they waited until I showed the motivation to get involved before engaging with me. Over email I would have remained a distant academic. In the pub I could craft puppets, hang out and get to know people. That is to say, I was a Seethinger. For Seethingers, community is not to be theorised but is to be enacted through interpersonal engagement.

Soon after the Lefi Parade I was invited to give a talk to the community on a Sunday afternoon in the pub. I talked about the ASP project, the Community Map and my intentions to conduct ethnography. I was aware of the tension inherent in the idea that I would, at the end of my PhD fieldwork, return to UCL to write up and be examined on my knowledge of a place which both had a constantly evolving history and, further, rejected the idea that any one person could be an authority on it. Amongst the Seething Villagers, knowledge of the community, its history and foundational stories is constantly being invented. I understood that I could not, then, do ethnography *of* Seethingers; rather I had to do ethnography *with* Seethingers.

Reflecting the value of local knowledge production, the community had recently formed (with characteristic wit) a local 'university' which would host my activity: the 'ancient Free University of Seething'. At the event at which I spoke, two other people (locals) also gave talks (on local myths and legends and local archaeology). So now I was not only a PhD student at UCL, I was also a fellow researcher at the Free University of Seething. As the project moved forward, this mode of collaborative research deepened, eventually resulting in collaboratively organised local walking tours, exhibitions, lectures and more. But for now, the Seethingers were interested in my project and showed interest in the maps. Whilst only a few said they would add information to the ASP map, most people encouraged me to attend their events and get involved in their work.

A few weeks later the ASP Community Map remained empty. The Seethingers insisted they had added information to the map. I went back to the UCL department responsible for moderating the map's content to ask for more information about why they could not moderate 'historical fact'. It was important to the moderators that information be clear and comprehensible to those not from the area. I was told that someone looking at the map from the outside 'might get confused'. The Seethingers had added a point of information over the pub. They had described it as the location of the now destroyed Mount Seething (see Box 1.1). The Seethingers asserted that this 'fact' was justified as it was local knowledge, and that local knowledge should be accepted on its own terms. Over a quiet lunch to discuss how the community might use the map following this incident, Steve and Andy asked me what the limit of fact is. They asked what would happen if users submitted information about places they insisted had religious significance (such as being the site of a vision) or if moderators would accept data on sites that were widely associated with well-known myths and legends (think of Glastonbury Tor, the sites associated with Arthurian legend, or Robin Hood's supposed stomping ground, Sherwood Forest).

I do not take it as my duty to work through this incommensurability and suggest a practical solution. Rather I treat this as an 'ethnographic moment'. I take this term from Marilyn Strathern, who uses it when describing how 'writing begins in the field'. In the field, she writes, 'the ethnographic moment works as an example of a relation which joins the understood (what is analysed at the moment of observation) to the need to understand (what is observed at the moment of analysis)' (Strathern 1999:6; see also Strathern 1996). The silence of the underpopulated map constituted a moment; it revealed that the two groups were incommensurable. At the time I did not overly concern myself with this moment, but as I went through the fieldwork I kept returning to it in my mind. As I thought about the actions, motivations, intentions and consequences of the work of the locals/Seethingers and the ASP, it became even more important to understand this moment. The incommensurability between social projects emerged as an orientation point for analysing life in late liberalism, and how the ethical substance of being a good local citizen is made.

The judgements and views of the people working within the ASP or the Seething community always occur within particular 'moral and political calculations' (according to their social projects), which correlate with what they consider most likely to bring about the good life. Notions of the good, and an imagined better future, proliferate in the rhetoric of the ASP and the Seething community. In many ways both groups are working to the same ends. They want the suburbs, in particular Surbiton, to be better, more successful places, with 'vibrant communities' and suitable material environments. However, they go about crafting this in different ways. The

ASP comprises a team of academics who are world-leading experts on architectural urban analysis (see Chapter 4). They can deal with complex data sets and calculate forms of value that lie 'hidden' within the fabric of the built environment. They are advised by, and in turn advise, a range of government think tanks, policy makers, and academic and professional practitioners. They go about making suburban areas 'better' by developing a deep understanding of the historical processes of change in the urban fabric and establishing a set of generalisable rules through which such areas can be understood. They aim to extend their forms of analysis and insight to guide national-level policy on urban development plans.

The Seethingers work at the local level. They are concerned with developing a strong sense of community, which is understood to be constituted by feelings of belonging, sense of purpose and togetherness for the people who live and work in the area. They prioritise face-to-face contact to establish personal and emotional relationships to each other and to the local area. They also want to ensure that the area benefits from 'appropriate' urban development (see Chapter 7), and they work to ensure that the area is protected from what they see as inappropriate development that threatens community assets. Their events and Seething tales are a distinctly local form of community building, but they also work with other communities around the country to share best practice.

The two projects largely considered themselves to be very different groups doing different things and were, to a large extent, able to ignore each other. They made little fuss about the moment of incommensurability concerning the information placed on the Community Map, and carried on with their own activities. The ASP continued its technical analysis and the Seethingers continued holding their community-building events. However, these two social projects do, and must, meet again, at planning meetings. Whilst the individual academics of the ASP were not involved in the Surbiton planning meeting, I argue that their social project manifested in this meeting. Within the context of the meeting, the locals and the ASP occupy the positions of citizen and state respectively. The tensions between the Seethingers and the ASP and the Seethingers and the council symbolise the tensions that occur between groups, not only in the making of place but in late liberal subjectivities. At these meetings each project asserts its notions of the good life. I argue that, whilst they seem to ignore each other, different social projects, such as the ASP and Seethingers, always operate in relation to each other, in less obvious ways. The ASP, the local council and planning committee are all required to consider and accommodate local opinions, values and desires in order to produce 'better' urban infrastructure in a democratically legitimate way, upholding prevailing models of local engagement. The Seethingers' aim to enhance the 'resilience' of their community meant they needed to interact with the dynamics of urban planning. A resilient community is forged from a group of like-minded people who value, care for and are willing to labour for the local area, which includes seeking to maintain or realise the material urban fabric they wish to see. Seething events lay the groundwork for a form of community familiarity, trust and care that enables those people to mobilise a political campaign when something threatens the community, such as the planning application. However, as noted earlier, my interlocutors categorically did not identify political action as part of what Seethingers did. In pursuit of resilience, locals need to be able to engage with, understand and respond to the systems of local governance and local government planning policy, and to engage in the procedures of local democratic decision making.

In summary, both projects are concerned with and invested in the relationship between the state and the demos (the common populace that makes up the democratic unit of the state). Both behave on the assumption that one must take on the recognisable identity and behaviour of a politically active citizen to maintain political agency in late liberal society.

Whilst the two projects map onto the dynamics of state–citizen relations, they come at the relationship from very different angles and represent different sides of the binary: the ASP is aligned with the state and the Seethingers with the citizen. The ASP enacts its role as a professional expert, contributing to the public good through the democratic development of knowledge of the built environment that eventually translates into public policy. The Seethingers/locals approach citizen–state relations in an embodied, passionate way via the workings of community inclusion. As an anthropologist I traversed between the two social projects as an active member of both groups. I situate my analysis here on the edge of these social projects. I believe an anthropology on the edge can illuminate the conditions and practices through which the ethical substance of being a 'good citizen' in late liberalism comes about. Specifically, I can illuminate the behaviours that define the parameters of 'local' or 'expert' in late liberalism by focusing my analysis on the moments when the ASP and Seethingers, or state and citizen, assert themselves in relation to each other, or on the moments when they decide to exclude, include or ignore something, as happened with the map.

This book, then, is less about the ways in which local urban infrastructure is made, and more about how dwelling in a particular moral and ethical subjectivity comes about in relation to other social projects, the wider ideological frames of late liberal ideals, and the particular material ecologies of everyday actions and their consequences. Going beyond the specific issues of local governance and urban planning, my analysis considers the broader ways in which people form relations to place, kin and themselves, via social projects. The book traces how enacting particular moral forms of citizenship produces particular subject positions and bodily experiences, and how the dynamics of late liberalism shape the forms of lived experience even at the level of the seemingly mundane practice of suburban living.

Wider critical issues and the structure of the book

The book takes the empirical detail of a long-term anthropological study of local subjectivity to think through some wider issues in contemporary anthropology and late liberalism. These issues are foregrounded in the next chapter to help the reader to scale out from the case study. I have separated the issues into three areas: firstly themes of *representation and inclusion*, secondly the values of *democracy and citizenship* and thirdly the practices of crafting *material and meaning*.

Representation and inclusion are the themes that run throughout both social projects. The ASP, the council and the Seethingers all talk of aiming to include all people and seek representation of many points of view. These are ideals that are central to late liberalism. The concepts of representation and inclusion have been widely discussed throughout the history of the anthropological discipline. The aim of this study is not to find more equitable ways to include or represent (although that is a concern) but rather to approach them as themes that emerge from the field site and therefore inform the moral calculations of my interlocutors. In this book issues of representation and inclusion are examined in the context of the field, but also in a self-reflexive manner, in terms of how the field is understood and approached, anthropologically, as field in the first instance (see Chapter 6).

The anthropological practice of participant observation is not simply the means by which data was gathered for this book; it informs the way in which knowledge is understood and represented. Fieldwork was conducted in a spirit of openness and epistemological democracy, and knowledge is represented in this book in the same spirit. For example, I take local myths, like that of Lefi, seriously. And I am sincere when I say that I undertook my studies as a student of/at the Free University of Seething. It both is, and is not, a joke. I take myths as valid parafictions and approach the Free University with the seriousness of the social intent from which it emerged (although the fact that it is stupid is part of that manifestation and, therefore, it should be laughed at). Seething's wild stories and its folk university play with notions of fact and truth, and with the idea of an authority to speak, and so raise interesting anthropological questions about representation and inclusion.

Democracy and citizenship are explored as core *values* that resonate through late liberalism. They manifest in the field via the practices of the ASP and locals/Seethingers as they seek to include people and their opinions in their respective processes. Both require a 'self-responsible' citizen. The democratic ideal explicitly informs the ASP's intention to involve the community in map making (see Chapter 3). It is democracy that drives the locals to assert their voices in the fight to save the water filtration site (see Chapter 7). Democracy, or at least the idea of equality of representation, is also found as an underlying value of the anthropological discipline. The ideals of democracy and citizenship, then, serve as key orientation points for moral action in both the field site and the academy. However, democracy is always in a state of becoming, of almost being achieved. Thus, democracy demands constant work, action and effort.

As Brown (2015) has noted, democracy and citizenship appear in new neoliberal formulations with market logics underpinning their operation. In the case of the locals, they felt the need to assert community and the value of the landscape to others or they would face the threat of the inevitable creep of neoliberal logics in the form of the development and commercialisation of local assets, increasingly isolated self-centred life, and the loss of neighbourliness.

Citizenship is a state of politically qualified life (following Agamben 1998). A person becomes or maintains themselves as an active member of a polis through the practice of certain behaviours, such as being part of the community, or taking an active role in democratic social life. I trace how the actions of Seethingers/locals work to maintain such qualifications of active citizenship and how this work structures much of their time, effort and identity.

Inclusion is an ideal that undergirds the notions of democracy and citizenship. To be a citizen is to be included. The ASP and the locals aim to include people in what they do to increase the democratic nature of their social projects. However, inclusion is also a condition of the internal logics of those social projects: one must play along with the Seethingers or stick to historical facts, with the ASP. Sometimes one cannot do both.

Material and meaning are explored as core *practices* through which the local, democratic inclusion and participation, and citizenship are made. The book emerges from a distinctly material culture approach to anthropology. This ranges from how the ASP works with historical and architectural data to produce images from which value can be read (see Chapter 4) through to how crafting a wicker sculpture of a lamp brings about a moral citizenship position (see Chapters 2 and 5). This material approach aims to trace empirically the processes through which locals and the members of the ASP construct their political efficacy through daily practices such as eating cake, shopping locally or making visualisations. It aims to trace how seemingly mundane acts are both informed by and constitute the practices of moral life of late liberalism. The most fundamental outcome of this approach is the politicisation of the material conditions of difference. The book argues that the ideal of recognition that underlies the democratic ideal (and which is also at the heart of the anthropological ideal, albeit in a different sense) is challenged by the stubborn materiality of existence. I aim to go beyond the trope that one should respect another's world view and that the acceptance of multiple world views is the end point of the anthropological project. I ask what happens when two social projects recognise each other and respect each other but have different ideas over what the materials they use to bring about their social life should do. To put it another way, you can respect others as much as you like, but either the water filtration site gets saved or it doesn't. This is more than an ontological issue of understanding the 'other'; it is also a political issue of material control. Materials through which we exist are finite in their ability to enable particular social worlds; land is either conquered, or it isn't. The materiality of existence brings the politics of difference into sharp focus.

These three areas do not represent a comprehensive overview of all the themes of the book. I foreground them to orientate the reader as to the wider anthropological and analytical points of the ethnography.

During the research process and writing I was concerned with the following key questions: 1) How do modern subjectivities emerge through the tension between social projects? 2) How are the conditions of a morally good life delimited through the expectations of a late liberal ideology? 3) What sorts of subjective experiences and exclusions emerge from the management of a social project and the pursuit of late liberal ideals? 4) What effect do late liberal ideals such as democracy, inclusion and active citizenship have on the psychological and physical ways in which we think about ourselves and our relation to others? 5) How influential are contestations over the right to speak on behalf of place on the development of a particular subjectivity?

This chapter has set out the context of the book, and the key actors, themes and approaches. The next chapter will outline the three theoretical themes introduced above in more detail, locating them in both long-standing and contemporary anthropological debates. The dense nature of this theoretical section allows the reader to work through the following ethnographic chapters with a solid idea of the wider conceptual frame in which the book was written. Chapter 3 focuses on the moment when the ASP refused to pass the Seethingers' data onto the map. It traces the emergence of 'localism' as a political policy and social phenomenon and sets out the motivations of both social projects within this context. Chapter 4 focuses on the ASP as a social project through an analysis of how they produce diagrams as visualisations of place. These diagrams require skilled doing in making, reading and explaining complex data. The chapter considers the work of becoming an expert and how particular forms of rationality are applied in the process of making places better. It illuminates why the ASP needed to refuse the Seethingers' data from the perspective of their own social project. Chapter 5 focuses on the community of Seething as a social project. In particular it looks at the Seething Freshwater Sardine Festival and analyses the use of play, invention and stupidity as mechanisms of crafting community. The chapter uses a semiotic analysis to get at how and why stupidity works to craft community and change the ways in which people interact with the local built environment and each other. Chapter 6 focuses on the ways in which locals engage with and alter the research process itself. Through adapting a research grant for walking tours, the Seethingers create the Free University of Seething, which opens up new spaces through which to do anthropology. Here the Seethingers enter into a mode of collaboration with the researchers (the ASP and myself) to generate data that allows further questions to be asked. This chapter also considers the ways in which people relate to the landscape through walking, both alone and with others. Chapter 7 focuses on why this all comes to matter as the locals campaign against a planning application to build on the old water filtration site. Through the objection process it is clear that the work of the Seething events comes to matter as the community mobilises. Groundwork for strong emotional and practical relationships has been laid through Seething events, enabling the community to motivate and organise locals in objecting. The chapter also focuses on how such involvement in community can lead to negative effects, as some interlocutors suffer personal issues ranging from ill health to marital breakdown. The chapter harks back to what 'a community that works' really means, as the labour needed to be a morally good local citizen in modern democracy is significant and clearly has significant effects. Chapter 8, the conclusion, outlines the subject positions of being a good citizen in a late liberal, consensus-based democracy. It outlines how citizenship (as politically qualified life) must be continually enacted. The book concludes with a reflection on the anthropology of the 'edge' through discussing the implications of recognition and inclusion in the making of people and place in late liberalism, before an afterword from an interlocutor.

Notes

1. 'Government launches Big Society programme'. Prime Minister's Office. 10 Downing Street, 18 May 2010. https://www.gov.uk/government/news/government-launches-big-society-programme--2 (accessed 21 April 2021).
2. 'Adaptable suburbs'. https://www.ucl.ac.uk/bartlett/architecture/adaptable-suburbs (accessed 21 April 2021).
3. Thames Ditton Island is the name of a real place in the middle of the River Thames on the edge of the suburb.
4. 'The Community Brain'. http://thecommunitybrain.org/ (accessed 3 June 2014).

References

Agamben, Giorgio. 1998. *Homo Sacer: Sovereign power and bare life* (trans. Daniel Heller-Roazen). Stanford, CA: Stanford University Press.
Brown, Wendy. 2015. *Undoing the Demos: Neoliberalism's stealth revolution*. New York: Zone Books.
Department for Communities and Local Government. 2010. *Decentralisation and the Localism Bill: An essential guide*. London: Department for Communities and Local Government.
Faubion, James D. 2012. 'Foucault and the genealogy of ethics.' In Didier Fassin, ed., *A Companion to Moral Anthropology*, pp. 67–84. Chichester: Wiley-Blackwell.
Foucault, Michel. 1985. *The History of Sexuality. Volume 2: The Use of Pleasure*. New York: Pantheon.
Hutchinson, Robin. 2010. *The Legend of Lefi Ganderson: The goat boy of Mount Seething*. [Surbiton:] Homage Publishing.
Kearns, Ade. 2003. 'Social capital, regeneration and urban policy.' In Rob Imrie and Mike Raco, eds, *Urban Renaissance? New Labour, community and urban policy*, pp. 37–60. Bristol: Policy Press.
Lambert-Beatty, Carrie. 2009. 'Make-believe: Parafiction and plausibility.' *October* 129 (Summer): 51–84. http://dx.doi.org/10.1162/octo.2009.129.1.51.
Ortner, Sherry B. 1995. 'Resistance and the problem of ethnographic refusal.' *Comparative Studies in Society and History* 37, no. 1: 173–93. https://doi.org/10.1017/S0010417500019587.
Ortner, Sherry B. 2005. 'Subjectivity and cultural critique.' *Anthropological Theory* 5, no. 1: 31–52. https://doi.org/10.1177/1463499605050867.
Povinelli, Elizabeth A. 2011. *Economies of Abandonment: Social belonging and endurance in late liberalism*. Durham, NC: Duke University Press.
Povinelli, Elizabeth A. 2013. 'The social projects of late liberalism.' *Dialogues in Human Geography* 3, no. 2: 236–9. https://doi.org/10.1177/2043820613495784.
Scott, Matthew. 2011.'Reflections on "the Big Society"'. *Community Development Journal* 46, no. 1: 132–7. https://doi.org/10.1093/cdj/bsq057.
Strathern, Marilyn. 1996. 'Cutting the network.' *Journal of the Royal Anthropological Institute* 2, no. 3: 517–35. https://doi.org/10.2307/3034901.
Strathern, Marilyn. 1999. *Property, Substance and Effect: Anthropological essays on persons and things*. London: Athlone Press.
Walker, Alan and Steve Corbett. 2013. 'The "Big Society", neoliberalism and the rediscovery of the "social" in Britain.' Sheffield Political Economy Research Institute, 8 March. http://speri.dept.shef.ac.uk/2013/03/08/big-society-neoliberalism-rediscovery-social-britain/ (accessed 21 April 2021).

2
The theoretical frames of the book

Representation and inclusion

My analysis of making the local considers the edges of the two social projects of the ASP and Seethingers. Furthermore, it is concerned with the contact point between the anthropologist as a producer of knowledge and those they aim to represent. Anxiety associated with the task of representing the 'other' lies at the core of the anthropological project. This enduring problem was given spectacular attention in what became known as the 'crisis of representation' in the 1980s (see Clifford 1988; Clifford & Marcus 1986), in which discomfort with the reified 'othering' (Eriksen & Nielsen 2001:146) of classical modernist anthropology led to a series of difficult questions. Concerned anthropologists questioned whose voice could be heard in anthropology and whose interests the discipline served. It has led anthropologists to ask whether it was productive to talk about a 'community', an 'other' or a 'whole' at all. They asked what such representations do, how they circulate and what they produce. They asked how these representations relate to bias in the ethnographic moment, which is the point at which the anthropologist decides something needs to be understood.

As the research for this book was being conducted, issues of representation, knowledge practices, colonial legacies and power inequalities in research were being hotly debated in anthropological forums. The response to Elizabeth Povinelli's 2014 keynote speech to the European Association of Social Anthropologists' conference is representative of this debate. A technical failure resulted in a loss of film audio, so that Povinelli talked over the film of her 'indigenous'[1] interlocutors in Northern Australia, delivering a complex philosophical analysis of her ethnography, whilst her interlocutors remained silenced. It prompted much discussion online about the comprehensibility of anthropological analysis – both to expert anthropologists and lay interlocutors. Halme-Tuomisaari and Billaud (2014) said the talk was an example of that which 'resonated' with or 'even strengthened' the 'troubling legacy' of the European/North American anthropological tradition, which 'has tended to exoticize the "other" and make him/her become the silent object of the anthropological gaze and Western knowledge consumption'.

Halme-Tuomisaari and Billaud indicate that anthropology 'at home' has the potential to erode this troubling (and long-standing) gulf between the (powerful) anthropologist and the (disempowered) interlocutor. Anthropology 'at home' is a term that I'm not particularly fond of (as it posits a non-home), but the term rose to prominence during the postmodernist movements of the 1980s, when a vibrant conversation amongst scholars such as James Clifford, George Marcus and Michael Fischer (see Clifford & Marcus 1986; Marcus & Fischer 1986) drew attention to the ways in which anthropologists had grown 'uncomfortable with the reified "othering" of classical modernist anthropology' (Eriksen & Nielsen 2013:146). These academics sought to redress this 'othering' through such things as experimental ethnographies, writing styles and modes of representation, as well as a radical critique of the idea of cultures as integrated wholes found in Boasian and more recently Geertzian ethnographies (see Eriksen & Nielsen 2013:146). They argued for an anthropology of home whereby anthropology seeks to defamiliarise the conditions of social life so as to expose the ways in which everyday social acts contribute to the production of social relations. This work could be considered an 'at home' form of anthropology. However, I wish to posit that it is about neither home nor non-home. This dichotomy rests on a notion of the anthropologist going to a place where knowledge economies are remarkably different from the ones the anthropologist is familiar with, or, conversely, to the anthropologist 'at home' performing a form of archaeology-like deep dig into the underlying, and somewhat hidden, workings of the knowledge economies that are familiar to them. Both these positions assume a relation to knowledge in which knowledge is a priori there to be got at. Instead, I want to foreground a form of anthropology as curation (see Chapter 6). Here the context and contingency of the anthropologist's position, in relation to those with whom they study, the academy and so on, are recognised. The anthropologist engages in happenings whereby different perspectives are brought together in moments of sharing, explaining and analysing. Hence, the knowledge generated by the anthropologist occurs in moments of curation. New spaces of knowing and relating are opened up as interlocutors, academics and the academy enter into specific constellations of relations (see Chapter 6). This book is less about a discrete group than it is about the particular practices of moral and ethical action that go into crafting late liberal citizenship, and this crafting always occurs in moments of curation and attrition with other groups and other ways of knowing.

The emphasis on practice enables political analysis because it helps us understand how some ways of being and particular subject positions become hegemonic, whilst others are delegitimised or excluded. Anthropology does indeed shine a spotlight on alternative ways of being, but, as Hage (2013) points out, anthropology's democratic credentials are flawed. They are based on its capacity to platform the existence of many points of view, but it has only done so 'as long as capitalism and nature … are left [as] one and unchallenged' within the discipline. They remain 'the fundamental realities on which everything stands'. Hage argues that whilst anthropology may cast a light on 'new spaces of possibility', they remain 'merely arenas of political struggle rather than counter-hegemonic modes of existence in themselves'. Fundamentally, all of these debates about the role of the anthropologist and our methods prompt us to ask if we take our interlocutors seriously enough. To do so we need to fundamentally examine the assumed position, roles and relations between the anthropologist, the academy and interlocutors within the extractive dynamics of ethnographic practice.

This ethnography does not deal with radical difference. I grew up in the UK. Whilst the place where I grew up was noticeably different from places like Surbiton in terms of race and class, the fundamental ontological orientations of life are familiar. I understood the styles and context of reference points for the jokes my interlocutors made. I understand the social dynamics of pubs, festivals and community events. I am familiar with the political landscapes, histories and power structures which orientate the activism I encountered. Whilst I am interested in the tensions between social groups, these tensions are not characterised by radical difference. The locals of Surbiton and the forms of power they encounter are familiar to each other. The locals are very much the type of citizen subject imagined by the local council, the ASP, and the late liberal democratic imaginary. They are the model citizen British systems of governance are built around; they are engaged, educated and motivated, and have the free time and skills to self-organise.

To reiterate: the ASP and the Seethingers/locals are not fundamentally different from each other. Some Seethingers make online maps for the UK civil service, and it's totally possible that some members of the ASP are involved in community work in their own private lives.

Both projects could be said to be working within the parameters of an ideological commitment to liberal democracy. Despite their fundamental similarities, they have different ways of managing inclusion and their relation to the built environment, the state and other people. And so this ethnography does not concern itself with reifying radical difference, but it is *about* the production of difference. It explores how difference is created, recognised, represented and dealt with. That is to say, it identifies the dynamics of difference as a set of practices. These practices are, I will argue, political acts.

Authors such as Elizabeth Povinelli (2011), Audra Simpson (2014), Glen Sean Coulthard (2014) and others have shown that recognition has been used as a method of organising difference and identity in liberal politics. In dealing with the questions of recognition in settler colonial states (settler Australia, the USA and Canada respectively), they have asked how recognition may be a 'cunning' tool of extending a colonial power's ability to define what a legitimate, politically qualified life is. For Povinelli this involves the Australian government's expectation that land should be inhabited and settled in particular ways, consistent with its notions of dwelling, childcare and work. Those who live in modes outside these parameters, in her case her 'indigenous' interlocutors, suffer disproportionately, experiencing poorer health and premature death. Povinelli calls for a recognition of 'worlds otherwise'. Simpson writes from the position of the Kahnawà:ke Mohawks, examining their refusal to recognise the US settler state. This, Simpson argues, demonstrates that the colonial project is incomplete. She recounts how she, as Mohawk, is told by a border guard (whose authority she does not recognise) that she requires a US passport to cross the border. Despite her having the official documentation of the settler state which recognises and asserts her right to cross the border as Mohawk, the guard does not recognise it. After some phone calls and legal clarifications Simpson passes through the border, but not without the guard turning to shout that she should just carry a US passport as she is 'really American'. Simpson traces the ways in which anthropological frames of analysis have misread aspects of Iroquois life and wrongly delineated the conditions of recognition that are extended to Iroquois peoples by the state, such as blood quantum (see also TallBear 2013), which are not the categories of identity that Iroquois peoples use themselves. The practices of recognition prefigure the ways the 'other' is measured, related to and controlled. Similarly, Glen Sean Coulthard, in his book *Red Skin, White Masks*, questions whether histories of destructive colonialism between the Canadian state and indigenous peoples can be reconciled through mechanisms of acknowledgement.

He asks if an alternative politics can be born from self-identification and a politics of refusal. Tracing the use of 'recognition' as a dominant mode of negotiation between the settler state and the indigenous nations of North America, Coulthard challenges the idea that contemporary difference and destructive colonialism can be reconciled through a process of acknowledgment, and assesses the role and effectiveness of self-recognition in indigenous resistance movements.

This book is clearly not a study of the continual oppression of indigenous peoples by colonial states. My interlocutors largely identify as a suburban white middle class (they even have a song about this), who believe in the social contract of the country in which they dwell. However, the politics of recognising difference and the conditions of valid social life are at play here, as are issues of how people form relations to each other, their own bodies and the state. In my work, tensions associated with these relations are subtle and the politics of recognition plays a minor, everyday or even banal role in their lives. Therefore it feels crass to align them with the colonial issues addressed by the writers discussed above. Such studies do, however, question the validity of the technocratic solutions to inclusion in terms of its political dynamics (as opposed to operational efficiency), in a way that is very relevant to the present study. Just as Coulthard has questioned the use of 'recognition' rhetoric, Wendy Brown asks if notions of inclusion and participation are deployed to delimit the politically agentive subject in the context of Euro-American democracies:

> Inclusion and participation as indices of democracy have been separated off from the powers and the unbounded field of deliberation that would make them meaningful as terms of shared rule. Put another way, while inclusion and participation are certainly important elements of democracy, to be more than empty signifiers, they must be accompanied by modest control over setting parameters and constraints and by the capacity to decide fundamental values and directions. Absent these, they cannot be said to be democratic any more than providing a death row inmate with choices about the method of execution offers the inmate freedom. Rather, this is the language of democracy used against the demos.
> (Brown 2015:128)

In this sense Brown asks if, in its neoliberal formulation, democracy becomes detached from politics and economics and is reduced to a form of citizenship 'buy-in' whereby people participate in finding technical practical solutions through a mobilisation of their 'responsibility' as a citizen. Here the citizen takes on the moral duty of problem solving (by taking responsibility for the maintenance of a vibrant high street or the provision of a good local park and so on) via active citizenship.

What these works have in common is the ways in which they draw attention to hegemonic ideological practices that create models of ideal citizens and delimit the forms of life that are possible. This book looks at the ongoing, everyday, banal practices of late liberal democracy in the making of the local. In the ethnography presented here there is no a priori cultural group asserting itself against state power. Rather, I focus on dynamic practices that lead to shifting constellations of what constitutes the morally good, politically efficacious citizen. In paying attention to the edges of social projects, to the moments of where knowledge and subject positions are legitimised or delegitimised, I trace the production of ethical substance, the crafting of 'a subject of a certain qualitative kind' (Faubion 2012:72).

Making the local emerges through the contestation between competing social projects via the radical singularity of materiality: that is, either you develop the land, or you don't. This approach acknowledges the limitations of platforming 'as many points of view as you like' and recognises how forms of life are closed down or opened up through material impositions. It is through attention to these processes that anthropology can do political work, since power works through these processes. My critical attitude towards the supposed co-existence of multiple points of view has been informed by my field site, where some possible futures for life in Surbiton are shut down, because of necessary limits of materiality, but also by recent discussion of the 'ontological turn' in anthropology. I will turn to this discussion to situate what I call the 'edge' anthropology foregrounded in this study, an anthropology that focuses on the ways in which life does not become, that locates analysis on the moments of attritions, contestations and exclusions that produce and delimit late liberal subjectivities.

Edge anthropology

The ontological turn has prompted vibrant conversation within anthropology (see Holbraad & Pedersen 2017; Paleček & Risjord 2013; Scott 2013). Proponents of the turn have argued that whilst the term 'culture' recognises the existence of many world views, it assumes a single, universal understanding of nature. Influenced by Eduardo Viveiros de

Castro's work on Amazonian perspectivism (2012), as well as the work of Roy Wagner (1981, 1986) and Marilyn Strathern (1988, 2005) on anthropological reflexivity and notions of culture, writings that have constituted the turn argue that anthropologists must take difference seriously. That is to say, they must go beyond recognising that people have different world views (an epistemological problem) to take seriously the idea that people may see a different world (an ontological problem). The turn advocates a radical methodological openness to difference of all kinds and 'poses ontological questions to solve epistemological problems' (Holbraad & Pedersen 2017:x). The 'signature move' of the turn, according to Holbraad and Pedersen, is to 'turn on its head the relationship, as well as the hierarchy, between ethnographic materials and analytical resources. Rather than treating ethnography as the object of analytical concepts and procedures, the turn to ontology treats ethnography above all as their source' (Holbraad & Pedersen 2017:6). Holbraad and Pedersen situate the turn within long-standing concerns about reflexivity in anthropology and ask how we can conceive of other ways of being by making our own assumptions clear and then challenging them through our ethnography.

Henare, Holbraad and Wastell explore solutions to the relativistic trap of an ontologically informed approach in *Thinking through Things* (2007) and advocate an analysis that works outwards from the objects discussed by their interlocutors and aims to take such objects seriously on their interlocutors' own terms. Nevertheless, escaping the confines of our ontological framing is a formidable, if not impossible, task; Ghassan Hage (2013) encourages caution whenever we feel we have successfully unshackled ourselves. Indeed, Henare, Holbraad and Wastell argue that we don't have the vocabulary to grasp the significance of objects in radically different contexts – at least not when we use a standard representational semiotic framework. They champion a radical emically orientated position:

> The mysterious-sounding notion of 'many worlds' is so dissimilar to the familiar idea of a plurality of worldviews precisely because it turns on the humble – though on this view logically obvious – admission that our concepts (*not* our 'representations') must, by definition, be inadequate to translate *different* ones. This, it is suggested, is the only way to take difference – *alterity* – seriously as the starting point for anthropological analysis. One must accept that when someone tells us, say, that powder is power, the anthropological problem cannot be that of accounting for why he might think that about powder (explaining, interpreting, placing his statement into

context), but rather that if that really is the case, then we just do not know what powder he is talking about. This is an ontological problem through and through. For its answer is patently not to be found by searching 'in the world' – maybe in Cuba? – for some special powerful powder. The world in which powder is power is not an uncharted (and preposterous!) region of our own ... It is a different world, in which what we take to be powder is actually power, or, more to the point, a third element which will remain ineffably paradoxical for as long as we insist on glossing it with our own default concepts – neither 'powder' nor 'power' but, somehow, both, or better still, the same thing.

(Henare, Holbraad & Wastell 2007:12; italics original)

Their position here is inspired by Marcel Mauss ([1925] 2002). In his work on Māori gift exchange, Mauss did not dismiss the existence of ancestor-artefacts and objects imbued with the personality of former owners as evidence of primitive animism or superstition. Rather, he embraced these unfamiliar entities in order to challenge assumptions and categories that were prevalent in his own society (see Henare, Holbraad & Wastell 2007:17). Mauss's interlocutor Ranapiri identified the taonga (valued articles) with hau (the 'spirit of the gift') and stated that 'the *taonga* is the *hau*'. This assertion troubled the categories of person and thing as separate. To see the 'artefact' as ancestor, one must perform an ontological switch to see the 'artefact' as agentive, not simply representative but fundamentally a different thing. This switch

illustrates the difference between epistemology and ontology as we understand it. While the former seeks to find ways to apply concepts that are already known to unfamiliar instances, the latter treats the unfamiliarity of those instances as an occasion to transform concepts, so as to give rise to new ones. It is not that 'persons' and 'things' have different referents for Māori – an epistemological question. It is that 'persons' and 'things' *are* different from that which animates Māori gift exchange – an ontological claim.

(Henare, Holbraad & Wastell 2007:18)

Attention to ontological difference requires one to understand the networks of relations that produce the meanings and social efficacy of materials. As outlined above, this book does not concern an anthropologist's encounter with a radically different social setting. Whilst my interlocutors may occupy a conceptual world familiar to myself and to each other, it is important to explore exactly how they mobilise, alter, challenge or ignore key concepts across social projects. Indeed, whilst the two groups I study may engage with concepts that seem identical, they actually interact with them in very different ways. Their practices work to open up or close down ways of being, in subtle ways that belie the apparent familiarity and uniformity of the field site. In this book my approach is less an attempt to understand the other's concept and more an attempt to see how concepts are mobilised, altered, challenged or ignored in order to open up or close down alternative ways of being.

This study is similar in its approach to many works associated with the ontological turn in that it focuses on the places where boundaries and meanings 'are precariously uncertain and unstable' (Ødegaard 2016:76). Jon Henrik Zieglar Remme uses the term 'the "otherwise within"' (2016:116) to refer to the forms of alterity that are closed down by hegemonic forces in the process of creating and maintaining worlds. A focus on the 'otherwise within' and constitutive exclusions of hegemonic modes of living aid an escape from what Kathinka Frøystad calls 'ontological prisons'. These 'prisons' emerge when an anthropologist's pursuit of clarity around a particular concept inadvertently causes the field to shrink, and makes 'overlaps, porousness, and crossings disappear almost completely from view' (2016:233). In this study I am less concerned with what something is – say, the powder or the 'local' – than with what it enables someone to do, particularly in terms of opening or closing down forms of socially liveable life. That is, I find it less important to comprehend the ontological basis of a material than to understand the forms of life an adherence to that ontological order engenders.

The work of Annemarie Mol has been much cited within the ontological turn and it is worth turning to her in regard to her approach to objects. In *The Body Multiple* (2002) Mol analyses how atherosclerosis is discussed and defined by various medical and health specialists across a range of health services and hospital departments. Mol moves away from perspectivist approaches (see Viveiros de Castro 2004) to assert that atherosclerosis is constantly (re)performed or enacted. Incommensurate ideas of the disease are maintained as patients move from practitioner to practitioner. What matters is not so much what atherosclerosis is – in fact the medical field maintains a range of understandings of what this is – rather, what matters is how, despite its being understood in multiple ways, there is sufficient shared understanding to enable the disease to be treated effectively.

Whilst Henare, Holbraad and Wastell are concerned with the analyst's ability to see how 'powder is actually power' (2007:12), I argue that we should also be attentive to the many ways powder is understood and examine how these competing meanings interact with each other to delimit the forms of life that can be lived. The key question then is less 'What is this?' than 'What is this doing?'. That is to say, we must be attentive to how making (and asserting) meaning is the means and effect of power and shapes the ethical substance of being. We must examine how particular practices delimit the conditions of life and death and prompt the expansion or contraction of social projects and ways of being human. Just as Mol explores which tools open the body to new configurations and understandings (the microscope, the lab and so on), we can seek to identify the tools of erasure that close down otherness in the pursuit of (false) totality. In our case this means a thorough investigation of the practices and rhetorics of late liberal citizenship around which legitimate personhood, moral action, local subjectivities, bodies and places are sculpted. Analytical attention is to be focused on the minor detail of that which is almost, but not quite, on the edge of social projects and modes of life as lived. As people campaign to save a water filtration site, to build resilient community, and to craft local social bonds, I trace the forms of citizenship being enacted, what futures are being imagined, and what futures are slipping away.

I pay particular attention to the ways material ecologies are contested. I work from a similar theoretical position to what Karan Barad (2007) calls the 'material-discursive', taking matter and meaning as intimately entwined, rather than separate, elements. But before we consider the relation between material and meaning later in this chapter, we must consider the values that underpin social action in making the local, namely democracy and being a good citizen. It is these ideals that make 'representation' and 'inclusion' important values in the first instance.

Democracy and anthropology

Within my field site, democracy works as an ideological symbolic operator, that is, a concept that underpins the core values of equality, inclusion and representation that guide the actions of my interlocutors and framed my research within the ASP. Democracy has also informed anthropology as a discipline and the field has been involved in the advancement of the democracy principle, particularly in the 1960s and 1970s (Paley 2002). In the 1980s and 1990s, informed by postmodern analyses of democracy's circulation, constructedness, discursive nature and implication in power relations, anthropologists became interested in how democracy manifested in multiple local forms. Universalist assumptions of Western democratic practices were scrutinised (see Comaroff & Comaroff 1997), as was the blending of cultural difference into universal projects of democracy (see Sabloff 2001 on Mongolia and Taussig 1992 on state fetishism). More recently, critical attention has been paid to the idea of democracy itself as a social organiser and ideal; however, most of this has come from political theorists.

Wendy Brown notes that Foucault-inspired scholarship has been excellent in focusing critical attention on biopower and disciplining practices. However, Brown notes that in such work the subject is often figured as either being governed or resisting being governed as 'individual subjects or as disciplinary bodies' and that 'There is no *political* body, no demos acting in concert (even episodically) or expressing aspirational sovereignty' (2015:73; italics in original). She notes that there is little reflection on the effects of neoliberal reasoning and logics on democratic political life and the configurations of citizenship.

In an era which has been labelled 'post-political' (see Mouffe 2005; Rancière 2010; Rancière, Panagia and Bowlby 2001; Žižek 1999), neoliberal ideology and forms of governance have been described both as saturating the socio-political imaginary and as inseparable from each other in their operation, that is to say, governance of social life occurs through a neoliberal, *homo oeconomicus* logic (see Boyer & Yurchak 2008). Nikolas Rose (1996) asserts that terms such as participation and inclusion are motivating discourses whereby neoliberal thinking extends from structural governance to individual thinking. Rose writes that the state 'conceive[s] of these actors in new ways as subjects of responsibility, autonomy and choice, and seek[s] to act upon them through shaping and utilizing their freedom' (Rose 1996:53–4). Rose paints a picture of how liberalism has gone beyond a social or economic philosophy and even beyond a perspective of governmentality and has become a formula for subjectivity. This occurs because the tools of governance (such as bureaucracy, expertise and state apparatus) have merged with the projects of individual subjects to craft themselves and community.

In her work on job seekers in the USA Ilana Gershon (2011, 2016) describes the reflexive nature of the neoliberal subject's agency. The neoliberal self is conceived of as a flexible bundle of skills capable of being managed as if it were a business. This enables the neoliberal subject to navigate neoliberal landscapes of risk. Gershon's work demonstrates how the responsibility for the ability to survive in late liberalism lies with the individual. It is intimately tied to the moral responsibility of the individual to sculpt themselves as the good worker and the good citizen. In the context of Surbiton, I trace how the notion of effective citizenship was embodied by the Seethingers/locals through their community work. I trace not only the social effects of this, in terms of how it reconfigures relations of kin, community and ethics, but also how it is felt through physical and mental health as the strain of being a 'good local' takes hold.

The motivations for crafting good citizenship in late liberalism intersect with technocratic propositions to solve what Jürgen Habermas (1990) would call the 'ideal speech situation'. Much discussed by advocates of radical democracy, this 'ideal situation' requires clear communication between all parties within a democracy, and vibrant public discussions. It serves the aim of bringing 'socially marginalized' groups into deliberative democracy (Calhoun 1992; Coombe 1998; Gal & Woolard 2014). This ideal underpins the ASP's 'auto-ethnographic' mapping project (see Chapter 3). Seethingers also wished to enact a democratic form of life in which all were included. Ultimately, then, both social projects share the same *telos*: to make better places and to do so through including as many people in their project as possible. Yet each held a very different understanding of how to do this. This resulted in incommensurable moments between the social projects. It is in these moments that social projects labour to assert themselves.

Democracy and hegemony

The ambition to realise consensus lies at the heart of the late liberal democratic ideal (or, at least, its rhetoric). Here we also find the paradox of universal inclusion. Democracy, in its pursuit of consensus, closes off forms of life that do not fit into a universal social whole. Derrida (2003) called this an auto-immune logic. The sovereign determines which forms of life are closed off and excluded (Schmitt 2008). Without sovereignty, the demos would be compromised by conflicting powers. The situation is complicated in late liberalism, in which the sovereign has become the demos; in modern Europe, the sovereign has shifted from the figure of the monarch to the collective of the people represented through government (Gunning 2013:145; see also Agamben 2005). In late liberal democracies citizens partake in decision making via their vote; that is to say, they contribute to deciding the conditions of exclusion. Derrida (2006) draws attention to a paradox of late liberal democracy, whereby universality must contend with and encompass the particular. He outlines how tense, i.e. social emphasis on the future, works as a strategy to avoid recognising this paradox. That we do not have truly full democratic representation in the present is a problem that can be overcome by the promise that it will come in the future. This 'democracy to come' explains why certain failures, such as the ASP's map, are not seen as such. Rather than representing the insuperable problem at the heart of democracy, the map represents a technical challenge that will eventually be overcome with further development. Seethingers also use tense. For them, the lost utopian past of the ancient village is the prefigured ideal to which they are striving. Crucially, these ideal democratic futures are always just out of reach and require constant labour to inch closer to them.

For Derrida, this gap between ideal and actual democracy is not a flaw in democracy but is intrinsic to modern democracies. It is part of how democratic societies maintain themselves. He writes:

> this failure and this gap also characterize, *a priori* and by definition, *all* democracies, including the oldest and most stable of so-called Western democracies. At stake here is the very concept of democracy as concept of a promise that can only arise in such a *diastema* (failure, inadequation, disjunction, disadjustment, being 'out of joint'). That is why we always propose to speak of a democracy *to come*, not of a *future* democracy in the future present, not even of a regulating idea, in the Kantian sense, or of a utopia – at least to the extent that their inaccessibility would still retain the temporal form of a *future present*, of a future modality of the *living present*.
> (Derrida 2006:81; italics in original)

The universal ideal of democracy requires clarity. This allowed the ASP to justify the exclusion of the Seething story. It was excluded on the basis that it was not fact, and so the story would have confused the nature of the data included on the map. The ASP made efforts to work on developing the map, adding other layers for 'myths'. However, the problem (the failure of inclusion) was seen as something that could be resolved in the future, as the map could be developed further, once funding had been secured.

The capacity of tense to resolve, or defer, the paradox (that is to say, the capacity of invoking democracy-to-come to obviate incommensurability) is troubled when it comes to material conflicts. The locals aimed to save a disused water filtration site. For all the recognition of the different voices and opinions over what to do with the site in the end there could only ever be one outcome: either the land would be built upon or it wouldn't.

The locals needed to state their case skilfully to the local council as to why the site should not be developed. This required marshalling the skills required to articulate the value of the site in formal and politically efficacious language. They needed to learn the languages, methods and skills of late liberal subjectivity. Locals also needed to talk in another register in order to communicate the value of the land, and the importance of the campaign, throughout the community. This would build popular support – an important currency within the context of localism.

One might observe that Surbiton, a largely white middle-class London suburb, is the typical setting of liberal democracy. In this late liberal heartland, we can observe an ongoing tension around the decisions of inclusion and exclusion, that is to say, which forms of social life and material environment are allowed to flourish, and which are not. Surbiton is another site of unresolvable tension between the universal aim of including all people and the particularity of including difference, a tension that is at the heart of liberal democracies (see Laclau & Mouffe 1985: xii–xiii). This tension gives purpose and energy to the forms of social life at work here; locals energetically assert their preferred forms of social life to perpetuate their validity and survival. To position themselves within the democratic-sovereign power, the locals must necessarily, constantly, perform their citizenship and active moral agency. They risk being excluded by and from the sovereign if they do not assert themselves. Following Giorgio Agamben (1998), we may say they are always in the process of making *bios*, a politically qualified life, and avoiding *zoë*, a life outside political efficacy or consideration. Therefore the parameters of a politically qualified life are made at the edge of a social project, at the site of contestations of legitimacy. Who has the powder is important.

Sovereignty and forms of life

Agamben (1998) contrasts the figure of the sovereign, the one who decides on the exception, with the figure of *homo sacer*, the 'sacred man'. *Homo sacer* is a figure in Roman law who can be killed by anybody, yet whose life is sacred, and so cannot be sacrificed in a ritual ceremony. The key aspect of the figure of *homo sacer* is that they can be reduced to nature (*zoë*). That is to say, they are placed outside cultural and political life. They can be expelled from the polis, from the realm of the politically active subject or citizen. In contrast to *zoë* Agamben calls the politically qualified life *bios*. Agamben calls the position of exclusion from politically qualified life 'bare life'. The ability to define the conditions of exclusion is what defines the sovereign. Agamben was writing about the conditions of making politically qualified life in the context of the Holocaust and the dehumanisation of people. Clearly there is nothing comparable in the suburbs of London. But in Chapters 7 and 8 my analysis demonstrates how Agamben's concepts can help us understand how various forms of life can be made more or less legitimate in this ethnographic context. We can trace how the practice of making yourself a morally engaged citizen in the London suburb can mark your life as socially valid, and helps you secure effective social and political power. The behaviour of the ASP and the Seethingers/locals represents a series of strategies for enacting political subjectivity and assuming sovereign power. On one hand, the ASP assumes sovereign power by acting as a knowledge-producing expert within policy-facing academia. On the other hand, local enthusiasts assert sovereignty through forming a resilient 'community that works'. Having said that, the practices associated with enacting good citizenship, in the pursuit of community sovereignty, can have negative effects. Some people spend less of their spare time at home, and instead of relaxing they volunteer to endure stressful situations. These (potentially damaging) social and embodied practices that produce the 'good local citizen' are informed by late liberal ideals. The local is never fully sovereign nor fully excluded, but occupies a precarious, and exhausting, position on the threshold between included and excluded. They must work to maintain themselves as politically valid life. My interlocutors, being relatively affluent and skill-rich, are particularly successful at this. My point is that the threshold position is one that is endemic to the practices of late liberal citizenship, by virtue of the requirement that the late liberal citizen self-organises and is 'responsible'. They must be involved in planning decisions, not excluded from them, in order to secure a future to come. The local is constantly enacting their *bios* and (by doing so) avoiding the threat of *zoë*. A central concern of my study of making the local is how *bios* is made from *zoë* in late liberal society. It considers how the constant need to perform *bios* from *zoë* gives life to particular forms: the suburban citizen, the ASP, and anthropology itself. Making a politically qualified life can be a banal and quotidian process, happening through everyday actions.

Material and meaning

This study of making the local is invested in exploring the connections between the production of material culture – particularly the built environment – and meaning. I consider how material and semiotic production are intimately entwined. This will provide the theoretical and analytical frames to analyse the way in which people develop and assert a political efficacy through daily practices of being local or expert. This approach is heavily influenced by, and contributes to, conversations in material culture theory in anthropology.

As Elizabeth Mertz (2007) notes, Charles Sanders Peirce has had a huge influence on the use of semiotics on material culture anthropology. A Peircean approach allows links to be made between the analysis of language and the wider social context. When introduced, this approach contrasted with the more static and synchronic semiotic approaches that were influenced by Ferdinand de Saussure. The latter's approach has been considered overly abstracted from the flexibility of language that can be found in everyday usage. In semiotics the sign is anything that communicates meaning that is not the sign itself to the interpreter of that sign. For Saussure, the relation between the signifier (the form the sign takes, like a noise, image or word) and the signified (the meaning of that sign) is essentially arbitrary and is defined by social convention. For Peirce, the sign was more contextual and open to interpretation and contestation. For Peirce, the sign is something that stands for something to someone (Danesi & Perron 1999). That is, for Peirce the interpreter of the sign is important, because they are agentive in reading meaning. Mertz celebrates the benefits that anthropologists reap from shifting analytical focus to the contextual connections between materials and meaning. This shift allows anthropologists to analyse language in a way that connects local grounded knowledge to wider structural, ideological and political forces. When considering the contestation of meaning of landscape in Surbiton, I seek to pay close attention to context on a range of scales.

For Alfred Gell, the work of Peirce was hugely important. Gell uses Peirce's ideas throughout his seminal work on material culture anthropology, *Art and Agency* (1998). In this book he inaugurated a shift from overly static notions of objects as representations in his search to understand what objects did as social agents. This returns us to the problem of how to understand that taonga *is* the hau rather than taonga *as* hau. Gell's use of Peircean semiotics aims to counter the dematerialisation of the sign associated with Saussurean analysis. Such an approach sets language apart from the material conditions from which meaning is generated and communicated. Such dematerialisation made understanding taonga *is* hau rather than *as* hau almost impossible. Gell's rematerialisation returns the agentive force of material and aesthetic form to the foreground of analysis (see Küchler & Carroll 2020). Such an approach allows us to consider how different social projects relate to the materiality of the built environment in emic terms. However, for Webb Keane, Gell doesn't go far enough. According to Gell, Peirce does not question the fundamentals of Saussure's structuralist model of language (see Keane 2005). In this model, sign is always assimilated to meaning and meaning to language. Therefore, Gell could never quite get beyond formulating taonga *as* hau, that is, that the taonga is a representation of, rather than is, the spirit. Further, Keane asserts that Gell 'doesn't fully explore the social and historical implications of the index. Instead he seeks a direct road to the transhistorical domain of cognition' (2005:186),[2] that is, how something comes to mean the thing that it does. There are questions to be asked of the historical social forces at work in establishing meaning. Keane notes Peirce's critique of Hegel, that he 'almost altogether ignores the Outward Clash' of the sign (Peirce 1958:43–4 in Keane 2003:413). That is, Hegel pays little attention to the contingency and vulnerability of the sign (that is, that its ability to index a particular meaning is contested in the social world). Peirce asserts that social context and acts of recontextualisation, and the very materiality of a thing, can give rise to new and transformative meanings and significations. Ultimately, Keane's reading of Peirce draws attention to the ongoing contestation of signs in both the social and material worlds. Peircean semiotics offers to reinvent and reorientate the anthropology of meaning, from describing *what* things represent to *how* things represent. Peirce-informed anthropology is an 'anthropology of possibility' (see Appadurai 2013), oriented towards the future, not only able to grasp how things come to mean something but how they could come to mean something else. It allows political analysis of how social projects work to establish worlds of meaning (and close others) through contestations of the material world. I encountered two discrete moments of meaning making that operated through such material contestations: the crafting of puppets to make community, and the making of diagrams to make expertise (see Chapter 4). Puppets and diagrams are politically effective by virtue of their symbolic and indexical power. Peircean semiotics allows us to see beyond this, and to understand their capacity to generate new meanings, and configure new relations of materials and meaning.

In Chapter 5 we will consider how Seethingers used 'stupid' as a social strategy to build community. Playing with the symbols of local government and authority (specifically the three fish that historically represent the area) is key to this strategy. Through crafting stories of historical fish, making and parading fish puppets and holding a fish festival the Seethingers realign the indexical qualities of the fish that can be found on the local council's crest. My interlocutors explained how they conceive of their citizenship differently after Seething events and consider the fish symbol to be theirs rather than belonging to the local authority. This realignment uses silliness, humour and semiotic excess to craft the social effects they desire. These political realignments are only possible because of the contingency of the sign on its social context – in moments of indeterminacy of the sign where realignments of meaning are made. Crucially, these realignments are a material practice.

Advocates of 'new materialism', such as Jane Bennett (2010), Timothy Morton (2013) and Karen Barad (2007), have drawn attention to the relation between the ways in which the materiality of the world is understood and the ways in which such materials are observed, measured and categorised. Such work has troubled the divide between the epistemological mode of knowing an object and the ontological problem of what that object is. Barad claims that there is no prior object but rather that objects become known through the intra-action of the material with an agent. Barad, in a development of the work of physicist Niels Bohr, moves the primary ontological units of empiricist study from 'objects' to 'phenomena' (see also Ingold 2013).

By focusing on the moments of the inherent instability that arises between matter and meaning (see the example of the visualisations in Chapter 4, or the fish in Chapter 5), this study asks how social projects seek to craft 'infrastructures of certainty' (Castoriadis 1987) around what place is and can be. This book asks how social projects go about crafting relations between meaning and material and why socio-material ecologies stabilise in particular forms. It also seeks to identify the exclusions and foreclosures upon which socio-material arrangements are predicated. My emphasis on the moment of tension between the ASP and the Seethingers draws attention to the practices that inform the establishment of legitimate ways to know place. In this way, the book considers social action as practices that open up and close down ways of being, and either reinforce certainty or introduce uncertainty.

Certainty and uncertainty

Ideas of semiotic flexibility and the relations between meaning and material are explored in the work of Judith Butler. In her book *Bodies That Matter*, Butler argues that theories of gender need to 'return to the notion of matter', more specifically the body (1993:10). Butler argues that power operates through the repetition and delimitation of social norms of sex and gender. She works through a performative, material and linguistic exploration of how bodies come to matter (in both senses of the word). Butler highlights the gaps between language and the materiality of the sign: 'The linguistic categories that are understood to "denote" the materiality of the body are themselves troubled by a referent that is never fully or permanently resolved or contained by any given signified' (Butler 1993:67). For Butler, the normative link between meaning and material is established through the iterative and regularised repetitions of associations which give some material-discursive arrangements greater 'discursive legitimacy' than others (8). However, there are 'gaps and fissures' (10), spaces of possibility, within these iterations, where forms of minor alterity may emerge. Rearticulation of the symbolic horizon is possible through the failure to reiterate in accordance with social laws. This failure to reiterate in accordance with social laws, or 'queering' (see also Halberstam 2011), is the linguistic function at the heart of a joke. In a similar way, Seething events play with the symbols of the local area, such as the fish, and create semiotic excess which is released through humour. This allows the Seethingers to make new associations with symbols, landscapes and local government. Whilst the politics of gender recognition and community work in suburban London may feel like different political arenas, they are united by politics of meaning and material and mechanisms of changing/ crafting the relations between them.

The purposeful loss of epistemological certainty through being 'stupid' forms a *minor* resistance to the ways suburbs, and the sorts of citizenship to be found there, are normally (re)iterated. However, the Seethingers do not totally resist the demands of late liberal democracies here. Rather, they adjust their position within this social context in a way that maintains, rather than nullifies, their position as socially valid, politically engaged active citizens. They are always working to assert their version of citizenship in a way that is broadly consistent with the wider context of state–citizen relations particular to the prevailing late liberal logic.

There is, then, always a tension between social conventions and the invention of new relations between meaning and materials. Roy Wagner's seminal work *The Invention of Culture*, which has had a significant influence on discussions around ontological difference, links culture to the ability to perform an act of significance (1981:4). Culture, then, can be invented through a play on the 'controlling context'. Controlling context is similar to Keane's 'semiotic ideology' (2005), a term he uses to describe how meanings are fixed, and of limited range, within normative culture. For Wagner, the controlling context describes the relation of the actor's intention and awareness to the judgements and priorities of the conventional world (1981:45). The ability to control context, then, is the ability to fix the inherently fluctuating nature of semiosis in a false stillness. This *masks* the potential to alter meaning, via contradiction (following Marx [1867] 1996:1064). This masking enables the establishment of rigid social logic and normative belief systems which appear natural and universal (following Eagleton 1991).

Invention always occurs in relation to the current (controlling normative) context of meaning. Play gives rise to novelty through re-territorialising meaning. Semiotic play extends existing meaning by substituting links in chains of association with new links, which produces realignments. Close examination of the value transformations associated with novel meaning, which Morten Nielsen (2012, 2013) calls 'obviational analysis' (compare Munn 1986; Appadurai 1996), can be instructive. It can demonstrate how, as Nielsen's study shows, workers in Mozambique realign their ethical relation to work through a concrete bag or, rather, through its potential: they buy it with their wages from road building, and pivot from labourer to future housebuilder/owner by turning their wages into concrete. This action for road workers resulted in the wage packet 'dropping the traces of its own origin' (Nielsen 2013:79). In a similar manner, when Seethingers do stupid things with fish (Chapter 5), we may say they are creating tiny realignments of the meanings of these local symbols, and by doing so enact a new type of citizenship position.

For Wagner, the idea of inherent meaning is a 'necessary illusion' (Wagner 1981:41), needed to provide semiotic coherence within a culture. For this reason, invention always occurs in relation to a controlling context. Whilst convention and invention are held in a binding dialectic, invention always pushes at the limits of the possible. Wagner's work enables an anthropological analysis to scale out from seemingly minor individual actions to larger social structures. His approach allows us, for example, to grasp how citizenship positions in late liberalism can be enacted by being stupid with fish symbols (see Chapter 5).

Establishing the context, establishing sovereignty

If alternative ways of conceiving one's ethical being involve constantly working to assert alterity in relation to the controlling context, then it pays for anthropological attention to be focused on the threshold of the symbolic. The exclusions that constitute the 'other' to hegemonic forms of life, such as particular sexualities or citizenship positions, are what Hegel, speaking through the figure of Antigone, describes as 'the eternal irony of community' (see Butler 2000:4). In her work on sovereignty and hegemony, Butler uses Sophocles' Antigone. Antigone's love for her brother is unable to be supported by current conditions of the symbolic. She both recognises and refuses the authority that maintains the symbolic realm. Butler asserts that recognition of one's sovereignty 'begins with the insight that one is lost in the Other, appropriated in and by an alterity that is and is not oneself, and recognition is motivated by the desire to find oneself reflected there, where the reflection is not a final expropriation' (Butler 2000:14). Antigone will suffer either a symbolic (social) death or bodily death (through law). Butler asks if there is any room for positions and relations outside universalising hegemonic terms. If kinship is the precondition of the human then, as Butler states, Antigone's claim occasions a 'new field', or reorientation, 'of the human' (82). That is to say, new ways of being human can be conceived when actors forcefully bring new relations into the realm of the possible; only when their possibility is demonstrated may these new relations be established as ethically legitimate.

As stated above, this book explores issues of recognition and inclusion in a social arena in which democracy and citizenship are established values. Here I have outlined a semiotic approach to analyse how new forms of subjectivity emerge in the gap between meaning and material. I situate my analysis less in radically alternative worlds than in the micro-contestations of materiality.

Having located my analysis at the point of evolving relations between meaning and material, I will now situate this strategy within a wider debate in anthropological theory, with reference to the notion of involution.

The moment of involution is the empirical detail of the obviatory mechanism, that is, the means by which actors realign meanings via material culture. Alfred Gell discusses the notion of involution through examples of nail fetishes in the Congo region and through acts of iconoclasm in the UK. Gell finds that the '"involute" character of the index, which may objectify a whole series of relations in a single visible form' (1998:62), links art and agency. Gell explains this by demonstrating how objects internalise the agency of one and several people/agents (such as women, patriarchy or, in the case of fish, the council and hierarchical authority) and also exteriorise this internalised agency (demonstrating power, meaning or intention) through the social actions that surround them. For example, Gell explains the twin gestures with reference to an attack on the Rokeby Venus. This painting was, says Gell, imbued with powerful agency via its depiction of what activist Mary Richardson called 'the most beautiful woman in mythological history' (Gell 1998:64). For Mary Richardson, a supporter of women's rights and an activist in the suffragette movement of the early twentieth century, it represented the oppression of women. By slashing it, Mary Richardson felt she was slashing the symbolisation of the oppression of women. It had internalised the agency of oppressed women, and this allowed its slashing to have wider social meaning and political efficacy as the act worked to externalise and challenge this meaning.

However, as Ludovic Coupaye notes, the concept of involution in Gell's work can leave the reader frustrated as it does not adequately work through the ways in which 'agency is *transferred* from the technician to the index' and it underplays 'the technical process itself to the profit of an almost immaterial transfer of intentionalities' (Coupaye 2013:270; italics added). In other words, Coupaye asks precisely how it is that a person can affect the meaning of an object and the ways in which interactions with such objects both internalise and externalise these meanings. This echoes Howard Morphy's critique of the 'major gap between the theoretical positioning of the book and the methods of analysis that Gell employs' (Morphy 2009:6; see also Arnaut 2001:206). For Morphy, whilst Gell proposes analysis that is attentive to the dialogical relations between materials and meanings, it says little about the process by which this dialogue functions, or how meanings are transferred, altered and crafted. Taking up Keane's call to focus on the 'outward clash' (Keane 2003:413) of the index, which gives rise to new and transformative modes of action and subjectivity, my analysis focuses on how people develop the motivation to participate and how they craft new indexes of relation (as we will see with the example of fish in Chapter 5). I wish to focus on how the meaning of an object can be changed through play, via involutionary mechanism. That is, I wish to think about how taking an established symbol, such as the council's fish, and repeatedly recontextualising it, allows its meaning to swerve (see Althusser 2006). The ideological force of materiality can be realigned through a series of brief encounters which rework both material form and its meanings.

Above, I have laid out the theoretical tools which have informed my analysis. Such perspectives allow me to analyse the actions of Seethingers and the ASP and relate their everyday social worlds to larger ideological forces to get at the empirical detail of crafting citizenship in late liberalism. Issues of representation and inclusion, democracy and citizenship, and meaning and material, represent the themes, values and practices of late liberalism seen in the field site presented here. These perspectives radiated in the background during the fieldwork and the writing up, from my enrolment in the Free University of Seething to a focus on cake. But first, we return to the map.

Notes

1 This term is one used by Povinelli rather than myself.
2 Gell defines the index as 'material entities which motivate abductive inferences, cognitive interpretations, etc.' (1998:27). He further explains that 'The index is the material thing which motivates abductions of an art-related kind' (28).

References

Agamben, Giorgio. 1998. *Homo Sacer: Sovereign power and bare life*. Stanford, CA: Stanford University Press.
Agamben, Giorgio. 2005. *State of Exception* (trans. Kevin Attell). Chicago, IL: Chicago University Press.
Althusser, Louis. 2006. *Philosophy of the Encounter: Later writings, 1978–87* (trans. G. M. Goshgarian). London: Verso.
Appadurai, Arjun. 1996. *Modernity at Large: Cultural dimensions of globalization*. Minneapolis: University of Minnesota Press.
Appadurai, Arjun. 2013. 'The future as cultural fact: Essays on the global condition.' *Rassegna Italiana di Sociologia* 14, no. 4: 649–50. http://dx.doi.org/10.1423/76023.
Arnaut, Karel. 2001. 'A pragmatic impulse in the anthropology of art? Gell and semiotics.' *Journal des Africanistes* 71, no. 2: 191–208. http://dx.doi.org/10.3406/jafr.2001.1277.
Barad, Karen. 2007. *Meeting the Universe Halfway: Quantum physics and the entanglement of matter and meaning*. Durham, NC: Duke University Press.
Bennett, Jane. 2010. *Vibrant Matter: A political ecology of things*. Durham, NC: Duke University Press.
Boyer, Dominic and Alexei Yurchak. 2008. 'Postsocialist studies, cultures of parody and American stiob.' *Anthropology News* 49, no. 8: 9–10. https://doi.org/10.1111/an.2008.49.8.9.
Brown, Wendy. 2015. *Undoing the Demos: Neoliberalism's stealth revolution*. New York: Zone Books.
Butler, Judith. 1993. *Bodies that Matter: On the discursive limits of 'sex'*. New York and London: Routledge.
Butler, Judith. 2000. *Antigone's Claim: Kinship between life and death*. New York and Chichester: Columbia University Press.
Calhoun, Craig J., ed. 1992. *Habermas and the Public Sphere*. Cambridge, MA: MIT Press.
Castoriadis, Cornelius. 1987. *The Imaginary Institution of Society* (trans. Kathleen Blarney). Cambridge: Polity Press.
Clifford, James. 1988. *The Predicament of Culture: Twentieth-century ethnography, literature, and art*. Cambridge, MA: Harvard University Press.
Clifford, James and George E. Marcus, eds. 1986. *Writing Culture: The poetics and politics of ethnography*. Berkeley: University of California Press.
Comaroff, John L. and Jean Comaroff. 1997. 'Postcolonial politics and discourses of democracy in southern Africa: An anthropological reflection on African political modernities.' *Journal of Anthropological Research* 53, no. 2: 123–46.
Coombe, Rosemary J. 1998. *The Cultural Life of Intellectual Properties: Authorship, appropriation, and the law*. Durham, NC: Duke University Press.
Coulthard, Glen Sean. 2014. *Red Skin, White Masks: Rejecting the colonial politics of recognition*. Minneapolis: University of Minnesota Press.
Coupaye, Ludovic. 2013. *Growing Artefacts, Displaying Relationships: Yams, art and technology amongst the Nyamikum Abelam of Papua New Guinea*. New York and Oxford: Berghahn.

Danesi, Marcel and Paul Perron. 1999. *Analyzing Cultures: An introduction and handbook*. Bloomington and Indianapolis: Indiana University Press.

Derrida, Jacques. 2003. 'Autoimmunity: Real and symbolic suicides – a dialogue with Jacques Derrida.' In Jürgen Habermas, Jacques Derrida and Giovanna Borradori (interviewer), *Philosophy in a Time of Terror: Dialogues with Jürgen Habermas and Jacques Derrida*, pp. 85–136. Chicago, IL: University of Chicago Press.

Derrida, Jacques. 2006. *Specters of Marx: The state of the debt, the work of mourning and the new international* (trans. Peggy Kamuf). Abingdon: Routledge.

Eagleton, Terry. 1991. *Ideology: An introduction*. London and New York: Routledge.

Eriksen, Thomas Hylland and Finn Sivert Nielsen. 2001. *A History of Anthropology*. London: Pluto Press.

Faubion, James D. 2012. 'Foucault and the genealogy of ethics.' In Didier Fassin, ed., *A Companion to Moral Anthropology*, pp. 67–84. Chichester: Wiley-Blackwell.

Frøystad, Kathinka. 2016. 'Alter-politics reconsidered: From different worlds to osmotic worlding.' In Bjørn Enge Bertelsen and Synnøve Bendixsen, eds, *Critical Anthropological Engagements in Human Alterity and Difference*, pp. 229–52. Cham: Palgrave Macmillan.

Gal, Susan and Kathryn Woolard, eds. 2014. *Languages and Publics: The making of authority*. London and New York: Routledge.

Gell, Alfred. 1998. *Art and Agency: An anthropological theory*. Oxford: Clarendon Press.

Gershon, Ilana. 2011. 'Neoliberal agency.' *Current Anthropology* 52, no. 4: 537–55. https://doi.org/10.1086/660866.

Gershon, Ilana. 2016. '"I'm not a businessman, I'm a business, man": Typing the neoliberal self into a branded existence.' *HAU: Journal of Ethnographic Theory* 6, no. 3: 223–46. https://doi.org/10.14318/hau6.3.017.

Gunning, Dave. 2013. *Postcolonial Literature*. Edinburgh: Edinburgh University Press.

Habermas, Jürgen. 1990. *Moral Consciousness and Communicative Action*. Cambridge, MA: MIT Press.

Hage, Ghassan. 2013. 'Critical anthropology as a permanent state of first contact.' Talk delivered to the American Anthropological Association, 25 November 2013. http://culanth.org/fieldsights/critical-anthropology-as-a-permanent-state-of-first-contact (accessed 23 April 2021).

Halberstam, Judith. 2011. *The Queer Art of Failure*. Durham, NC. Duke University Press.

Halme-Tuomisaari, Miia and Julie Billaud. 2014. 'Persistent point of first contact – Povinelli and EASA2014.' *ALLEGRA lab – Anthropology, Law, Art & World*, 22 August. http://allegralaboratory.net/persistent-point-of-first-contact/ (accessed 23 April 2021).

Henare, Amiria, Martin Holbraad and Sari Wastell, eds. 2007. *Thinking through Things: Theorising artefacts ethnographically*. Abingdon: Routledge.

Holbraad, Martin and Morten Axel Pedersen. 2017. *The Ontological Turn: An anthropological exposition*. Cambridge: Cambridge University Press.

Ingold, Tim. 2013. *Making: Anthropology, archaeology, art and architecture*. London: Routledge.

Keane, Webb. 2003. 'Semiotics and the social analysis of material things.' *Language & Communication* 23, nos 3–4: 409–25. http://dx.doi.org/10.1016/S0271-5309(03)00010-7.

Keane, Webb. 2005. 'Signs are not the garb of meaning: On the social analysis of material things.' In Daniel Miller, ed., *Materiality*, pp. 182–205. Durham, NC: Duke University Press. https://doi.org/10.1515/9780822386711-008.

Küchler, Susanne and Timothy Carroll. 2020. *A Return to the Object: Alfred Gell, art, and social theory*. Abingdon: Routledge.

Laclau, Ernesto and Chantal Mouffe. 1985. *Hegemony and Socialist Strategy: Towards a radical democratic politics*. 2nd edn. London and New York: Verso.

Marcus, George E. and Michael M. J. Fischer. 1986. *Anthropology as Cultural Critique: An experimental moment in the human sciences*. London and Chicago, IL: University of Chicago Press.

Marx, Karl. [1867] 1996. *Capital. Volume 1: The process of production of capital* (trans. Ben Fowkes), Harmondsworth: Penguin.

Mauss, Marcel. [1925] 2002. *The Gift: The form and reason for exchange in archaic societies* (trans. W. D. Halls). Abingdon: Routledge.

Mertz, Elizabeth. 2007. 'Semiotic anthropology.' *Annual Review of Anthropology* 36: 337–53.

Mol, Annemarie. 2002. *The Body Multiple: Ontology in medical practice*. Durham, NC: Duke University Press.

Morphy, Howard. 2009. 'Art as a mode of action: Some problems with Gell's *Art and Agency*.' *Journal of Material Culture* 14, no. 1: 5–27. https://doi.org/10.1177%2F1359183508100006.

Morton, Timothy. 2013. *Hyperobjects: Philosophy and ecology after the end of the world*. Minneapolis: University of Minnesota Press.
Mouffe, Chantal. 2005. *The Return of the Political*. London: Verso.
Munn, Nancy D. 1986. *The Fame of Gawa: A symbolic study of value transformation in a Massim (Papua New Guinea) society*. Durham, NC: Duke University Press.
Nielsen, Morten. 2012. 'Roadside inventions: Making time and money work at a road construction site in Mozambique.' *Mobilities* 7, no. 4: 467–80. https://doi.org/10.1080/17450101.2012.718428.
Nielsen, Morten. 2013. 'Analogic asphalt: Suspended value conversions among young road workers in southern Mozambique.' *HAU: Journal of Ethnographic Theory* 3, no. 2: 79–96. https://doi.org/10.14318/hau3.2.006.
Ødegaard, Cecilie Vindal. 2016. 'Alterity, predation, and questions of representation: The problem of the Kharisiri in the Andes.' In Bjørn Enge.Bertelsen, and Synnøve Bendixsen, eds, *Critical Anthropological Engagements in Human Alterity and Difference*, pp. 65–87. Cham: Palgrave Macmillan.
Paleček, Martin and Mark Risjord. 2013. 'Relativism and the ontological turn within anthropology.' *Philosophy of the Social Sciences* 43, no. 1: 3–23. https://doi.org/10.1177%2F0048393112463335.
Paley, Julia. 2002. 'Toward an anthropology of democracy.' *Annual Review of Anthropology* 31: 469–96. https://doi.org/10.1146/annurev.anthro.31.040402.085453.
Peirce, Charles Sanders. 1958. *Collected Papers of Charles Sanders Peirce. VIII: Reviews, correspondence, and bibliography*, ed. Charles Hartshorne and Paul Weiss. Cambridge, MA: Belknap Press of Harvard University Press.
Povinelli, Elizabeth A. 2011. *Economies of Abandonment: Social belonging and endurance in late liberalism*. Durham, NC: Duke University Press.
Povinelli, Elizabeth. 2014. 'Downloading the Dreaming? All of it extinguished but none of it dead?' Keynote speech at the 13th EASA biennial conference, Tallinn, Estonia, 11 September.
Rancière, Jacques. 2010. *Dissensus: On politics and aesthetics* (trans. Steven Corcoran). London and New York: Continuum.
Rancière, Jacques, Davide Panagia and Rachel Bowlby. 2001. 'Ten theses on politics.' *Theory & Event* 5, no. 3. doi:10.1353/tae.2001.0028.
Remme, Jon Henrik Zieglar. 2016. 'Chronically unstable ontology: Ontological dynamics, radical alterity, and the "otherwise within"'. In Bjørn Enge Bertelsen and Synnøve Bendixsen (eds.), *Critical Anthropological Engagements in Human Alterity and Difference*, pp. 113–33. Cham: Palgrave Macmillan.
Rose, Nikolas. 1996. 'Governing "advanced" liberal democracies.' In Andrew Barry, Thomas Osborne and Nikolas Rose (eds.), *Foucault and Political Reason: Liberalism, neo-liberalism and rationalities of government*, pp. 37–64. Chicago, IL: University of Chicago Press.
Sabloff, Paula L. W. 2001. *Modern Mongolia: Reclaiming Genghis Khan*. Philadelphia: University of Pennsylvania Museum of Archaeology and Anthropology.
Schmitt, Carl. 2008. *The Concept of the Political*. Expanded edn. Chicago, IL and London: University of Chicago Press.
Scott, Michael W. 2013. 'The anthropology of ontology (religious science?).' *Journal of the Royal Anthropological Institute* 19, no. 4: 859–72. https://doi.org/10.1111/1467-9655.12067.
Simpson, Audra. 2014. *Mohawk Interruptus: Political life across the borders of settler states*. Durham, NC: Duke University Press.
Strathern, Marilyn. 1988. *The Gender of the Gift: Problems with women and problems with society in Melanesia*. Berkeley and Los Angeles: University of California Press.
Strathern, Marilyn. 2005. *Partial Connections*. Updated edn. Walnut Creek, CA: AltaMira Press.
TallBear, Kim. 2013. *Native American DNA: Tribal belonging and the false promise of genetic science*. Minneapolis: University of Minnesota Press.
Taussig, Michael. 1992. *The Nervous System*. London and New York: Routledge.
Viveiros de Castro, Eduardo. 2004. 'Perspectival anthropology and the method of controlled equivocation.' *Tipiti: Journal of the Society for the Anthropology of Lowland South America* 2, no. 1: art. 1.
Viveiros de Castro, Eduardo. 2012. *Cosmological Perspectivism in Amazonia and Elsewhere* (HAU Masterclass Series, 1). Manchester: HAU Network of Ethnographic Theory.
Wagner, Roy. 1981. *The Invention of Culture*. 2nd edn. Chicago, IL: University of Chicago Press.
Wagner, Roy. 1986. *Symbols that Stand for Themselves*. Chicago, IL: University of Chicago Press.
Žižek, Slavoj. 1999. *The Ticklish Subject: The absent centre of political ontology*. London: Verso.

3
The making of an unused map: moments of incommensurability

This chapter focuses on a moment of incommensurability between the two social projects, when information about the Surbiton/Seething landscape, provided by locals, was rejected from the ASP's map. This moment of data refusal was, in a Strathernian sense, an ethnographic moment, the point at which I needed to understand what was happening. Throughout the fieldwork period I would frequently work with the ASP at the UCL campus in central London and then travel to the suburb, around 45 minutes away, for an evening of community meetings. As I moved between these two distinct, but linked, sites, I developed an understanding of their respective knowledge economies, and how they could have such different understandings of the same landscape, namely Surbiton. The tensions between these social projects became manifest and comprehensible via the technology that connects them, the map.

For the ASP, rejecting Seething information from the map was necessary to maintain the overall coherence of data, particularly across other scales and communities. For the Seethingers the assertion of 'facts' was part of a mechanism to assert one's authority over the narration and control of place, and, as I will argue, their status as citizens. This chapter will explore the political value of 'coherence' in the context of late liberalism, considering the map as emblematic tool of late liberal governance. It does so as part of a wider reflection on the designation of knowledge as legitimate or otherwise, and the importance of such an epistemological manoeuvre to the support of hegemonic power. The chapter starts by outlining the wider ideological and technological context of the use of public-participation mapping and the idea of 'active citizenship' as tools and citizenship positions of late liberalism.

Active citizenship in the suburbs

'Active citizenship' is a buzzword used frequently in legislation and policy discourse that relates to individuals who engage in public life, particularly at the local level. The term can be found throughout local and national government policy briefs. The so-called 'active citizenship agenda' (Raco 2007), which has taken various forms under successive governments, aims to create and mobilise communities and citizens through local volunteering, democratic participation and strong social networks at the neighbourhood level, encouraging community self-help (Seyfang 2003). The 'active citizenship agenda' and the wider move to localism were understood as a new settlement between the government, communities and individuals. The 'New Labour' government sought to rebalance economic and political power by re-establishing the rights and duties of citizens (Woodcraft 2019). The duty of citizens was further foregrounded in David Cameron's 2010 election manifesto pledge to kickstart a so-called 'Big Society' based on volunteerism and ground-up community organising in areas previously controlled by the state. Described as a post-welfare political ideology (McGuirk and Dowling 2011), active citizenship is intended to encourage citizens to take greater responsibility for their own welfare and that of their communities on the grounds that 'more developed communities and communities with more capacity are safer and healthier places to live' (Kelly, Caputo & Jamieson 2005:308).

The actions and motivations of the ASP and the Seethingers/locals are reflective of wider political shifts in the ways citizens and the state have related to each other in the UK over the past 20 years. Localism as a political agenda asserts that services are delivered best when government is decentralised and when individuals and communities take responsibility for the management of the local area. Policies of localism, which were enacted by the Localism Act of 2011 (Department for Communities and Local Governent 2010), were heralded as being more democratic in nature, in that they increased citizens' direct influence on decision making. This political ideology gave form and intent to the actions of both the ASP and the Seethingers/locals.

In 2003 the New Labour government launched the Sustainable Communities Plan, which formed part of a wider urban renewal agenda in the UK (Raco 2007). Reordering the relation between citizens and the state, the policy shift was a rejection of both Thatcherist neoliberal individualism and old Labour's understanding of the welfare state (McGuirk and Dowling 2011). New Labour moved away from faith in the efficacy of the big state and towards the idea that empowered local communities could not only run their neighbourhoods more effectively but also act as vehicles of freedom and self-betterment. 'Social capital' was key to the power of this reinvented version of community; it was the fuel that would drive the moral restoration of society (Woodcraft 2019). The term 'social capital' gained prominence through influential urban theorists such as Jane Jacobs ([1961] 2016) and Robert Putnam (2000); it refers to the connections amongst individuals and social networks that work within an economy of reciprocity, trust and mutual support. The basic premise is that 'interaction between people builds communities, shared values and virtues, behavioural and social norms and a social fabric in which a society and an economy can function more effectively' (Westwood 2011:692). A policy that foregrounds social capital plays firmly into the ideals of greater levels of individual autonomy and accountability that neoliberal forms of governance desire (Baron 2004). Localism was attractive to communities and to the Tony Blair and David Cameron governments (spanning the years from 1997 to 2016) and those that followed as a way to counter the widely perceived fragmentation of urban life, and rehabilitate the concept of 'society' after Thatcher denied its existence (Imrie and Raco 2003; Putnam 2000).

Ade Kearns (2003) notes that in what is known as 'third way' politics, the roles of the state and the market are combined. The private, voluntary and community sectors are used to deliver services and partnerships. New working relations are created between the state, businesses, and the voluntary and public sectors. Here, not only do the responsibilities of the state change, but so do those of the citizen. 'Third way' or stakeholder politics places a much stronger emphasis upon the 'responsible and responsive individual – the notion of a developmental self, and the idea that through help and education people can improve' (Richards and Smith 2002:237). The Department for Communities and Local Government (2010:7) argued that localism allowed communities to 'bid for the ownership and management of community assets', and reformed the planning system to enable local communities to shape their own locales. Critics argued that such policies of participation and inclusion are disingenuous, since they are given on terms dictated by those outside the community (Diamond 2001:277) and, as Brown (2015) argues, such policies fail to offer genuine openness.

This political ideological agenda informs the actions of the ASP and the Seethingers/locals. It was in this context that members of the community in Surbiton had, since at least 2009, been active in organising community events. They had established two community interest companies (CICs), 'the Community Brain'[1] in 2010 and the Friends of Seething Wells (FoSWA) in 2012. CICs emerged following the Audit, Investigations and Community Enterprise Act 2004.[2] They are often run by volunteers and make no profit. Their primary concern is the community, and they aim to use business solutions and structures to deliver a public good. The Community Brain was established in order to foster, in their words, 'community resilience'. 'Resilience' was seen to be needed to protect the community against the perceived threats of modern life, such as the loss of history, ecology and community spirit, unchecked urban development and the increased isolation of individuals. On its website, the Community Brain stated that its objectives were:

> to carry on activities which benefit the community[,] in particular anyone who believes they are outside of a perceived, meaningful community. This could be people isolated by culture, geography, poverty, disability or simply a lack of connection with the people around them.[3]

The Community Brain gave structure and form to the activities of the wider community. It emerged out of, and helped organise, the regular Seething parades, festivals and associated events. Whilst they state that the events have no explicit political purpose, as I will show in Chapter 5 they serve to foster an economy of trust and familiarity that lay the foundations for community political action elsewhere. Members of the community get to know each other, and share skills, stories and concerns about the local area. This network can then be mobilised effectively in more explicitly political forms, such as in the campaign to save the water filtration site, led by the Friends of Seething Wells (see Chapter 7). In the next section I will outline how the pervasive ideology of localism informed the design of the ASP's map through the ideals of local inclusion and citizen participation but did so in a manner that was incommensurable with those same ideals in the Seething community. Before getting to the map, I will outline the policy-facing role of the ASP and detail how the map was envisaged within the project.

The Adaptable Suburbs Project

Adaptable Suburbs was a four-year project, based at UCL's Bartlett School of Architecture. It aimed to develop 'an understanding of the workings of small scale, "below the radar" economic and social suburban activities'.[4] The ASP's 'Case for Support' (CFS) document,[5] instrumental in securing funding from the UK's Engineering and Physical Sciences Research Council (EPSRC), claimed that insufficient policy attention had been given to London's suburbs. In this document, they said the ASP would seek to develop 'an integrated theory of how town centres evolve by developing knowledge on urban sustainability, patterns of social and economic behaviour and how places adapt and change over time'. Further, it aimed to develop an '[u]nderstanding [of] how suburban space fits within urban complex spatial systems: ... to improve our understanding of the relationship between individual actions, small and large-scale spatial order and change and emergent morphological changes' through measuring 'the impact of small-scale activities on the built environment'.

The ASP, as a social project, is informed by the history and moral politics of city planning. The rise of the role of the state, and its administrative and bureaucratic machinery, in managing, policing and designing urban environments goes hand in hand with the rise of modern governance (see Rabinow 1989). The ASP is an extension of this machinery. The stated aim to develop 'integrated' knowledge sets, by combining data that had not previously been combined, would allow value to be seen where it was once unseeable (see Chapter 4). A holistic approach was taken so that changes to the material conditions of the city at one location, such as a road being built, could be measured in terms of the effect on the workings of other parts of the city.

The ASP relied heavily on a 'space syntax' methodology which is based on the work of Bill Hillier and Julienne Hanson (Hillier & Hanson 1984). Founded on structuralist logic (influenced by the work of anthropologist Claude Lévi-Strauss), this method assumes that a 'morphic language' of the built environment emerges from culturally delimited 'generative rules'. Hillier and Hanson say that these rules can be determined through syntax analysis, and that they can and should inform planning policies, producing 'better' design. In short, for Hillier and Hanson, the form of the built environment emerges in line with social rules. For example, a village in France has a specific built form which reflects the social rules that govern the community. The social rules of a village in England or Germany differ from those of this French village, and this is why places look different. Once these social rules are understood, analysis can determine how material changes within one part of the built environment (understood as an integrated system) generate changes in other parts. I will go into more details of the specifics of this method in Chapter 4. The point here is that the ASP aimed to fill a gap in knowledge about the workings of London as a system through a detailed analysis of its suburban areas. The ASP contributed to a regulatory planning policy framework by generating knowledge of how material changes on a micro-scale maintain or change the whole. The ASP fits neatly into state planning apparatus; it shares its aims and methods.

The ASP sought to make urban management processes more efficient, which would help suburbs 'realise their untapped potential'.[6] The ASP had an advisory board and 'letters of support' from a number of governmental organisations, think tanks and policy groups, including Centre for Cities, the Greater London Authority, English Heritage, the Outer London Commission and Arup. These organisations would both learn from the ASP's findings and help guide the ASP through the research process through annual feedback reports and meetings. The ASP asserted that its study was justified because it aimed to comprehend aspects of the built environment which had previously always been studied in isolation, namely the relations between different areas of London and those between different aspects of the built environment, such as building shape and use (see Chapter 4).

At the core of the project is a desire to help certain decision makers ('local planning bodies, government agencies, civic society and the "Third Sector"'; CFS) make places *better*, at a variety of scales. This requires understanding (based on robust data) of the relations and activities that enable places to be sustainable and adaptable to economic changes. The ASP's emphasis on 'realising untapped potential' of the built environment through its analysis was firmly linked to the value of a strong local business economy. I have outlined how the ASP's motivations and intentions extend those of the state by merit of its contribution to policy development. I will examine how the citizen relates to state planning policy in Chapter 7, but here I examine how the state engages the citizen, via the participatory ideals of the ASP in the form of the online map.

The ASP was a continuation of an older project – 'Towards Successful Suburban Town Centres' – that pre-dated my involvement. This project laid the groundwork for an understanding of the suburbs as centres of economic activity.[7] The ASP used the data gathered by that project (such as the extent of the business activity in an area) and overlaid further sets of data, such as foot traffic. This layering of data sets was seen as the key to revealing relationships between built form, business activity and social and economic life in the suburbs. A 'social layer' of data was to be gathered through a 'web-based profiler of spatially-related socio-economic data' or, more simply, the 'Community Map' (CFS). The Case for Support document only mentions this map briefly, as a tool to develop understanding of 'the way in which people use their area'. This data could be layered over architectural and historical data to reveal hidden value. But the map needed citizens to be active and engage with it, which is where I, as an anthropologist employed to 'roll out' the map, came in.

The Community Map

The map (see Figure 1.1) was not prominent in the project's Case for Support, and it never did emerge as a key topic in team meetings held over the course of the project. As I started my work, I searched the ASP's 'research task record', which outlined the primary research objectives and aims of the project and hinted that the map was needed to help 'understand the built landscape as a social place, to reveal *meaning, values, symbols*' (CFS; emphasis added). My role on the project, as the anthropologist, was to supplement the architectural data with a collection of local testimonies about the area and high street as a 'social place'. My studentship description[8] stated:

> The ethnographic basis of the study will be provided by the systematic examination of local history sources (in both text, pictures and representative objects) and the assembly of an oral history archive in which the 'remembered' history of the suburb is recorded. It will also include work on an 'auto-ethnographical' project, in which local inhabitants will be asked to report and tag their local activities and networks on the project website. It is intended that the findings of the PhD research will help inform the research project's overall aim of understanding processes of socio-economic adaptation in smaller settlements.

The ASP hoped that 'layering' ethnographic information over an architectural analysis would reveal the social 'meanings, values, symbols' of the built environment, allowing planners to understand how they might be utilised. The map was also a tool for democratising the project, since it was the means by which local voices would be included in urban policy making. The map was conceived in a mode of democratic participation that echoes Jürgen Habermas's ideal speech situation (1990:40), in that the map was imagined to be an arena in which different voices could be heard.

The description of the map as 'auto-ethnographic' implied that map users would be able to select what information was important to them to share on their own terms. In other words, they would be writing about themselves, as they liked, keeping 'the subject (knower) and object (that which is being examined) in simultaneous view' (Schwandt 2007:16). This capacity to describe the landscape of the suburb in local terms and communicate this to urban planners was to be actively enabled by the map. The ASP hoped that such maps would, in the future, be widely used as a method of including people in local decision making. The ASP used an associated UCL company, Mapping for Change, to design and maintain the map. Mapping for Change outlined the ideals of such maps on its website: 'The concept behind community mapping is to move away from "top-down" mapping that so often fails to reflect the needs of people'.[9]

This 'bottom-up' approach is fuelled by a commitment to consensus-based participatory democracy. The map belongs to a technological family of maps called public participation geographic information systems (PPGIS). These maps display information in an interactive way and are written and used by the public. The Community Map has its origins in the wider field of geo-engineering and the development of geographic information systems (GIS) and information and communications technologies (ICTs). The ASP incorporated GIS not only as a way of representing data but as a way of increasing participation and sharing information between experts working on state policy and citizens of that state. These tools were designed to contribute to the democratisation of knowledge, particularly that gathered by policy-facing research. This was appropriate and desirable since the ideals of democracy and inclusion were embedded in the mission of the ASP. An overview of the emergence of PPGIS helps us understand the relationship between technologies and the democratic ideals they seek to reflect and enact. The enactment is particularly interesting, since the practice of democracy reveals, as I will discuss, the paradox of democracy, namely that voices are always necessarily excluded from decision making, however democratic it aspires to be. PPGIS are no exception – they are imperfect democratic tools.

PPGIS

Public participation geographic information systems aim to bring the practice of GIS mapping to the local level to facilitate inclusive knowledge practices. The use of PPGIS has been widely discussed in development and planning literatures, particularly in regard to their promise to facilitate wider participation and inclusion.

In the 1980s a focus on participation grew as the failures of development initiatives designed by 'outsiders' became apparent. The development of participatory appraisal methods transformed international development initiatives. The contributions of indigenous knowledges to development, planning and interventions in land use were sought more often (Agrawal & Gibson 1999; Brosius et al. 1998). New technologies emerged that could help involve local people in natural resource management and reorient policy processes from 'top-down' to 'bottom-up' (Conquest 2013). Although participation was the 'new orthodoxy' (Henkel & Stirrat 2001:168) of the 1990s, by the late 2000s a more critical review of ICTs was emerging. Parfitt (2004) claimed that the idea of participation had become a dogma without meaning, a means to an end: to continue imposing outsider-conceived objectives on local people.

Critics focused on how power relations permeated participatory techniques. They interrogated categories of information that had remained unexamined until that point and reflected on the ways knowledge was framed and delimited in mapping processes. They questioned various values inherent in prevailing cartographic paradigms, such as notions of territory, Euclidian space and the scales of assessment, and began to think about maps in a reflexive manner (see Kapoor 2002). Cooke and Kothari (2001) argue that previous approaches to participation had misunderstood power, obscured its dynamics, and in many cases actively depoliticised the development process. They call this the 'tyranny' of participation, arguing that such approaches operate to deliver the same top-down, outsider-driven initiatives as before, but in a manner designed to reduce local opposition and create an appearance of greater democracy (see Hildyard et al. 2001). For these critics, participatory projects reinforce the interests of the powerful by bringing marginalised populations within the reach of centralised state control and the market. Williams summarises: 'If development is ... an "anti-politics machine" (Ferguson 1994) ... participation provides a remarkably efficient means of greasing its wheels' (Williams 2004:557).

Chantal Mouffe refers to this 'anti-politics machine' when she describes the gap between ideal and actual radical democracy. For Mouffe, technocratic solutions, such as the PPGIS map, to the problem of creating an ideal speech situation in consensus-based democracies inevitably force the commensuration of values into a single register. This eliminates ideological diversity, subsuming alternative perspectives into a hegemonic whole. She states:

> The cosmopolitan project is therefore bound to deny the hegemonic dimension of politics. In fact several cosmopolitan theorists explicitly state that their aim is to envisage a politics 'beyond

> hegemony'. Such an approach overlooks the fact that since power relations are constitutive of the social, every order is *by necessity* a hegemonic order.
>
> (Mouffe 2005:106; italics original)

A community map manifests the epistemological conundrum at the heart of this apparently post-hegemonic cosmopolitanism. By professing they can represent all points of view on equal terms, map makers promise they can, via technocratic means, host the ideal democratic forum. However, the authors of the map aggressively invalidate some types of knowledge, delimiting the views that the map is able to represent. When this is raised as an issue, the supposed technical development of the map maintains the promise of a 'democracy to come'. This delimitation is the means by which a hegemonic order of knowledge is fashioned. Map makers, through framing what is and is not legitimate, 'perform territory' with 'ontological authority' (Perkins 2004; Kitchin et al. 2009). As Mitchell states, 'all maps, like all other historically constructed images, do not provide a transparent window on the world. Rather they are signs that present "a deceptive appearance of naturalness and transparence concealing an opaque, distorting, arbitrary mechanism of representation, a process of ideological mystification["]' (Mitchell 1986:8; see also O'Mahony 2014).

Some optimistic scholars have suggested that appropriately designed digital mapping technologies can present a 'third space' (Turnbull & Chambers 2014:167) or a 'third translating domain' (Verran & Christie 2014:66) where disparate knowledges can come together to be 'worked together', on even terms, without being subjugated to a single, technologically mediated, Western tradition. The question of *who* participates in mapping projects here shifts to *how* people participate in such projects. New technologies (particularly Web 2.0 and 3.0) promise to have the capacity to engage with alternative forms of knowledge production. Rather than just visualising alternative forms of knowledge, such technologies seek to involve others in the design of the technological platform itself (see Haklay et al. 2008; Leach et al. 2008; Kleine & Unwin 2009; Tacchi 2012; Haklay 2013). Within such projects there is a recognition that there is no 'one size fits all' solution, and each iteration of a PPGIS technology is tailored to a specific project (see Jeevendrampillai with Conquest 2021). That is, design is seen as contingent and from somewhere, rather than promising neutrality. However, within each PPGIS project commensality is ultimately required, so that data can remain coherent across the different users of that map. In reality it was neither practical nor doable to build a 'third space' where the ASP and the

Seethingers can both display knowledge about the suburban landscape on the same platform. The two groups take radically different epistemological approaches to knowing place. As Mouffe demonstrates, exclusions are necessary in the building of a clear way of knowing. Analytical attention to the ASP's map reveals the banal, almost unnoticeable gestures that constitute undemocratic exclusions, exclusions which shield their nature as ideological acts in the name of epistemological clarity.

Seethingers could only add their data to the ASP map if they either 'outed' their story as 'not really fact', or if the ASP categorised it as 'alternative facts'. In the end, neither happened. The Seethingers largely ignored the ASP map and made their own maps instead. However, I argue that the map did not fail but rather was put to work in a different way. The ASP understood that their ethical commitment to participatory knowledge production was uncompromised, and that the inhospitality of the map to local knowledge could and would be resolved through future changes to the map's design (which would come with the next round of funding). I question the integrity of this assertion (which I believe was made in good faith). I argue that this deferral demonstrates how points of view can be excluded through the use of the future. That act of tensing, placing a solution into the future (a 'democracy to come'), allowed both the ASP and the Seethingers to maintain themselves as separate projects which could exist alongside each other without having to confront the epistemological aporia between them, that is, incommensurate (or even mutually aggressive) modes of knowing and narrating place. However, as I and all parties found, such a refusal to engage has limits with regard to material reality. Competing narratives confronted each other once again at the planning meeting about the fate of the water filtration site (see Chapter 7).

The moment

The ethnographic moment I seek to interrogate was constituted by failed communication. A series of disjointed conversations, mistranslations and avoidances generated a silent and largely unacknowledged gap between the understanding of the meanings and value of place as expressed by the ASP on one side and the Seethingers on the other. The Community Map was accessible via the project website, and was a basic Google application program interface (API), commonly known as a Google map, with a specifically designed 'wrap', a tailored design specific to the ASP. Each of the ASP's four field sites had its own 'mini-site' that could be tailored to the community's needs as the project developed. To share information, a user (imagined as a local community member of one of the suburbs) would register an account using their email address and a password. Once this had been moderated by Mapping for Change, the user could log in, upload text, photo or video and attach this information to a point on the map. The user could assign a pre-designated category to their data. Initially the categories of information – 'historical fact', 'cycling and transport', 'green space' and so on – were designed by the ASP, but they were flexible. There was an expectation that they would change following a period of consultation (i.e. my fieldwork) with the communities. It was hoped that the community would eventually take over the moderation of the map and that it would be a widely used forum for discussing and displaying oral histories of the area; the ASP envisioned it would become a living, evolving user-managed archive.

I introduced the map to around 40 or more Seethingers at a Free University of Seething (FUS) lecture a few months into my fieldwork. I had asked a few of my most familiar interlocutors to test the usability of the site and to try adding a piece of information. After some time had passed, I assumed that enthusiasm for the map was low: no new information had appeared (apart the test points I had added myself). However, when I asked my informants if they had added information, Steve said that he had submitted a point about the Mount of Seething, but that the point hadn't appeared on the map. He assumed I hadn't moderated, and approved, the post yet. Steve was one of the most prominent Seethingers and had been very interested in the ways in which the map might be able to help the community at large. He had, in the past, and still a little now, worked closely with the local council on community engagement.

I promised Steve I would find out why the post hadn't yet appeared on the map. I returned to UCL and made an appointment to speak with Flo, the co-director of Mapping for Change. Flo was not part of the ASP but had, along with two of the ASP co-investigators, developed the project's maps and was responsible for overseeing its moderation and development. An experienced map designer, she would be working with Mapping for Change to ensure that community maps would be developed in the future. Along with the ASP maps she was working with other university projects on maps that tracked forestry in the Congo basin, air quality in London, noise pollution around airports, and much more. In our meeting Flo explained that the post did not pass moderation because it was entered under the label 'historical fact', but it was not – according to her understanding of the term – historical fact. For her, the Mount of Seething was a myth. Flo was vaguely familiar with the Seething stories, parades and festivals. We shared a workspace and although she was usually very busy we had 'water cooler' moments where we could talk about our work informally. Flo seemed to enjoy the tales of how Seethingers played with local history, invented stories and created spectacular events. But, for her, the information added to the map was not fact. Flo expressed her concern that people from other areas, other users of community maps, would not be sufficiently socialised into the heritage and history of Seething and would therefore be unable to distinguish 'fact' from 'fiction'. Flo offered to create an extra 'layer' on which information could be added with the label 'myths and legends', but this was refused by the Seethingers. They had a different understanding of 'facts'.

Seething facts

As outlined in Box 1.1, the Seething events largely revolved around an ethos of inclusivity that is represented and promoted through the story of Lefi Ganderson, the goat boy of Mount Seething. Lefi is the icon of difference for the community, and indeed his name stems from his left-handedness, a marker of his difference. Whilst the Seething group has been active (from around 2009) the Seethingers have developed a number of stories that all relate to the local history and landscape of Surbiton. All these stories are designed to support particular morals (in a manner similar to children's stories): they feature characters learning to be kind and peaceful, to share with others and to be in touch with their local community and feel connected to place.

For example, 'The tale of the last sardine' tells of a child who is visited by a fish as she stares into the dirty, polluted and overfished local river. The fish tells her to find the old fisherman who used to care for the river. After becoming disenchanted with people who did not care for the river, he had become a recluse. When she finds him, the girl's fresh perspective, optimism, hope and childish innocence persuade him to come and help clean the river. Soon the people realise that they need to care for the river and eventually it becomes clean and once again full of fish. This story is celebrated with a parade that starts on the bank of the River Thames on the west side of the suburb. People walk behind a catch of 'Seething freshwater sardines' from the river to a local park, where people share fish sandwiches (see Chapter 5).

'The king's soup' is a tale of a king who was mean but learnt to be good. He was shown kindness by an old lady who helped him when he fell

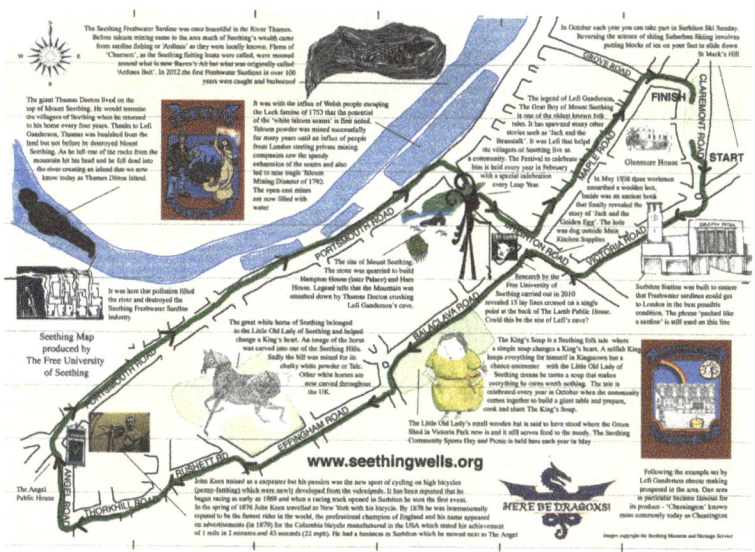

Figure 3.1 A map to show the stories of Seething (with cycle route). Thames Ditton Island is at the upper left of the image. Courtesy of Seethingers, 2014.

from his horse and became lost in a forest. The Seethingers hold a festival, again in a park, where people make a giant pot of soup and share it out. These stories play with the local landscape and history. For example, the local river island, Thames Ditton Island, features in the story of Lefi as the place where the giant fell. So Seethingers tell people that Thames Ditton gets its name from Thamas Deeton the giant, not the other way round.

These stories reference the local landscape (see Figure 3.1). So, when Steve was asked to add information to the map it was no surprise that he added a point of information about the location of the local community pub that stated that the pub was the site of Mount Seething. The mountain had 'long been destroyed by the giant' but Seethingers assert as 'fact' that it was once there.

'Fact' is a term Seethingers actively play with in order to bring people into the community. As outlined in the Introduction, the Seethingers aim to include all people in the community; all may belong. This is a challenge in an area that is often considered a commuter town to London. As such, its population is largely composed of busy professionals. Some people have long historical family connections to the area, but many do not. Seethingers understood that knowledge of the local area and long family connections can assign authority to narrate and speak on behalf of a place. Seethingers sought to destabilise claims to authority and expertise through a different understanding of historiography. One Seethinger outlined to me, and I paraphrase, that 'if history is made up then nobody can be an expert'. Such a perspective explains the value of stupid stories not based in 'true fact': anyone can fashion them, and so they constitute a mechanism for inclusion on an egalitarian footing. Whilst telling stupid stories does not require existing knowledge, it does require a commitment to play (see Chapter 5). When confronted with a Seething fact from the stories, say, how Thames Ditton Island came to be, or that the area used to be home to a 'freshwater sardine factory', one is presented with a choice. Does one choose to ignore the story, sticking only to what one believes to be historical fact, or does one accept the story, maybe even add a 'fact' of one's own? This moment invites an ethical commitment to the productive capacities of the Seething 'state of mind' (see Figure 3.2) and the mechanisms of play and being 'stupid'. Through this process, one takes on the ethical substance of Seething, its moral commitment to others in the community, to making a place better and to developing a community of familiarity and trust.

Seethingers perform a semiotic manoeuvre with regard to the nature of a fact. They *obviate* the conventional meaning of a fact. I use the term obviation in a Wagnerian sense. Roy Wagner finds that 'meaning does not float free' (1979:x) but is grounded in the conventions of a culture. Social processes of obviation enable new meanings to emerge.

Figure 3.2 'I live in Seething. It's a state of mind' t-shirt featuring the Mount of Seething. Author's own, 2014.

Wagner explains: 'Obviation is the effect of supplanting a conventional semiotic relation with an innovative and self-contained relation; it is the definitive paradigm of semiotic transformation' (31). For Wagner, acts of differentiation often take the form of improvisations and involve putting an unconventional element in place of one that one might expect. Thus the 'novel expression ... intentionally "deconventionalizes" the conventional (and unintentionally conventionalizes the unconventional): a new meaning has been formed (and an old meaning has been extended). The novel expression both amplifies and controverts the significance of the convention upon which it innovates' (31)

The Seethingers obviate 'fact' and make it work in new ways. Rather than generate authority through knowledge and expertise, Seething facts (that is, facts that have undergone a transformation in meaning and purpose by means of obviation) generate egalitarian social relations.

The obviation of conventional meaning is the performative essence of parafiction. As Lambert-Beatty writes, parafictions 'intervene in what Jacques Rancière calls the distribution of the sensible: the system of inclusions and exclusions that determine what can be sensed; the literally common sense about what can be said, thought, seen, felt, and who can say, think, see, and feel it'. Hence, 'a new distribution of the sensible has, at least temporarily, been brought into being' (2009:64). Seething stories oscillate between fact and fiction, maintaining deliberate fluidity and openness. The stories often stretch conventional meanings and relations of what is a fact. In their own words, they deploy 'stupidity': a distinct and deliberate lack of sense that opens up new spaces of meaning and relating to people and place. People are brought into the community through this mechanism of playing and storytelling. No one person can hold the authority over narrative in the parafictional mode; they demand a collaborative approach to making knowledge.

For Mount Seething to be rejected as 'not fact' was simply not permissible according to Seethingers. They had gone to great efforts to promote the 'fact' that Mount Seething had been there and had been destroyed. In early 2010 the 'British Society of Antiquarians and Archaeologists'[10] conducted an archaeological dig at the site where Mount Seething once stood. The site was found using archival evidence and oral history and through following 'an uncanny convergence of over 15 ley lines' that met at the back of the local community pub. The dig was widely advertised as a family day, and children, parents and different members of the community came to the pub to dig in the garden. Throughout the day various characters, including ministers from the 'Department of Safety and Research' and 'archaeological experts' 'dropped in' to the pub as Seething TV (this was Steve filming on his mobile phone to upload the event to YouTube later) filmed the dig. The dig was overseen by Anton from the 'famed cable TV programme on ancient burial mounds "Dead Boring"'. Excavations by young archaeologists and their parents found 'rare compressed flint, similar to that found at Stonehenge', bringing these 'sites of significant interest' into alignment. They also found a key in the shape of Lefi, a stirrup-shaped piece of metal possibly from the white horse of Seething, and many other 'artefacts'. Experts 'with the equipment' gathered evidence whilst dressed in white coats, masks and holding readers that looked and sounded like Geiger counters. They assured the young archaeologists it was safe to dig. The dig used full archaeological methods of labelled pieces, square trenches, scientists and explorers. Scientific method, the supervision of 'scientists' (one Seethinger just happened to be a professional archaeologist) and the testimonies of subject specialists on ley lines, archaeology and exploration ensured the work and methods met the standard of the British Society of Antiquarians and Archaeologists (BSAA).[11] After the dig, the location and heritage of Mount Seething were well established as 'fact' via the proper performative procedures of science and research. The history is well known throughout the community, and whenever the location of Mount Seething is alluded to in a conversation other Seethingers will interject (regardless of whether they were part of the original conversation) and shout 'FACT' at the end of a statement.

It may not come as a surprise that lively conversation ensued amongst the Seethingers when I reported that everything apart from 'historical facts' would be excluded from the ASP map. Sitting in the local pub on a weekday lunchtime, the ASP research assistant, Rich, and I met a couple of the Seethingers who had added the information to the map. Rich was heavily involved in the development of the map and worked closely with Flo on behalf of the ASP to ensure the map data would be developed and be commensurate with the other architectural data layers of the ASP.

The Seethingers Leon and Steve were key interlocutors and had been designated 'community champions' by the ASP. This meant they were given some travel expenses to come into UCL and look at the development of the maps and gain a greater understanding of the project. Through this they had both become very interested in the mapping process. We met in the pub which Leon owned. He had taken over control of the pub with the help of the community. Most Seething meetings happened there and the space, particularly the garden, was used for craft days, storage, meetings and much more. We sat at a quiet table with some food Leon provided from his pub. The atmosphere was friendly, relaxed and positive. Rich opened the conversation fully aware that the Seethingers and the ASP have different ideas of what can be added to the map, and arrived with possible solutions that will ensure the community's needs can be met.

Rich: Just as we have made a Surbiton mini-site we can actually make you a mini-site that is called Surbiton historic walk … Now we have a fine line with – to tread [as] regards what goes on this, if we are working within this platform … and I don't want to open a can of worms here but the head of Community Maps, the head of Mapping for Change, is not too keen on the idea of putting in, as she put it, 'false histories'. … I really don't want to get into this, I'm not behind any of this, I think technology should be there for the people and however they want to use it. This is more a political thing, this is why we have talked about a more disconnected option where people can go out and collect factual information and we can draw a link between the two. We can make a mini-site called Seething, as Seething is not a real place …

Table: Errrmmmmm …

Rich: (quickly interjects and throws his hands up): Don't kill the messenger …

Steve: (places his hand on the table and leans back and slowly but assuredly interjects): No. The nice thing is not to be precious about any of it. It's a fascinating idea that from her perspective that if you were in Nottingham and you wrote 'home of Robin Hood' then that would have to be dismissed because there is no actual proof to say that's true or not. Which I bet she wouldn't, she would say that's absolutely right as there is enough folk and legend around it to make that 'a truth'. So it's at what point does someone figure out what is a truth? When you lay it over the business of architectural spaces etc. … then legend and myth are massive influences and if you miss that off then you'll have no concept of what an area is about.

Leon: If she is precious about this legend and myth then let's just use a separate platform.

The conversation explored what a fact was and could be. The Seethingers were interested in making the map work but wished to maintain their own practices of narrating place. Rich and Leon talked about other possible technologies to achieve the aim of sharing stories in keeping with the 'spirit of Seething', including using different platforms, apps, augmented realities, Bluetooth technologies and other emerging ICTs. But, in the end, we lacked the funding, the resources and the will to pursue these avenues of interest.

Rich, working to advance the ASP, focused the conversation on the PPGIS platform and suggested that information about Surbiton and Seething stories be separated. However, this was dismissed by Seethingers as it defeats the purpose of their stories in the first instance. I was also not keen on a separation, as such a move to determine what a 'fact' is moves away from the 'auto-ethnographic' ideals of the map, whereby users present information on their own terms. Leaving the Free University of Seething campus and returning to UCL, Rich and I talked through altering the PPGIS to meet the community's needs. We were unable to find a way for Mapping for Change to create a site which can avoid the concerns over 'misinformation' and at the same time meet the community's need to tell Seething stories. Over the course of the project the ASP seemed little concerned with the continued silence of the map. The subject rarely, if ever, came up in meetings or annual reviews. In discussions over the possible development of the map I was told there was neither the money nor the time to develop the platform within the ASP and that the designer did not 'realise the degree to which anthropologists spent time in the field with participants'. There was a failure to anticipate, recognise, or respond in a serious way to the alternative 'meanings, values, symbols' that ethnographic engagement might present to the ASP. There was little momentum to accommodate alterity in the map as this would not be translatable into national policy. Project managers attributed the silence of the map not to their insistence on commensurable data but rather to a lack of usability and community training, issues which would improve with time and money. There were other attempts to reinvent the map in other forms (such as the walks outlined in Chapter 6), but by the end of the fieldwork period the map remained little used. However, the map was not seen as a failure. It was seen as a flawed work in progress which would, with time and technological endeavour, be perfected. Thus this technology promises 'democracy to come'; rather than resolve problems, it continually defers the realisation of democracy, masking the inextricable paradox at its heart.

Conclusions: being on the threshold

This chapter has taken a careful look at a largely unused map. This unused map represents, I have argued, a point of incommensurability between two projects, and the resulting exclusion of one project's contribution to the understanding of a place. These exclusions represent the hard-to-see machinations of hegemonic power, and how orders of legitimate knowledge are produced. Whilst the ASP's map did not accomplish its stated aims, the map was not a failure. Carroll et al. outline how failure functions as a moral accusation that arises when 'objectification ceases to adhere' (2017:2). That is to say, failure is contingent, and not inherent in material or technical objects such as the map. Objects, materials, technical assemblages exist within a social nexus of expectation. Failure, then, is an accusation that a thing does something other than what one expects of it. In the case of the map, it was not a success but nor was it a failure from the point of view of the ASP. Whilst unused, it helped the ASP to promise 'democracy to come'; it supported the ideal of a future participatory democracy. For the ASP, the non-use of the map was due to a technical problem rather than a systemic one related to any central flaw in the democratic project. Therefore the map supported, rather than threatened, the ideals of late liberal democracy (i.e., decentralised governance, which is participatory and inclusive). For the Seethingers the map didn't fail, as it wasn't their map. They gave it a go and moved on. Their priorities were being 'stupid' and playing, and they refused to let these be compromised. They put their energy elsewhere. Their activities enabled them to build community and active citizenship (see Chapter 5). Both the ASP and the Seethingers, through the map and the Seething events, showed their commitment to their own versions of active citizenship and localism. The ASP had made efforts to develop tools to include people, and the Seethingers/locals had made efforts to participate. However, in the end, Seething facts (parafictions which produce obviations in the authority of knowledge) were incommensurable with the ASP's ideals (of clarity and translatability of information across the scales). The 'meanings, values, symbols' of the socio-material landscape could not be translated into a common metric. This incommensurability is illuminating. Espeland and Stevens note that:

> Commensuration can change our relations to what we value and alter how we invest in things and people. Commensuration makes the world more predictable, but at what cost? For Aristotle, a price too high [as it eliminates passion]; for Plato, an essential sacrifice [to the moral need of a democratic project]. The homogeneity commensuration produces simultaneously diminishes risk and threatens the intensity and integrity of what we value.
> (1998:319)

Both projects remained in control of their exclusions and inclusions. This is a way of remaining sovereign. But, since they both work to influence the use and form of the suburban built environment, they cannot retain their sovereign power. Further to the constant policing of the forms of knowledge that are considered legitimate, I assert that acts of epistemological contestation are at the heart of both social projects. Both groups work to maintain their legitimacy against the spectre of being excluded, via such things as unobjective research or by failing to be a good, resilient local community.

Each group foregrounded information that had a value to the legitimacy of their social project. As David Graeber outlines in his discussion of the politics of value, 'politics is always ultimately about: not just to accumulate value, but to define what value is, and how different values (forms of "honour," "capital," etc.) dominate'. In what he calls the 'ontological gambit' Graeber asserts that ontological claims are 'a kind of political move' that 'tend[s] to be made in the context of competing claims of value' (2013:232). Thus it is social values that guide what come to be taken as fact, as 'the pursuit of facts ... can only be a consequence of certain forms of value' (232, n. 11). The debate about 'fact' between the ASP and the Seethingers, played out on the map, is what brought my attention to a moment of attrition between two social projects. Here the projects do not commensurate, or recursively try to understand place through the other's epistemological mode; rather they assert their own 'gambit'.

As both projects work to assert their legitimacy, they do so haunted by the threat of exclusion. That is, they work as an expert or an active citizen on the threshold between politically qualified life and exclusion from the polis. This position on the threshold is the defining social force of late liberal subjectivities. One must take individual responsibility for one's political inclusion. This demands that one cultivates and asserts a politically qualified self through maintaining a legitimate and authoritative voice. This expectation shapes the forms of moral action and ethical substance of being in late liberalism.

Oren Yiftachel (2009) has applied the idea of the threshold position to land conflicts. He discusses 'grey' spaces in Israel/Palestine, Sri Lanka and South Africa, where expanding zones of urban informality position bodies 'between the "whiteness" of legality/approval/safety, and the "blackness" of eviction/destruction/death' (2009:88). Grey space is neither fully integrated into nor fully eliminated from urban planning frameworks. These spaces differ from urban informality, since they are the product of systemic and structural power. This has concrete implications for people who are either defined as legitimate citizens or relegated to a 'state of exception'. I do not wish to assert that the experiences of loss, harm and struggle experienced in the spaces of Yiftachel's analysis are equivalent to the experiences in the ASP or Surbiton. However, the distinction Yiftachel makes between politically qualified life and those excluded from it (using Agamben's terms *bios* and *zoë*) is useful. The dynamics of inclusion in Surbiton are interesting precisely because it is not a place of perceived conflict and suffering. Rather, these dynamics of working to maintain a politically qualified life are at work, in a subtle sense, in the heart of the affluent suburbs, typical liberal democracies. Yiftachel argues that commentaries on urban planning have referred to the 'public' in an uncritical way, obfuscating acts of exclusion. He also critiques the preoccupation with the Habermasian project of creating an ideal speech situation for modern democracy, and the failure to interrogate the validity of such a project (Yiftachel 2000). Such commentaries, he asserts, have been overly focused on agency within the nexus of participation, rather than stepping back to engage in structural analysis of the nexus itself. Rather than approach the map as something to be developed or something that can deliver a solution to issues of inclusion and participation, I have approached the map as an ethnographic object that emerges from these late liberal ideals and have worked through how the practice of making an ideal speech situation inherently requires epistemological exclusions.

This chapter has shown how the ASP and the Seethingers seek to maintain their positions as politically qualified subjects. Their actions, and their ethical and moral purviews, are shaped by the demand made of them by late liberal ideals of being a democratically involved subject. Richard Rorty, in his discussion of the formation of liberal subjectivities, argues that the 'ideal liberal subject' must suffer doubt and anxiety, as liberal democracy is predicated on the exclusions of other forms of being. He states: 'the process of socialization which turned [the ironist] into a human being by giving her a language may have given her the wrong language, and so turned her into the wrong kind of human being' (Rorty 1989:75). Elizabeth Povinelli responds directly to this point, saying 'Her doubt is born from the knowledge that all truths are the contingent values of linguistic functions; that no one "vocabulary" is closer to reality than another; and that the values one cleaves to most dearly may well be harmful to others' (Povinelli 2001:328). Whilst one may recognise the contingency of values, and so look at how else they could be, one also needs a common language for them to be articulated. However, this common language demands commensuration, which in turn demands exclusions. As Laclau and Mouffe explain (1985), a hegemonic social project requires an appearance of universality, that it encompasses everything. Thus a hegemonic social project will, of necessity, foreclose that which is incommensurable with it. However, this is an ongoing project; the line between legitimate and illegitimate is always being negotiated. Supposedly universal knowledge is always contingent. This being so, it is contestable. That which is excluded always comes back to haunt hegemony (see Butler et al. 2000). The instability and ongoing work needed to maintain the subject position at the heart of the democratic ideal is what allows new forms of being to emerge. But this takes work. A subject must find a language and action through which they can not only assert themselves but be taken seriously by others.

Graeber (2013) argues that the anthropological discussion around ontology implies that most people care about the 'ultimate' nature of reality when, in practice, they don't. Rather, most action is situated in the immediate and everyday value regimes of political contestation. Following Graeber, I assert that social projects become established through ongoing performance of value. That is, they are concerned with increasing their political efficacy through developing and demonstrating an understanding of what is valuable and worthwhile action.

The next chapters will outline in more detail how the ASP and the Seethingers cultivate and promote their values in relation to the built environment of the suburb. We will see how the ASP promotes an empirical analysis of place which led to the necessity of excluding Mount Seething from the map and how the Seethingers are motivated by building a community through being stupid.

Notes

1 'The Community Brain'. http://thecommunitybrain.org/ (accessed 3 April 2013).
2 Companies (Audit, Investigations and Community Enterprise) Act 2004. http://www.legislation.gov.uk/ukpga/2004/27/part/2 (accessed 23 April 2021).
3 http://thecommunitybrain.org/ (accessed 2 August 2021).
4 ASP 'Case for Support', p. 1. EPSRC reference number EP/I001212/1. 1 November 2010.
5 https://gtr.ukri.org/projects?ref=EP%2FI001212%2F1 (accessed 25 June 2021).
6 Quoted from the ASP 'Case for Support' document.
7 http://www.sstc.ucl.ac.uk/sstc_index.html (accessed 24 April 2021).
8 'Three PhD Studentships in "Adaptable Suburbs"', 13 August 2010. https://uclsstc.wordpress.com/2010/08/13/three-phd-studentships-in-%E2%80%98adaptable-suburbs%E2%80%99/ (accessed 26 June 2021).
9 http://www.mappingforchange.org.uk/services/community-maps/ (accessed 3 July 2013).
10 http://www.youtube.com/watch?v=qulpWZY9aUg&noredirect=1, http://www.youtube.com/watch?v=MGRGv2FbP2Y (both accessed 24 April 2021).
11 A society Seethingers had just invented.

References

Agrawal, Arun and Clark C. Gibson. 1999. 'Enchantment and disenchantment: The role of community in natural resource conservation.' *World Development* 27, no. 4: 629–49. https://doi.org/10.1016/S0305-750X(98)00161-2.

Baron, Stephen. 2004. 'Social capital in British politics and policy making.' In Jane Franklin, ed., *Politics, Trust and Networks: Social capital in critical perspective*, pp. 5–16. London: London South Bank University.

Brosius, J. Peter, Anna Lowenhaupt Tsing and Charles Zerner. 1998. 'Representing communities: Histories and politics of community-based natural resource management.' *Society & Natural Resources* 11, no. 2: 157–68. https://doi.org/10.1080/08941929809381069.

Brown, Wendy. 2015. *Undoing the Demos: Neoliberalism's stealth revolution*. New York: Zone Books.

Butler, Judith, Ernesto Laclau and Slavoj Žižek. 2000. *Contingency, Hegemony, Universality: Contemporary dialogues on the Left*. London and New York: Verso.

Carroll, Timothy, David Jeevendrampillai and Aaron Parkhurst. 2017. 'Introduction: Towards a general theory of failure.' In Timothy Carroll, David Jeevendrampillai, Aaron Parkhurst and Julie Shackelford, eds, *The Material Culture of Failure: When things do wrong*, 1–20. London and New York: Bloomsbury Academic.

Conquest, G. 2013. 'Dodging silver bullets: Opportunities and challenges for an "extreme citizen science" approach to forest management in the Republic of the Congo.' Unpublished MA dissertation, UCL.

Cooke, Bill and Uma Kothari. 2001. 'The case for participation as tyranny.' In Bill Cooke and Uma Kothari, eds, *Participation: The new tyranny?*, pp. 1–15. London: Zed Books.

Department for Communities and Local Government. 2010. *Decentralisation and the Localism Bill: An essential guide*. London: Department for Communities and Local Government.

Diamond, John. 2001. 'Managing change or coping with conflict? Mapping the experience of a local regeneration partnership.' *Local Economy* 16, no. 4: 272–85. https://doi.org/10.1080%2F02690940110078274.

Espeland, Wendy Nelson and Mitchell L. Stevens. 1998. 'Commensuration as a social process.' *Annual Review of Sociology* 24: 313–43. https://doi.org/10.1146/annurev.soc.24.1.313.

Ferguson, James. 1994. *The Anti-Politics Machine: 'Development', depoliticization, and bureaucratic power in Lesotho*. Minneapolis: University of Minnesota Press.

Graeber, David. 2013. 'It is value that brings universes into being.' *HAU: Journal of Ethnographic Theory* 3, no. 2: 219–43. https://doi.org/10.14318/hau3.2.012.

Habermas, Jürgen. 1990. *Moral Consciousness and Communicative Action*. Cambridge, MA: MIT Press.

Haklay, Muki. 2013. 'Citizen science and volunteered geographic information: Overview and typology of participation.' In Daniel Sui, Sarah Elwood and Michael Goodchild, eds, *Crowdsourcing Geographic Knowledge: Volunteered geographic information (VGI) and practice*, pp. 105–22. Dordrecht: Springer.

Haklay, Muki, Alex Singleton and Chris Parker. 2008. 'Web mapping 2.0: The neogeography of the GeoWeb.' *Geography Compass* 2, no. 6: 2011–39. https://doi.org/10.1111/j.1749-8198.2008.00167.x.

Henkel, Heiko and Roderick Stirrat. 2001. 'Participation as spiritual duty; empowerment as secular subjection.' In Bill Cooke and Uma Kothari, eds, *Participation: The new tyranny?*, pp. 168–84. London: Zed Books.

Hildyard, Nicolas, Pandurang Hegde, Paul Wolvekamp and Somasekhare Reddy. 2001. 'Pluralism, participation and power: Joint forest management in India.' In Bill Cooke and Uma Kothari, eds, *Participation: The new tyranny?*, pp. 56–71. London: Zed Books.

Hillier, Bill and Julienne Hanson. 1984. *The Social Logic of Space*. Cambridge: Cambridge University Press.

Imrie, Rob and Mike Raco. 2003. *Urban Renaissance? New Labour, community and urban policy*. Bristol: Policy Press.

Jacobs, Jane. [1961] 2016. *The Death and Life of Great American Cities*. New York: Vintage Books.

Jeevendrampillai, David with Gill Conquest. 2021. 'The role of the digital anthropologist in citizen science and public participation mapping projects: A case study or two.' In Haidy Geismar & Hannah Knox, *Digital Anthropology*, 2nd edn, pp. 288–306. Abingdon: Routledge.

Kapoor, Ilan. 2002. 'The devil's in the theory: A critical assessment of Robert Chambers' work on participatory development.' *Third World Quarterly* 23, no. 1: 101–17. https://doi.org/10.1080/01436590220108199.

Kearns, Ade. 2003. 'Social capital, regeneration and urban policy.' In Rob and Imrie and Mike Raco, eds, *Urban Renaissance? New Labour, community and urban policy*, pp. 37–60. Bristol: Policy Press.

Kelly, Katharine D., Tullio Caputo and Wanda Jamieson. 2005. 'Reconsidering sustainability: Some implications for community-based crime prevention.' *Critical Social Policy* 25, no. 3: 306–24. https://doi.org/10.1177%2F0261018305054073.

Kitchin, Rob, Chris Perkins and Martin Dodge. 2009. 'Thinking about maps.' *Rethinking Maps: New frontiers in cartographic theory*, pp. 1–25. Abingdon: Routledge.

Kleine, Dorothea and Tim Unwin. 2009. 'Technological revolution, evolution and new dependencies: What's new about ICT4D?' *Third World Quarterly* 30, no. 5: 1045–67. https://doi.org/10.1080/01436590902959339.

Laclau, Ernesto and Chantal Mouffe. 1985. *Hegemony and Socialist Strategy: Towards a radical democratic politics*. London: Verso.

Lambert-Beatty, Carrie. 2009. 'Make-believe: Parafiction and plausibility.' *October* 129 (Summer): 51–84. http://dx.doi.org/10.1162/octo.2009.129.1.51.

Leach, Melissa, Andy Sumner and Linda Waldman. 2008. 'Discourses, dynamics and disquiet: Multiple knowledges in science, society and development.' *Journal of International Development* 20, no. 6: 727–38. https://doi.org/10.1002/jid.1492.

McGuirk, Pauline and Robyn Dowling. 2011. 'Governing social reproduction in masterplanned estates: Urban politics and everyday life in Sydney.' *Urban Studies* 48, no. 12: 2611–28. https://doi.org/10.1177%2F0042098011411950.

Mitchell, W. J. T. 1986. *Iconology: Image, text, ideology*. Chicago, IL, and London: University of Chicago Press.

Mouffe, Chantal. 2005. *On the Political*. Abingdon: Routledge.

O'Mahony, Eoin. 2014. 'Problems with drawing lines: Theo-geographies of the Catholic parish in Ireland.' *Journal of the Irish Society for the Academic Study of Religions* 1, no. 1: 48–65.

Parfitt, Trevor. 2004. 'The ambiguity of participation: A qualified defence of participatory development.' *Third World Quarterly* 25, no. 3: 537–55. https://doi.org/10.1080/0143659042000191429.

Perkins, Chris. 2004. 'Cartography – cultures of mapping: Power in practice.' *Progress in Human Geography* 28, no. 3: 381–91. http://dx.doi.org/10.1191/0309132504ph504pr.

Povinelli, Elizabeth A. 2001. 'Radical worlds: The anthropology of incommensurability and inconceivability.' *Annual Review of Anthropology* 30: 319–34. https://doi.org/10.1146/annurev.anthro.30.1.319.

Putnam, Robert D. 2000. *Bowling Alone: The collapse and revival of American community*. New York: Simon and Schuster.

Rabinow, Paul. 1989. *French Modern: Norms and forms of the social environment*. Chicago, IL: University of Chicago Press.

Raco, Mike. 2007. *Building Sustainable Communities: Spatial policy and labour mobility in post-war Britain*. Bristol: Policy Press.

Richards, David and Martin J. Smith. 2002. *Governance and Public Policy in the United Kingdom*. Oxford: Oxford University Press.

Rorty, Richard. 1989. *Contingency, Irony, and Solidarity*. Cambridge: Cambridge University Press.

Schwandt, Thomas A., ed. 2007. *The SAGE Dictionary of Qualitative Inquiry*. 3rd edn. Thousand Oaks, CA: SAGE.

Seyfang, Gill. 2003. 'Growing cohesive communities one favour at a time: Social exclusion, active citizenship and time banks.' *International Journal of Urban and Regional Research* 27, no. 3: 699–706. https://doi.org/10.1111/1468-2427.00475.

Tacchi, Jo. 2012. 'Digital engagement: Voice and participation in development.' In Heather A. Horst and Daniel Miller, eds, *Digital Anthropology*, pp. 225–41. London: Berg.

Turnbull, David and Wade Chambers. 2014. 'Assembling diverse knowledges: Trails and storied spaces in time.' In James Leach and Lee Wilson, eds, *Subversion, Conversion, Development: Cross-cultural knowledge exchange and the politics of design*: 153–82. Cambridge, MA: MIT Press.

Verran, Helen and Michael Christie. 2014. 'Postcolonial databasing? Subverting old appropriations, developing new associations.' In James Leach and Lee Wilson, eds, *Subversion, Conversion,*

Development: Cross-cultural knowledge exchange and the politics of design, pp. 57–78. Cambridge, MA: MIT Press.

Wagner, Roy. 1979. *Lethal Speech: Daribi myth as symbolic obviation*. Ithaca, NY: Cornell University Press.

Westwood, Andy. 2011. 'Localism, social capital and the "Big Society"'. *Local Economy* 26, no. 8: 690–701. https://doi.org/10.1177%2F0269094211422195.

Williams, Glyn. 2004. 'Evaluating participatory development: Tyranny, power and (re)politicisation.' *Third World Quarterly* 25, no. 3: 557–78. https://doi.org/10.1080/0143659042000191438.

Woodcraft, Saffron. 2019. 'Void potential: Absence, imagination and the making of community in London's Olympic Park.' PhD thesis, UCL.

Yiftachel, Oren. 2000. '"Ethnocracy" and its discontents: Minorities, protests, and the Israeli polity.' *Critical Inquiry* 26, no. 4: 725–56. http://dx.doi.org/10.1086/448989.

Yiftachel, Oren. 2009. 'Theoretical notes on "gray cities": The coming of urban apartheid?' *Planning Theory* 8, no. 1: 88–100. https://doi.org/10.1177/1473095208099300.

4
How to make a suburb. Part 1: diagrams, expertise and cake

The production and maintenance of a coherent data set is fundamental to the ASP's ability to function as an academic project; it requires scholarly coherence to maintain validity. Coherent data is also vital to the ASP's ability to function as a social project, as the state management of people and place requires experts who can work with moral authority and perceived legitimacy. The ASP excluded local knowledge from the Community Map on the basis that such stories threatened the ASP's ability to form a coherent data set that was universally comprehensible. In keeping with pervasive neoliberal ideologies of state governance, the ASP sought to reveal the relationships between the built environment and socio-economic activity in the suburbs of the UK in order to find and release the 'untapped potential' (ASP Case for Support document, henceforth CFS[1]) of such places. The data that the ASP gathered, shaped and presented would inform urban design and planning policy for the suburbs. The ASP used Surbiton as a case study of an archetypal suburb and the data from this study was to be generalised as a set of rules that can work for suburbs across the country. Taking its cue from the ethnographic moment in which local data was rejected from the ASP's map, this chapter does not take the objectivity of data for granted. It examines the ASP's method of producing data. It traces the method by which raw information, gathered on the ground in Surbiton, is abstracted into a form of data, predominantly manifest through diagrams, that can be read as analogues for suburban built environments. My interest here is in how the ASP foregrounds particular aspects and relations of the built environment through these diagrams. The suburb becomes known through aesthetics and the associated forms of value that these diagrams highlight. In this way the suburb becomes known as an enactment of knowledge, a phenomenon. That is, it is less an object 'out there' or a material reality and more an enactment of knowledge that comes about through the curation of different properties into relation with one another in such a way that they can be read as a pattern with an underlying set of rules. These rules are then applied to all urban areas.

The chapter begins by outlining the history and development of the space syntax method and shows how the ASP used it in their work. This allows us to follow how the ASP produced diagrammatic maps of Surbiton using data, surveying techniques and data modelling. The chapter then considers how the position of 'expert' comes about through this practice. A fundamental aspect of this work is the ability of the ASP team to trace the transformation of information about materials, such as a street, into the images we see on the maps. The chapter works through the importance of the traceability and movability of data in the production of expertise. Tracing data allows the idea of suburb to be maintained as the reference in talking about both the materiality of Surbiton and abstract visualisations. The chapter highlights how important objectivity is for the ASP, which helps us to understand how being an 'expert' depends on producing coherent data and managing one's relation to it. Counter to how we might understand the production of objective knowledge, we shall see how experts feel and sense data, using intuition and managing personal relations when processing it. The chapter concludes by returning to the Community Map to examine the ASP's maintenance of epistemological clarity, with regard to which data and 'facts' went on the map (and which did not).

Making order

The ASP team consisted of a group of academics from the fields of architecture, geography, engineering and anthropology. The team collectively agreed broadly on which types of data should be gathered, how it should be processed, which data required further investigation, and which should be rejected. However, the principal investigator (PI), Vera (a pseudonym[2]), led the team, and made all final decisions on these matters. Vera was based at the 'Space Group', a research group within UCL's School of Architecture that specialises in complex analyses of urban areas, particularly using the 'space syntax' method. Vera was aided by four co-investigators (CIs): Gareth, a lecturer, also based at the Space Group, a specialist in the historical development of urban areas; Hans, a professor of geo-engineering and a specialist in PPGIS; Elsa, a lecturer from the engineering department, and a specialist in urban analysis and data management; and Benni, a professor of material culture studies within the anthropology department. The group also included a research assistant, Rick, who later did a PhD in GIS, and two PhD students, Dave, a data visualisation analyst based in the Space Group, and Claire, who looked at local businesses on high streets. Finally, there was me, a PhD student whose brief was to engage local people and gather an oral history of locals' relationship to the built environment.

Meetings were held every two weeks over three years in the Space Group 'laboratory' on the UCL campus, which consisted of an open-plan workspace and a set of forgettable off-white academic meeting rooms. Each meeting had a formalised agenda, an ordered list of discussion points that ranged from the ongoing aims and objectives of the project in the short, medium and long terms to the specifics of data work on the project, such as how best to technically analyse an urban area. The focus of the meetings could be very specific (drilling down into fine details) or very broad (exploring overall approaches). I engaged with the ASP as another field site complementary to the one in Surbiton and approached the meetings using classic anthropological participant observation techniques.

The work of this group was driven by the aim of making order and sense of suburban spaces by getting at the underlying rules that direct their development. Gareth stated, 'A town centre will not survive if it is chaotic … these are highly structured spaces.' Gareth repeatedly said that 'getting at' this (otherwise hidden) structure was key to the team's work, and by implication to the ASP's claim to authoritative knowledge. Whilst the ASP used multiple techniques and data sources to develop its understanding of suburbs, the most influential technique was the space syntax method. This focused on analysis of the movement of people in city streets, understood as a 'network'. Data on movement was visualised alongside data on land use, which was drawn from business classification types, and the corresponding building shapes. Through these means, space syntax aims to reveal correlations and relationships between movement and land use. The visualisations created as part of space syntax methodology help investigators to, in Gareth's words, 'get at what is going on'. The ASP sought to identify the rules that made places particularly productive and resilient to wider changes in socio-economic conditions (e.g. a recession) or in the structure of the physical network (e.g. a new road being built). Throughout this process, the ASP's analysis shifted scale frequently; it would zoom in towards the particularities of a suburb, Surbiton, but also zoom out in order to assess the general rules that make up a 'resilient' place. As Marilyn Strathern (1991) notes, a change in the scale of analysis involves a change in the amount of information present in that analysis. For example, think about zooming in and out of an online digital map or focusing a microscope: with each change in scale some information is lost. The ASP scales in and out repeatedly (see Yaneva 2005), in order to establish the contextual rules and relations between things, for example a street and the city, that make the suburb knowable as a phenomenon.

I take the term 'phenomenon' here from the 'new materialist' theorist Karen Barad and the science and technology theorist Bruno Latour, in particular from their works *Meeting the Universe Halfway* (2007) and *Pandora's Hope* (1999) respectively. Both authors are concerned with the relation between words and the world, or rather between discourse and matter, and work through realist and constructionist positions of how the world is. Realism posits that an object is really out there in the world and that objects are ontologically independent of our conceptual schemas, whereas social constructivism posits that objects cannot exist independently of the social meanings we give them. So a cup, for example, is less a cup than a collection of materials, with properties that can be utilised, such as its ability to hold liquid. It is only after a social interaction and naming that those materials become understood as 'cup'. That is, it is socially learnt that the word 'cup' is understood as the signifier that refers to that material form of porcelain, cup. Both authors present an analysis that doesn't fit neatly into either of these positions. Rather, they argue that there is no dividing line between nature and the social. Thus when they use the term 'constructivist', they are referring to how the collectives of human and non-human actors are assembled and are drawn into a relation with each other that is both materially real and socially produced. Hence the suburb comes into being as a 'thing' in a particular sense, that is, as a place that can be understood through the measurements of the ASP, through the knowledge practices of measuring it. These practices, using particular methods and techniques, allow the ASP's phenomenon of 'suburb' to move through networks of urban planners and policy experts.

Barad proposes a theory of 'agential realism' whereby the world emerges in a particular understandable and enduring form through the very practices of observing the world. Barad works through Heisenberg's famous experiment in particle physics, in which light is refracted through slits to show how light particles behave. In this experiment, if one changes the mode of observation it appears as though the behaviour of light, acting either as waves or as particles, retroactively changes. Barad states that light displays the properties of a particle or a wave, depending on how it is observed, and therefore can be understood as either. The act of observation emphasises a particular aspect of light, such as velocity or position. However, you cannot measure velocity and position at the same time, as one precludes the other. That is, if you measure velocity you measure the movement as light flows, therefore you can only see it as a wave, but if you measure position then you need to take a snapshot of the light, freezing the frame during measurement and so can only see light as a particle.

Barad's point is that observation limits the possibility of what constitutes an object. Thus she aims to move the focus of empiricist study from objects (such as light particles) to phenomena (such as light) that can have different properties depending on your knowledge-making practice. Phenomena, for Barad, 'do not merely mark the epistemological inseparability of observer and observed, or the results of measurements; rather, *phenomena* are the *ontological* inseparability of agentially intra-acting components' (2007:33; emphasis added); 'our ability to understand the physical world hinges on our recognizing that our knowledge-making practices, including the use and testing of scientific concepts, are material enactments that contribute to, and are a part of, the phenomena we describe' (2007:32). Following these insights, this chapter traces the knowledge practices of the ASP as they engage material aspects of Surbiton (the streets, the buildings, etc.) and categorise, topologise and record them in order to transform them into representations (maps). These processes serve to delimit what a suburb (as phenomenon) is to the ASP and what counts as knowledge when considering suburbs. The ASP selects particular aspects and properties of the material landscape, emphasises particular forms of value relations between materials, and therefore shapes what a suburb is and can be in planning discourses. This notion of knowledge as phenomenon has implications for ethnographic practice which are outlined further in Chapter 6.

Whereas Barad draws attention to the contingency of objects through analysing the practices of knowing, in *Pandora's Hope* Bruno Latour draws attention to how practices of knowing enable knowledge to move from a local engagement with materials to a universal general discussion and consideration of those materials as phenomena. In his work with scientists in the Amazon, Latour works through the myriad steps soil scientists go through to transform materials (the dirt of the earth) into items of scientific knowledge (soil types). Scientists take soil and hold it next to cards to categorise it. As they sort soil into types, categories and codes, the dirt changes from being dirt in the ground to a type in a table of comparison, or on a chart. The name of a soil type, for example 'terra preta', bears no resemblance to the dirt in the ground. One must know to which sign 'terra preta' refers. Latour traces how the scientists enact a series of processes, a chain of transformations, that allow a circulation of that reference, 'terra preta', to move between the dirt found in the ground and the term used internationally by scientists. Each transformation away from the particularity of the local results in a loss of information but also in an ability of that information to work in a more universal way. Latour argues that it is the ability of such scientists to understand, follow and trace these transformations of dirt to soil (or in our case streets to diagrams), up and down a series of such transformations, that enables their position as experts.

As the material of the local (which in the case of the ASP is the streets of Surbiton) is worked into data it becomes something else. It becomes categories, lines, colours. As it becomes transformed into categories, through an emphasis on a particular aspect of its properties, it can be understood as a phenomenon representing a set of relations for suburban environments. Latour calls the selection of properties that move up and down the series of transformations the 'circulating reference'. That is, scientists can move back and forth along a chain of transformations to investigate their samples or the processes of analysis and description, from diagram to street. Reference does not run directly from the diagram to the street, or the word 'terra preta' to the dirt, but rather circulates along a chain of transformations. Whilst the name of a soil or the coloured line on a space syntax map may bear no resemblance to the world it represents (the dirt or a street), the 'sign' *'takes the place of the original situation'* (Latour 1999:67; italics original) so that it can be integrated with other information. Instead of corresponding to the world, it has been manipulated for specific purposes through multiple processes of transformations, from the particular and local to the standardised and universal. The line can be compared to other lines, the soil type to other soil types, it becomes comparable and transferable. Knowledge, then, for Barad and Latour is less 'out there' to be discovered than an activity to be done through focusing in on certain properties and relations. In this chapter I trace the processes by which information on the ground in Surbiton is transformed into diagrams representing an idea of a suburb as a phenomenon, as a set of relations, and as an entity that can be used analogously to talk about 'suburbs' in general.

The space syntax method and skilled doing

Space syntax is a theoretical and methodological approach to understanding the spatial organisation and social life of built environments. It is outlined in Hillier and Hanson's *The Social Logic of Space* (1984), a book which has had significant influence on design and planning methods internationally. It has spawned a whole form of urban analysis practice and its use is prevalent in UCL's Bartlett School of Architecture (particularly within the Space Group). Space syntax seeks to mobilise a deeper understanding of the relationship between the material of the built environment and social forms of life there to achieve 'better design'. Hillier and Hanson note:

> It has become clear that a lack of understanding of the precise nature of the relationship between spatial organisation and social life is the chief obstacle to *better* design. ... The obvious place to seek such an understanding is in the disciplines that are concerned with the effect of social life on spatial organisation – how spatial organisation is in some sense a product of social structure. This has long been a central concern for geographers, but recently anthropologists (Lévi-Strauss, 1963; Bourdieu, 1973, 1977), theoretical sociologists (Giddens, 1981) and archaeologists (Ucko et. al., 1972; Clarke, 1977; Renfrew, 1977; Hodder, 1978) have become aware of the spatial dimension in their subject, and its importance to questions of social morphology and structure.
>
> (Hillier & Hanson 1984:x; emphasis added)

Space syntax emerged from a structuralist background. This theoretical position has informed both architectural and anthropological analysis; both have sought to uncover the underlying rules that organise social life. Hillier et al. (1978) made clear that the space syntax method is neither maths nor language but borrows properties from each in its pursuit of the 'everyday world of practical pattern recognition' (Hillier et al. 1978:344). This 'everyday world' is readable through a 'theory of patterns' which are built up from 'intuitive formal principles' based on 'real evidence' (Hillier et al. 1978:345).

The technique aims at 'getting at' (as the ASP team would say) a 'rule structure' (Hillier et al. 1978:346) that underlies relations between objects such as houses, streets and bodies that give form to human settlements. In 'getting at' these rules one can uncover the 'order' that informs a settlement understood as a system, which allows the analyst to elucidate the 'principles of knowability'. The method and its structuralist logic aim at moving urban architectural analysis beyond what Hillier called 'Aristotelian essences' that reduced spatial form to an output of universal behaviour principles. Space was positioned as an active agent amongst a network of influences that offered 'an alternative basis for encounters, other than those dictated by social structure' (Hillier et al. 1978:376). For Hillier and Hanson, if space was an active agent in directing the forms of social interactions that could be encouraged in a settlement then the governance of urban space was seen as integral to the governance of social life. By the 1980s and 1990s, structuralism had largely fallen out of favour within anthropology because it failed to give adequate accounts of subject and agency (Hodder 2004; Eriksen & Nielsen 2001), but it continued to underpin the logic of space syntax analysis, which thrived in town planning and urban analysis. Hillier and Hanson's ideas about urban movement economy, that is, how people move around the urban environment and interact socially, have been seen as particularly useful for the ASP, especially in its work on recommending planning policy to encourage business development on suburban high streets.

The ASP examined how a change in the road network impacted the socio-economic functioning of a settlement (a suburb) via associated changes in buildings and their uses that followed from such things as a new motorway being built. The ASP assumes that *better* design can be achieved by correctly aligning human movement, building type and building use or, as Gareth writes, by examining the 'conditions that give rise to' a healthy mix of movement, building type and use. The ASP worked to draw attention to these properties, arguing that they have been underexamined in UK planning policy. They argue, 'Understanding more about how the movement economy operates in different social and historical-geographical contexts is necessary to help local policy-makers and investors in making better decisions to support its aptitude for "mixing"' (Vaughan et al. 2013:239).

From streets to lines

Space syntax analysis understands urban environments as systems and sees the city as a network of spaces through which people move. These spaces, or 'segments' (for example, a street), are taken as individual units that are studied in terms of their connectivity to one another. Mathematical algorithms model the likelihood that a person would move through any given segment when traversing from any point (A) to any other point (B) in the system. Every possible journey must be considered, which requires a great deal of computational power. The calculations give each segment (usually a street or a line drawn over a section of a street – see Figure 4.2) a value which relates to the likelihood of movement in that segment in comparison to the other spaces in the network. These movement values are assigned a colour in the visualisations for easy and quick readability, typically using a red (hot) to blue (cold) scale to relate to high and low movement potentials (see Figure 4.1).

The calculations are based on two assumptions. Firstly, that people will walk the fastest route; this is the 'choice' measurement. Secondly, that people will walk the route with the smallest number of turns, or the simplest route; this is the 'integration' measurement (Klarqvist 1993; Hillier & Hanson 1984; Hillier 1996). The ASP used both the choice and integration measures to indicate which spaces are most likely to induce 'co-presence'. Co-presence is the effect a network has in encouraging bodies to meet in a particular space (such as a shopping street).

The segments are derived from existing, conventional maps. Different types of maps (or 'base maps') provide different conditions in which lines of movement can be drawn. Therefore, these different base maps and different ways of assessing movement produce different space syntax maps and show different relations between aspects of the network (see Dhanani et al. 2012 for the technical detail). The most commonly used base maps in space syntax are from the Ordnance Survey (OS). The OS is a non-ministerial government department in the UK, and one of the largest producers of maps in the world.

Mapping emerged as a method of state surveillance to facilitate tax collection in the eighteenth century. It sought to make taxable lands visible and quantifiable, enhancing the state's ability to extract value from land, and to manage populations (following Foucault [1986] 1990). State-led cartography in the UK can be traced to the mapping of the Scottish Highlands in 1747, which allowed the government to manage the territory more effectively following the Jacobite rebellion of 1745 (Hewitt 2010). Around the same time, pioneering cartographer John Rocque had produced maps of London and the surrounding counties (see his map of London of 1746 (Laxton 2004)). Rocque's maps are regarded as the first significant detailed maps of modern London. Also around this time, the OS, influenced by Rocque's methods, began to map at a national scale. The 1836 Tithe Commutation Act had prompted the production of highly detailed six-inches-to-the-mile surveys of England and Wales, which enabled surveillance of taxable lands at a national scale, which replaced the ancient system of collecting taxes. The Ordnance Survey Act of 1841 allowed surveyors to enter private lands, enabling unprecedented coverage. The Ordnance Survey remains the standard map source for national planning and land law. The career of state-sponsored cartography

Figure 4.1 Images of Surbiton analysed using axial, ITN and OSM lines at different scales. Blue lines indicate low movement and red high. Adapted from figures 7–21, Dhanani et al. (2012). © Adaptable Suburbs Project, UCL (EPSRC grant ref: EP/I001212/1), with permission.

in the UK stands in stark contrast to the history of mapping in other countries, where the surveying of land has often been a contested practice (Hewitt 2010; Schellenberg 2010). The ASP does not just work within this lineage of state-led governance of territory; it also consolidates the governmental power of cartographic technology via innovations such as the Community Map and the use of that information with other data sets. The work of the ASP can be thought of as a small step in the long history of governance of populations through mapping processes. The ASP's approach to the built environment, as a system to be understood and managed, is part of the wider naturalisation of state-led governance via expertise, bureaucracy and technology.

I use the term 'governance' here in the Foucauldian tradition. Foucault uses the term 'governmentality' to refer to the various practices and discourses that constitute governance, that is, the calculated means of directing how people and populations act. For Foucault ([1978] 1998) governmentality was not limited to state politics. For him, it was less about enforcement of law and more about the establishment and normalisation of ways of doing things and the socio-political, moral and ethical discourses that managed the people. This was linked to concepts such as biopolitics (the policing of bodies). Expertise and bureaucracy were deployed as a form of power, via knowledge, to maintain the authority of disciplinary institutions such as schools, prisons and asylums. Governmentality in the age of neoliberalism sees people take an active role in their self-government. Individuals self-discipline to align themselves with the various norms and power structures of society. Examples include the self-improvement required to get a job (see Gershon 2016, and active citizenship (see Brown 2015) whereby people take an active role in public life as 'responsible' citizens. Cartography has long been a strategy of governmentality. As Harley (1989) notes, state mapping practices extend and reinforce legal and authoritative jurisdiction over territory. However, in the age of neoliberalism the state has delegated the power of mapping to individuals and publics (Kingsbury & Jones 2009). Here the public gaze, where everyone is potentially involved in the mapping of the urban environment, acts as disciplinary power. The rise of public-participation GIS systems is a demonstration of the ways in which people take on moral responsibility for public order and for the creation and sharing of certain kinds of knowledge.

For the ASP, the rise of digital technologies and PPGIS (see Chapter 3) has led to the availability of alternative base maps, such as Open Street Map (OSM), the world's largest crowd-sourced mapping platform.[3] The data that informs the OSM is compiled, moderated and managed by its users (see Flanagin & Metzger 2008), and is itself enabled by the ready availability of global positioning systems (GPS) on smartphones. The user-generated nature of the maps results in uneven global coverage. Whilst there is low detail in some areas, other areas, of high technical capability, such as London, are well covered (Dhanani et al. 2012). In some places, coverage is more up to date and comprehensive than that offered by OS maps (Haklay & Weber 2008). This open-source map has the advantage of being able to show locally known routes that OS missed or did not recognise as routes, such as small paths. OSM is free and open to all, whilst OS seeks to generate revenues by monetising its data, selling it to private companies. The promise of OSM is entwined with so-called citizen science (see Haklay et al. 2008), which uses web technologies to enable participation in science and data gathering on a huge scale. Citizen science relies on active users to feed data into a platform. The 'public' that provides the OSM data is a knowledgeable, skilled and motivated public, but is largely made up of people with a particular interest in mapping. The ASP's Community Map apes this model, and the ASP and OSM are both underpinned by the same ideal, the democratisation of knowledge. The use of the OSM base layer for space syntax measurements would not only generate more accuracy but would also be congruous with the ASP's democratic and participatory principles.

The different base maps generate different data sets and visualisations (see Figure 4.1). The ASP compared the data generated by OS, OSM and Integrated Transport Network (ITN) maps, in order to decide which was the most appropriate base map. The ITN map is 'primarily a representation of the *road* network' (Dhanani et al. 2012:29) and is similar to the OS maps but focuses on transport routes, including official walking and cycling paths. In contrast to OS maps, OSM and ITN maps have lines that correspond to the centres of roads ('road centre lines'), consisting of as few straight lines as possible. The other type of line is the 'axial line' which has to be drawn over OS maps. This is based on the line of sight along a road, drawn in a straight line as far as possible regardless of the road's centre. The axial line aims to re-create the navigational technique employed by a hypothetical monadic walker. Space syntax practitioners have traditionally used axial lines because of their perceived indication of social behaviour, that is, how people walk.

Rather than discuss the relative merits of each mapping technique (see Dhanani et al. 2012) I want to emphasise the selections and decisions that informed the ASP's map production methods. The line, when drawn, does not correspond to a world 'out there', that is, to the materiality of the suburb. Instead, these lines create the suburb as phenomenon. The production of lines is a key process of transformation for the ASP, as the focus of analysis moves between the materiality of Surbiton and the aesthetics of the diagrams. A network of relations does not simply connect people and places but rather creates them (Riles 2001; Brodsky Lacour 1996; Latour 1999).

As Martin Jay notes, diagrams 'never duplicate a reality external to them, nor are entirely the result of pure imagination, but somehow fall productively between the two' (2010:158). They are a visual device that presents particular relations and values. Ro Spankie notes that the diagram 'shifts the emphasis from physical form or appearance to latent structure, offering a tool to "draw out" or reveal unseen qualities' (2019:30). These 'unseen qualities' map onto the forms of value the ASP desires in line with its wider social project, which in this case is 'resilience' in the built environment in terms of the economic functionality of places.

The process of making a diagram requires that data be processed, cleaned and made commensurate within a common matrix (Espeland & Stevens 1998:314); it must be standardised. In the process of making alignments between data sets and making categories of information, data is cut or excluded. Data must be considered stable and reliable by all involved for it to have efficacy (see Latour 2010) and for the visualisation to remain coherent and readable. However the data is abstracted by the ASP, it must recognisably refer to the suburb. When looking at the diagram one can still say that it represents a suburb. The word 'suburb' is the reference that circulates up and down the transformations of data. To summarise, then: the ASP's diagrams constitute an aesthetic that links to the materiality of the suburb but represent certain values in such a way that the diagram, and the reading of it, can circulate amongst ASP analysis, academic publications, think tanks and government. As legible data, it can inform policy and 'work' to effect material change in the built environment. This mobility and widespread legibility enables the data's legitimacy (and that of its author, the ASP).

The choice of base map and other variables used depends upon what values the ASP wants to show. It may wish, for example, to include fine-grained local information about all footpaths. Or it may only consider roads, to scale out to a regional rather than a local network. Different methodological choices emphasise different properties of the suburb as a network. The resulting visualisations may prompt different policies, and design recommendations. Aware of this, the ASP spent a significant amount time debating the relative merits of different methods. This was always done in a way that allowed the analysis of Surbiton to be applied to other places. That is, the ASP was more interested in finding the best

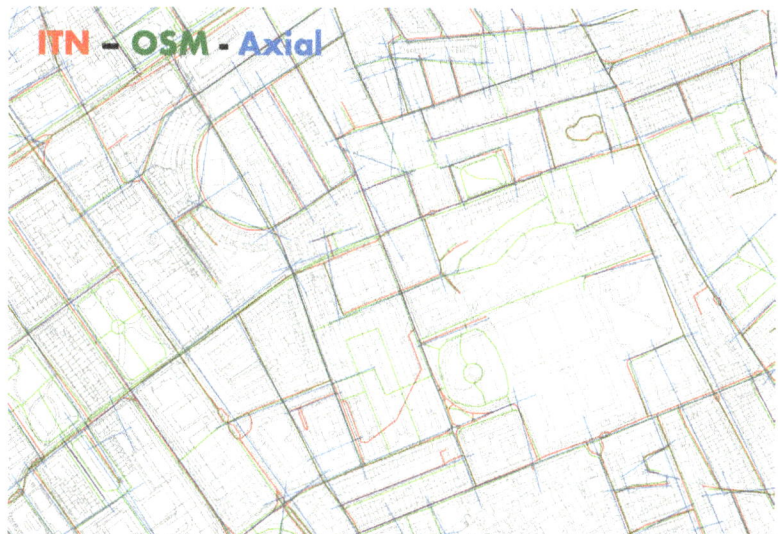

Figure 4.2 Overlaid image of axial (blue), ITN (red) and OSM (green) network models adapted from figure 5, Dhanani et al. (2012). © Adaptable Suburbs Project, UCL (EPSRC grant ref: EP/I001212/1), with permission.

method of analysing suburban environments in general (the universal) than they were in doing an analysis of Surbiton in isolation (the particular). They sought the measure that could best visualise 'latent structures', get at 'generative rules', and work as a universal method. Such a method would best inform national work policy recommendations.

When choosing a method, the ASP had to decide what it wanted to make visible. It had to choose whether to represent or hide various aspects of the material-built environment. These decisions had to be evaluated, calculated and traced at various scales. They ranged over where to draw the boundary of London, which base map to use, and what kinds of lines to draw. Each decision had an implication. For example, the type of lines chosen would affect the measurement of things such as street corners, roundabouts or footpaths (see Figure 4.2).

The lines, representing lines of movement, were coloured according to the frequency of use. Such lines could only show their value relative to other lines in that particular analysis of the network. That is, it is only possible to say that street X is more likely to have movement than street Y in that network, on that map. They don't have independent values.

The ASP had to decide where the end of the 'network' was before it ran an analysis. Where London ends is debatable; it cannot truly be called a contained network. In order to produce a repeatable and objective methodology, the ASP drew boundaries around street networks according to different scales of movement. Eight hundred metres was considered a local walkable distance, 3000m was considered the furthest walkable distance or a short drive and n was the entire city or system. In the case of London, the limit was determined by the greenbelt area, which produces a break in dense road structures. The use of these different scales allowed comparisons to be made of how a network would be affected by, for example, a new motorway, at the local, city and regional levels.

In 2013, during the ASP's analysis, the Ordnance Survey released new, previously unavailable data. The 'Ordnance Survey Urban Paths'[4] (OSUP) showed paths that had mostly been absent from OS and ITN data but present in OSM. After a period of discussion, the ASP decided that road centre lines should be chosen over axial (line-of-sight) lines owing to the fact that the axial line, as an assumed line of sight, was an uncertain measure. Lines were imported from the new OSUP data that now included smaller paths. In one of the many meetings about line data, axial lines caused some confusion. In one of the regular meetings Rick said, 'I don't know where to draw the line.' Gareth responded in a joking manner, 'It doesn't matter, the line is arbitrary.' This niche insider joke alluded to the embodied, on-the-ground perception involved in drawing a line of sight over a top-down, Cartesian cartographic representation of a place. Drawing (axial) lines of sight in relation to a street to which you had never been was flawed: although it might look like a legitimate line of sight on a map, there could be a tree or some other obstacle blocking the view. This had been discussed previously but everyone accepted it as a flaw in an otherwise useful method. This is why Gareth jokingly dismissed the line as 'arbitrary'. Another project member turned to me as the 'on-the-ground anthropologist' and joked, 'You should give your participants an axial line,' at which the room laughed.

Why was this funny? ASP researchers recognised that the line is neither tangible nor relatable to the lived experience of the people in the places being analysed. The joke worked precisely because the line bears no resemblance to reality, because the lines were so abstract, and because expertise was required to make the maps in which they were used. Following the joke Vera explained, 'You're not supposed to use this method unless you've been there and know the space.' But she then said, 'The challenge of doing network analysis embedded in the real world is that it is not straightforward. In a sense these problems are what we want.' Why would they want challenges? Because the essence of being an expert lay in the ability to meet such challenges. Experts can abstract and topologise information and make rational the judgements required to create appropriate images. Expertise comes from having the 'epistemic competence' to manage and create a methodology that maintains the links, the trace, between matter and representation without the data becoming unstable. Only an expert can avoid the intrusion of subjective experience. Experts are able to move up and down the series of transformations and follow the circulating references that make the maps and the actual place of Surbiton a 'suburb'. In this sense 'the problems that we want' are problems that can be overcome by expertise that reaffirms the position of the expert in their ability to provide detailed universal methods for measuring the built environment.

Eventually, the ASP chose to use the OSUP as the base map. Although the axial line is the most common measure in space syntax, it was dropped from the analysis, and road centre lines were used. In deciding not to use the axial line the ASP also lost its link to the assumed social behaviours associated with axial lines, namely that the line of sight was a predictor of pedestrian movement. However, whilst road centre lines were less capable of predicting pedestrian movement, they were the most useful measure in terms of 'rolling out' the ASP's method to a national scale, as such maps could be used by others easily. It was determined that axial lines failed to be consistent, clear and justifiable to someone who might critique the methods, as the people doing the analysis can't possibly have been to every street. The ASP felt that using the axial line as a method would raise too many questions about its accuracy and reliability if someone were to repeat the method. The ASP managed each transformation between streets and maps carefully to ensure that all the subsequent data that emerged from an measurement or analysis made sense and that the reference of 'suburb' could be maintained between each transformation.

This 'skilled doing', in which a rational objective practitioner can develop the correct techniques to make data commensurate and moveable, gives moral authority to such intellectuals and their outputs (Boyer 2005, 2008). The ASP team members become skilled in reading otherwise abstract images of coloured lines through a long process of learning complex analytical processes. Epistemic jurisdiction is established via producing, knowing and reading data such as the diagrams. The team develop knowledge, not only of the language of analysis but also of how terms, techniques and practices come to be used. They have a sense of the chains of transformations data has been through, how a street becomes a line. The team members thus have what Boyer (2008:39) calls a 'semiotic-epistemic competence'; they can read the images with authority. But this is more than a matter of understanding an analytical technique. Contrary to the popular understanding of the disembodied, coolly intellectual nature of technical expertise, this 'competence' involves phenomenological engagement with the suburb. The expert must have the capacity to translate phenomenological experience into data. The ASP team members use their bodies to sense and feel data using intuition when walking streets and 'eyeballing' data. This sensing of data, whilst corporeal and felt, must be rational and controlled if an objective approach to the work is to be maintained. Hence the ASP team members practise a form of Foucauldian self-discipline in managing their bodily experiences and desires. They police each other's engagement with the data. To outline this further we will look at the production of analysis boundaries around suburban areas and the practice of looking at the data.

Land use and boundaries

As well as producing maps that measured the relationship of potential movement in streets, the ASP wanted to determine how such movement affects the sorts of economic activity found in a particular street. The theory goes that a street that is highly integrated into a local network will have more local businesses, such as food shops, and that streets more closely linked to a wider regional network will see regional shops, such as specialist trade shops. The ASP used historical data to ascertain whether changes in the physical street network resulted in changes in the distribution and type of economic activity seen in certain areas. It was my job to gather data from three historical periods, using business directories. Directories were originally compiled by private companies for commercial reasons; they showed the addresses and professions of locals. In the 1960s they were superseded by phone books (Schlichtman & Patch 2008). Early directories organised their information according to the order in which the surveyor walked the area. A surveyor would start at one side of the settlement and walk up and down each street, often using the main 'high street' as an axis. Later, the directories were organised by alphabetical order of the street name in each area. An area was delimited by means of an assessment of where commercial activity came to an end. This relied on the local knowledge of the person making the directory. Directories were often prefaced with a page of description about the area. Of the two areas for which I was responsible for collecting data (of four within the ASP), South Norwood was always clearly defined in directories. Surbiton, however, was a more recent suburb (it arose after 1836 following the arrival of a railway line) and was catalogued as an area of

Kingston, the larger town to Surbiton's north, until 1956, when it had a sufficiently large enough business population to demand its own cataloguing and its own boundary definition.

I visited the local archives in person and transferred the directory information into a database and then into specialist GIS software. Back at UCL the information was visualised over historic OS maps (the only maps available for the period), with points on the maps relating to data in the spreadsheet. Different types of information could be selected from the spreadsheet to be visually represented on the GIS. This meant different aspects of data could be brought into relation with each other on different visualisations. I became deeply familiar with historical directory records and thus became the expert within the ASP on this matter. This meant I was also expected to point out possible anomalies, such as a local shop being somewhere where it was not expected to be, for example on a road aligned to a city-wide network. My knowledge was used to explain or 'clean' data points. Through the extensive 'clean-up' process data was standardised to produce an objective, repeatable method.

As there were no contemporary directories, Claire (the PhD student interested in local business relations) surveyed the areas on foot. She would determine the boundary of economic activity (and so her survey) by intuition. This proved to be a difficult thing to standardise: two people doing the same analysis might mark the boundary differently. However, this intuitive method mimicked the method used in the historical record. The ASP data document, which compiles all data methodology to ensure methods could be replicated and transformations traced, stated that the 'area was surveyed as long as it showed possible non-domestic use; after which, if there was *a feeling* that the area was wholly residential, the researcher turned back and moved on to another area' (emphasis added). It was the phenomenological *feeling* of place that guided the measure of a boundary.

The analysis showed that areas changed significantly over time in regard to their building density, size and distinctness from neighbouring areas. The ASP drew a 'comparative boundary ... defined as the lowest spatial common denominator for the areas, covering all time periods (1880s, 1910s, 1960s, and 2013)' to produce consistency across time periods. After debating questions like 'Will the boundary encompass both sides of the road?' and 'Will it cut through buildings?', the team eventually established a set of rules to enable a consistent method. Sometimes these rules were reworked as new issues arose. In addition to the fieldwork boundary, drawn through a mapping process based on walking, and the comparative boundary, which considered the historical period, a third 'town centre boundary' was used to link the ASP data to previous research. Created by the Department for Communities and Local Government (DCLG), this boundary allowed the ASP to compare their data with official data sets, such as census data, and with other research.

As with the lines, there were many issues with the data relating to economic activity. There were conversations as to what measures to use, and how to overcome obstacles to a 'clean' method (such as historical maps not aligning with business directory data or historical maps needing digital restoration). These issues were worked out over time, and solutions were recorded to ensure that the method was repeatable. The recording of the process of developing a method of analysis was to ensure that the method could be traced back to justifiable decisions and clearly demonstrate objectivity in the ASP's processes. The ability to read data and understand its generation, meaning and relation to other aspects of the data and the materiality of the world 'out there' is a key aspect of maintaining the position of expert. It is the expert's ability to trace the reference of the suburb up and down transformations of information into various forms of data, from street to map, that maintains their authority.

Through the various decisions described above, the ASP produced visualisations correlating potential movement (expressed as lines) with business activities (classified into types, such as manufacturing and retail) in various areas at different scales and over time (see Figure 4.3).

These maps made forms of value in the built environment visible. The production of visibility was not, however, considered the point at which answers were achieved. Rather, the maps are a starting point from which forms of relationality can be conceived and acted upon. Through such diagrams urban environments can be made readable as a network of properties which reify those relations as ones to be considered in the management of the built environment. As Green, Harvey and Knox state in their study of the development of communication networks, it is the production of a network of relations that enables a form such as a suburb to emerge as a thing to which action can be orientated. They note:

> everyone involved in the networking projects in which we participated was well aware that this idealized network did not exist, or not entirely. However, this did not make it potentially less 'real': it was a fantasy in Žižek's terms, and if backed up by sufficient official and aesthetic power fantasies [idealised networks] have a habit of making themselves felt as ontologically real.
>
> (Green, Harvey & Knox 2005:817)

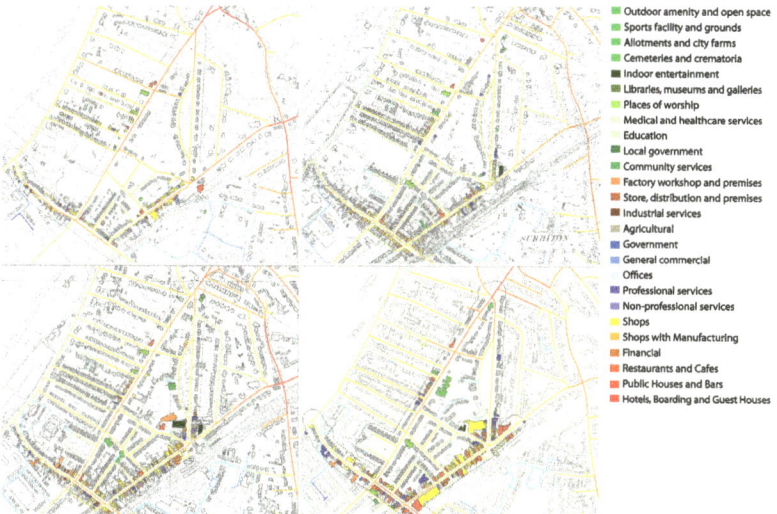

Figure 4.3 Built form and land uses in Surbiton in 1880, 1910, 1960 and 2013 (top left to bottom right), overlaid with segment angular integration 800 metres. © Crown Copyright/database right 2013. Map scale 1:1500. From Laura Vaughan, *Suburban Urbanities: Suburbs and the life of the High Street* (London: UCL Press, 2015).

These diagrams, which require much labour to produce and read, maintain a potency and authority as they circulate between academics, policy makers and urban planners and have real power to affect the ways in which the urban environment will be managed, what values are sought in design decisions and how the environment is altered. Experts must get to know the suburb not so much through its transformation *into* phenomena but *as* phenomena. That is, the suburb as a diagram becomes an abstracted form of relations that can be understood in relation to all other places and to a degree as other places. They must relate to the suburb through a diagram that shows relations and networks, which is why members of the ASP can talk on behalf of places that they may not have been to themselves.

However, just as some team members walked around the suburbs to feel the boundaries, other team members (who may not have been to these places) said that they needed to 'eyeball' the data. Thus the diagrams are a starting point for intuition; they are 'gestures that invite further gestures' (Burrows 2014 following Châtelet 2000).

Eyeballing the data

Over time a notable dynamic emerged between those ASP team members who generated the technical aspects of the visualisations and those who looked at the results and theorised the meaning of the diagrams. The latter group would ask for new images to be made which utilised different aspects of the data. Time and resources were limited and so each decision to run a new visualisation was discussed thoroughly before it was run. During one meeting a visualisation that had been requested was not ready, as the data it used had not been 'cleaned'. Gareth asserted that his request for a revised visualisation was part of a process that is 'difficult to anticipate as it is so unintuitive' (he needed to argue for this revision, in the light of the significant labour required to make even minor changes to the data parameters). Intuition was positioned as a central methodological tool in the research process, both on the ground, feeling boundaries, and in the lab, looking at the diagrams. Justifying his request for more reruns, Gareth explained, 'You don't really know what you want until you can see what it is you have. ... I'd like to just get it down so we can really *eyeball the data* and ask questions of it.'

Team members would invest time in explaining technical aspects of their conversations to others through hand drawings improvised in meetings. These scribbles aided communication whilst we were discussing visualisations and creating a shared language. Thus they aided team building: unless all team members understood and were invested in the value and necessity of visualisations, conversations would falter. Building consensus around how and why the visualisations are made was a process of maintaining team cohesion; it ensures that each member of the team is, to a degree, able to follow the trace of the suburb as it moves through data transformations. The process of explaining is a process of maintaining the expertise of the team. Each team member must be able to understand the nuanced journey from street to diagram, and the various merits of different translations as new data sets are made. At each stage, the team must be able to rationalise and justify the way information is cut or ignored, or given preference, through a lens of objective practice. This labour of making transformations of information in an objective way lends the diagrams their potency.

Diagrams and objectivity

According to Daston and Galison the diagram has become the standard-bearer of the objective method, 'superior to all other modes of expression'

(1992:116, translating Marey[5]), supposedly free of individual or artistic violation. In their study of the history of anatomical depiction, Daston and Galison demonstrate how 'objective' study requires the creation of an image that can be used universally (see also Galison 1998). The image must not be too particular to a specific individual's anatomy but rather must demonstrate a set of rules that apply to all forms of that anatomy. The diagram, as a universal image, emerged as a key tool for the scientific method because it maintains its authority through its objective relation to a phenomenon rather than focusing on a particular version of a thing. That is, the diagram can show rules, relations and value, and, therefore, can be used to 'think with' rather than be taken as a direct representation. Daston and Galison outline how anatomical paintings and sketches were deemed too subjective, and photographs too particular, by medical professionals. In conveying a reproducible and useful representation 'without a political agenda' the diagram emerged, in the mid-nineteenth century, as a useful conduit of morally sound objectivity. A failure to make objective images is a failure of sober judgement, a failure to control emotions and desires (see Foucault [1986] 1990). Therefore the ability to make objective images is a commitment to serve a social project beyond one's own desires; objective images contribute to the functioning of the ASP's social project, which is deeply tied to the state management of the built environment. The ASP sought to employ an objective method in its work. Yet, as Daston and Galison note, visualisations may purport to be 'standard bearer[s] of objectivity', but they also bear political and moral values (1992:98). In their study of historical images in early scientific atlases, Daston and Galison demonstrate how the mimetic quality of standardised images produces a perceived form of objectivity through the suppression of idiosyncrasies, obviating the need for interpretive judgement. Maintaining objectivity was associated with 'professionalism' within the ASP. Each component of objectivity is opposed to a form of subjectivity, as it 'attempts to eliminate the mediating presence of the observer' (1992:82), requiring self-discipline, honesty and restraint. It was the PI's job to ensure that people selected and worked with the data in a way that was right for the project and didn't, for example, hang on to data because they had spent a lot of time on it.

Maintaining objectivity, which involved making decisions to cut data or rerun data sets, came along with the need to be attentive to personal relations within the team. Whilst the team approached their work professionally, they were also keen to acknowledge the time and effort each other had spent working on data visualisations that may have taken a long time to produce yet might be discarded. The team often made jokes about poor computerisation speeds, shared personal stories at the start and end of meetings, and ate cake. To most meetings, the principal investigator brought excellent home-baked cake. The cake, as a gift offering and shared experience, produced cohesion and reaffirmed respect for each other's work. At the start of one meeting, I was typing my ethnographic notes as usual. The meeting proper had not started. People were getting tea, saying hello and complimenting the PI on the cake. One team member jokingly said, 'Busy on Facebook, are we?' as I typed. I explained that I was making field notes, as it had been agreed with the team that I would. They replied inquisitively, 'But the meeting hasn't started. What are you making notes about?' And so I explained that I was making notes about the room, the agenda, the atmosphere. They seemed surprised I might be interested in such detail and jokingly said, whilst eating, 'As long as you don't start all your notes by talking about cake.'

However, I *was* starting my notes with cake, as I had been doing for some time (with permission given). The cake was indicative of this need to build team bonds. The cake eating cannot be seen as separate from the process of making data but is itself, as an exercise in team building, a key aspect of maintaining the ability of the ASP to work cohesively and objectively on the data. The objectivity and rationality required by ASP team members generates ethical substance, it drives the forms of moral reflection in which the 'expert' self is cultivated. Despite the prominent role of the body in the production of knowledge, experts seek to exclude the body from their outputs (see Boyer 2005). Bodies are important not only in the research itself, for example through their role in sensing boundaries or eyeballing data, but are also involved in gestures and the maintenance of personal relations. This maintenance enabled objective judgement calls to be made over and above personal relations with data sets.

Lines as second-order affects

I argue that such diagrams, or rather the lines within them, are 'second-order affects', as it is these that are the starting point for intuition and judgement about what the suburb, as a phenomenon, is. As members of the ASP noted, it is only when they can see a visualisation that they are able to 'feel' something and 'get at' what a good suburb is. The assessment of a good suburb is deeply related to feeling, mood and bodily instinct. In this sense it is affective (see Chapter 5). These visualisations emerge after a series of abstractions that reflect not only what is in the suburb but what the ASP desired to see. Whilst the ASP images may seemingly produce an objective image, Carr (2010) argues that objectivity itself is a cultural concept, and that objective images, and the associated expertise that produces them, are deeply ideological.

> Expertise is ... always ideological because it is implicated in semistable hierarchies of value that authorize particular ways of seeing and speaking as expert. Expertise is arguably the exemplar of what Silverstein calls *'second order indexicality'* ... – that is, historically constituted and contingent metadiscursive practices (e.g., rationalizations, evaluations, diagnoses) that mediate between would-be experts and some set of cultural goods.
>
> (2010:18; emphasis added)

The type of visualisations created by the ASP function as a form of language which is neither mathematical (as practitioners of space syntax may argue), linguistic nor morphic. Rather, it is aesthetic (see Sharman 1997). Value is inferred from seeing an image, as the aesthetic brings things into relation and does more than represent data but also brings new forms of relationality into being. The aesthetic provides an affective bridge between the worlds of the seen and the unseen. The line, as aesthetic, draws its efficacy from its ability to promote particular ways of seeing. The line is onto-epistemological. I use this term, borrowed from Barad (2007), to refer to the line's ability not simply to represent the world but rather to enable a particular conceptualisation of it. This conceptualisation is more than an epistemological approach to knowing the world 'out there'; rather, through foregrounding certain properties and relations, it enables a world to emerge as an ontologically real 'thing'. That is to say, a world does not so much become known through observation as it becomes real and distinct as a 'thing' through practices of observation. The line enables distinctions. It is both the basis and the articulation of language through which a world emerges. However, a world emerges through very particular, selected and managed lines. The line does not simply show, but produces, the relations and consequential actions. Anthony Vidler, in his work on diagrams, asserts: 'Operating between form and word, space and language, the diagram is both constitutive and projective; it is performative rather than representational' (Vidler 2000:6). Vidler discusses how the digitisation of the diagram has affected how diagrams work as a performative actor. The ability to make many visualisations, use complex data sets and bring many aspects of data together means that diagrams can be understood less as icons (such as anatomical drawings) and more as blueprints for worlds, since they emphasise and prefigure values and relations. He states:

> the intersection of diagram and materiality impelled by digitalization upsets the semiotic distinctions drawn by Charles Sanders Peirce as the diagram becomes less and less an icon and more and more a blueprint – or, alternatively, the icon increasingly takes on the characteristics of an object in the world. The clearest example of this shift would be the generation of digital topographies that include in their modeling 'data' that would normally be separately diagrammed – the flows of traffic, changes in climate, orientation, existing settlement, demographic trends, and the like.
>
> (Vidler 2000:17)

In their work, the ASP team are not simply 'getting at' *the* world out there but are making *a* world. They are doing so by creating complex digital topographies in which they aim to combine different forms of data in order to run multiple analyses of relations between data sets. The diagram as a blueprint is a political act that has real force in its ability to shape the materiality of place and, therefore, affect what forms of social life are encouraged within a place such as Surbiton.

Conclusions

The work of the ASP, whilst it has been operating under objective and rational rubrics, has been analysed here as a social project that foregrounds the management of people and place in the name of the common good. The ASP, as a social project, is deeply tied to histories of state mapping and governance. In order to maintain its coherence, it must ensure clarity and consistency in its methodological approach. The establishment of epistemological hegemony, which decides what information counts, results in exclusions such as the dismissal of Seething 'facts' as facts. These exclusions are seen as inherent to the process of making data commensurate and making and using it rationally and objectively.

This chapter has outlined how the ASP goes about making its social project through making better places. Central to its practice is the objective and reasoned production of knowledge that transforms the suburb 'on the ground' into a visualisation. This visualisation allows the ASP to understand the suburb as a network of relations and as a phenomenon produced through 'generative rules'. The ASP produces and reads these visualisations in order to understand how particular forms of value may be encouraged by managing the built environment in a particular way. It passes this knowledge on to urban planners and policy makers, who in turn influence how suburban built environments are managed.

This process produces the 'expert' as a rational subject. ASP team members carefully manage their personal relationships with the data and each other in order to maintain a cool, rational, objective approach. However, the production of expert knowledge necessarily involves corporeal ways of relating to the work, from feeling boundaries to eyeballing data. Being expert is a lived and felt subjectivity which involves the disciplining of the self in order to contribute effectively to a social project of late liberalism. This social project works through objective, rational and democratic procedures of knowledge production through scales, from the local to the national, and firmly establishes the state as a governor of place.

Returning to the 'moment' of the ASP's refusal to moderate the Seething story, we can now understand this as a moral act. It seeks to uphold the social project of the ASP. By excluding unclear or untraceable information from the map (such as the 'fact' that a mountain was destroyed by a giant in the area), the ASP maintains clear, transferable data throughout its data set. The ASP team needed to be able to account for and explain all data. It is this knowledge that is fundamental to their position as experts and to the ability of their knowledge to move through the domains of policy makers and urban planners. However, expertise was fundamentally antithetical to the social project of the Seethingers. They, as we shall see in the next chapter, use stupidity to ensure that no one person can be an expert.

Notes

1   Quoted from the ASP 'Case for Support' document. EPSRC reference number EP/I001212/1. 1 November 2010.
2   The work of the ASP team is a matter of public record and is cited within this book. People have been anonymised in references to private conversations, but real names are used when I refer to matters on the public record.
3   http://www.openstreetmap.org/ (accessed 25 April 2021).
4   This was the term used by the ASP. The data can also be called 'OS MasterMap Highways Network – Paths'. https://www.ordnancesurvey.co.uk/business-government/products/mastermap-highways-path (accessed 28 June 2021).
5   E. J. Marey, *La Méthode graphique dans les sciences expérimentales et principalement en physiologie et en médicine* (Paris: G. Masson [1878]) III).

References

Barad, Karen. 2007. *Meeting the Universe Halfway: Quantum physics and the entanglement of matter and meaning*. Durham, NC: Duke University Press.
Boyer, Dominic. 2005. 'The corporeality of expertise.' *Ethnos* 70, no. 2: 243–66. https://doi.org/10.1080/00141840500141345.
Boyer, Dominic. 2008. 'Thinking through the anthropology of experts.' *Anthropology in Action* 15, no. 2: 38–46. https://doi.org/10.3167/aia.2008.150204.
Brodsky Lacour, Claudia. 1996. *Lines of Thought: Discourse, architectonics, and the origin of modern philosophy*. Durham, NC: Duke University Press.
Brown, Wendy. 2015. *Undoing the Demos: Neoliberalism's stealth revolution*. New York: Zone Books.
Burrows, David A. 2014. 'Negative Space in the diagrammatic imaginary of science and art.' Talk delivered in the 'Wonderments of Cosmos' series at UCL on 12 April 2014. Transcript available at http://blogs.ucl.ac.uk/woc/2014/04/12/negative-space-in-the-diagrammatic-imaginary-of-science-and-art-by-david-burrows-slade-school-of-fine-art/ (accessed 26 April 2021).
Carr, E. Summerson. 2010. 'Enactments of expertise.' *Annual Review of Anthropology* 39: 17–32. https://doi.org/10.1146/annurev.anthro.012809.104948.
Châtelet, Gilles. 2000. *Figuring Space: Philosophy, mathematics, and physics*. Dordrecht: Kluwer Academic.
Daston, Lorraine and Peter Galison. 1992. 'The image of objectivity.' *Representations* 40 (Autumn): 81–128. https://doi.org/10.2307/2928741.
Dhanani, Ashley, Laura Vaughan, Claire Ellul and Sam Griffiths, 2012. 'From the axial line to the walked line: Evaluating the utility of commercial and user-generated street network datasets in space syntax analysis'. In Margarita Greene, José Reyes and Andrea Castro, eds, *Proceedings: Eighth International Space Syntax Symposium*. Santiago de Chile: PUC. https://discovery.ucl.ac.uk/id/eprint/1308812/ (accessed 26 April 2021).
Eriksen, Thomas Hylland and Finn Sivert Nielsen. 2001. *A History of Anthropology*. London: Pluto Press.
Espeland, Wendy Nelson and Mitchell L. Stevens. 1998. 'Commensuration as a social process.' *Annual Review of Sociology* 24: 313–43. https://doi.org/10.1146/annurev.soc.24.1.313.
Flanagin, Andrew J. and Miriam J. Metzger. 2008. 'The credibility of volunteered geographic information.' *GeoJournal* 72, nos 3-4: 137–48. https://doi.org.10.1007/s10708-008-9188-y.
Foucault, Michel. [1978] 1998. *The History of Sexuality. Volume 1: The Will to Knowledge* (trans. Robert Hurley). London: Penguin Books.
Foucault, Michel. [1986] 1990. *The History of Sexuality. Volume 3: The Care of the Self* (trans. Robert Hurley). London: Penguin Books.
Galison, Peter. 1998. 'Judgement against objectivity.' In Caroline A. Jones and Peter Galison, eds, *Picturing Science, Producing Art*, pp. 327–59. New York: Routledge.
Gershon, Ilana. 2016. '"I'm not a businessman, I'm a business, man": Typing the neoliberal self into a branded existence.' *HAU: Journal of Ethnographic Theory* 6, no. 3: 223–46. https://doi.org/10.14318/hau6.3.017.
Green, Sarah, Penny Harvey and Hannah Knox. 2005. 'Scales of place and networks: An ethnography of the imperative to connect through information and communications technologies.' *Current Anthropology* 46, no. 5: 805–26.
Haklay, Muki, Alex Singleton and Chris Parker. 2008. 'Web mapping 2.0: The neogeography of the GeoWeb.' *Geography Compass* 2, no. 6: 2011–39. https://doi.org/10.1111/j.1749-8198.2008.00167.x.
Haklay, Mordechai (Muki) and Patrick Weber. 2008. 'OpenStreetMap: User-generated street maps.' *IEEE Pervasive Computing* 7, no. 4: 12–18. https://doi.org/10.1109/MPRV.2008.80.
Harley, John Brian. 1989. 'Deconstructing the map.' *Cartographica* 26, no. 2: 1–20. https://doi.org/10.3138/E635-7827-1757-9T53.
Hewitt, Rachel. 2010. *Map of a Nation: A biography of the Ordnance Survey*. London: Granta.
Hillier, Bill. 1996. *Space is the Machine*. Cambridge: Cambridge University Press.
Hillier, Bill and Julienne Hanson. 1984. *The Social Logic of Space*. Cambridge: Cambridge University Press.
Hillier, B., A. Leaman, P. Stansall and M. Bedford. 1978. 'Space syntax.' In David R. Green, Colin Haselgrove and Matthew Spriggs, eds, *Social Organisation and Settlement: Contributions from*

anthropology, archaeology and geography, Part 2, pp. 343–81. Oxford: British Archaeological Reports, International Series (Supplementary) 47.

Hodder, Ian. 2004. 'The "social" in archaeological theory: An historical and contemporary perspective.' In Lynn Meskell and Robert W. Preucel, eds, *A Companion to Social Archaeology*, pp. 23–42. Malden, MA, and Oxford: Blackwell Publishing.

Jay, Martin. 2010. '*The Culture of Diagram* (review).' *Nineteenth-Century French Studies* 39, no. 1: 157–9. https://doi.org/10.1353/ncf.2010.0018.

Kingsbury, Paul and John Paul Jones III. 2009. 'Walter Benjamin's Dionysian adventures on Google Earth.' *Geoforum* 40, no. 4: 502–13. https://doi.org/10.1016/j.geoforum.2008.10.002.

Klarqvist, Björn. 1993. 'A space syntax glossary.' *Nordisk Arkitekturforskning* 2: 11–12.

Latour, Bruno. 1999. *Pandora's Hope: Essays on the reality of science studies*. Cambridge, MA, and London: Harvard University Press.

Latour, Bruno. 2010. *The Making of Law: An ethnography of the Conseil d'État* (trans. Marina Brilman and Alain Pottage). Cambridge: Polity.

Laxton, Paul. 2004. 'Rocque, John (1704?–1762).' *Oxford Dictionary of National Biography* (online edn). Oxford University Press. https://doi.org/10.1093/ref:odnb/37907.

Riles, Annelise. 2001. *The Network Inside Out*. Ann Arbor: University of Michigan Press.

Schellenberg, Rosie, dir. 2010. *Maps: Power, Plunder and Possession*, episode 1: 'Windows on the World', 23 April, BBC4. https://learningonscreen.ac.uk/ondemand/index.php/prog/0154E088?bcast=45441625 (accessed 16 June 2021).

Schlichtman, John Joe and Jason Patch. 2008. 'Contextualizing impressions of neighborhood change: Linking business directories to ethnography.' *City & Community* 7, no. 3: 273–93. https://doi.org/10.1111/j.1540-6040.2008.00261.x.

Sharman, Russell. 1997. 'The anthropology of aesthetics: A cross-cultural approach.' *Journal of the Anthropological Society of Oxford* 28, no. 2: 177–92.

Spankie, Ro. 2019. 'Revisiting Sigmund Freud's diagrams of the mind.' *Social Analysis* 63, no. 4: 20–42. https://doi.org/10.3167/sa.2019.630402.

Strathern, Marilyn. 1991. *Partial Connections*. Cambridge: Cambridge University Press.

Vaughan, Laura, Ashley Dhanani and Sam Griffiths. 2013. 'Beyond the suburban high street cliché – A study of adaptation to change in London's street network: 1880–2013.' *Journal of Space Syntax* 4, no. 2: 221–41.

Vidler, Anthony. 2000. 'Diagrams of diagrams: Architectural abstraction and modern representation.' *Representations* 72 (Autumn): 1–20. https://doi.org/10.2307/2902906.

Yaneva, Albena. 2005. 'Scaling up and down: Extraction trials in architectural design.' *Social Studies of Science* 35, no. 6: 867–94. https://doi.org/10.1177/0306312705053053.

5
Being stupid in the suburbs: life in the state of Seething

Introduction

This chapter examines the practice of being local from the perspective of the Seething Villagers. By looking at how and why Seething Villagers endeavour to host events that are *stupid*, this chapter will demonstrate how such events are a vital part of supporting the goals of their social project. We will trace how Seething events are organised, and how they craft a new, horizontal and more equitable relation to the civic through such processes. Specifically, we will look at the Seething Freshwater Sardine Festival in more depth in order to understand how Seethingers play in the gap between materials and their meaning. We will see how such play realigns the index of particular public symbols, such as (in the case of the Sardine Festival) the fish, which appears three times on the local authority's official crest. We will see how the fish comes to stand for different ideals and alters feelings of citizenship and relations to local authority. I will argue that Seethingers enact their role as active citizens through these stupid events; through them, they craft their community and build its 'resilience' to external threats. The chapter will conclude by considering how the Seethingers realise their *bios* through these events, using them to craft a form of life that is vibrant and enjoyable, and aligns with their ideals and notions of citizenship. Finally, we return to the ASP Community Map to show how the Seethingers could only ever present facts to the map in a Seething way.

Before we take a closer look at the Seething Freshwater Sardine Festival, I will trace the way the suburb manifests in the popular imagination in the UK: I do so because Seethingers use stories, myths and 'facts' to counter the prevailing perception of suburbia. We will look at how such suburbs emerged as a key locus of social life in the UK. I will provide a historical architectural overview of British suburbia, and a brief history of Surbiton and its built environment more specifically. Overall, this chapter demonstrates that Seething events constitute a typical (whilst also particular and peculiar) late liberal manifestation of ground-up community action in the UK's suburbs. This sort of community action is the sort required and idealised by the localism rhetoric and policy agendas we looked at in Chapter 3.

The suburbs

On its website, the Community Brain (the CIC that was established to promote a stronger sense of community in Surbiton) states that it aims to create a 'resilient' community. It does not explicitly state what they are building resilience to. However, from my time spent with the group, I ascertain that this resilience seeks to counteract the perceived increasing individualism, loneliness and greed associated with contemporary life in the UK. These threats are embedded in neoliberal economic modes of living, and need to be kept in check through community work. During my fieldwork, locals frequently asserted that they did not want the area to be known as a suburban commuter town. Surbiton is a pleasant suburb with a fast connection to central London. It is ideal for those wanting a city career but also a home for a family, as suburbs are more affordable, spacious and calmer, and are perceived as safer. This led to a fear that the area could turn into what one local called a 'dormitory suburb', where people come to sleep between commuting to work. Locals talked of wanting to live in a place where you can walk down the main street and say hi to people you know, a place where you can know your neighbours. The Seething Villagers worked hard to prevent Surbiton becoming a suburban cliché and a neoliberal dystopia, both in the way the area is perceived and in terms of what it is like to live there.

Whilst London might be famed for its grand historic buildings, museums and vibrant urban culture, the majority of its residents live in its outer regions, in its suburbs. Vaughan et al. (2009) state that around two-thirds of London's population, and over 80 per cent of the UK's population, live in suburbs. The cultural imaginary of suburban life is of a dull, lifeless, middle-of-the-road England. Jim McClellan of the *Big Issue* magazine reported that suburbs are 'where the life of the mind curls up in front of the fire in a comfy pair of M&S slippers,[1] it's a brain-dead blizzard of matching carriage lamps and mock Tudor details' (McClellan 1999:16–17). Surbiton has become known as the 'Queen of the Suburbs' and has become a central figure of all things suburban in the UK's popular imagination. David McKie writes, 'The name sounds so much like "Suburbia". When some joker on the stage or the television screen says Surbiton, what we all subliminally hear is Suburbiton' (McKie 2004). Surbiton has frequently been intimately associated with the dominant image of the suburbs: dull, ahistorical and acultural places. Audaciously, in a bid to market itself as distinctly urban and cultural, in 1995 Liverpool City Council 'seriously considered adopting "Liverpool – it's not Surbiton" as a marketing slogan' (Statham 1996). Surbiton was even used in a sketch by perhaps the most famous comedy collective in English TV history, *Monty Python's Flying Circus* (Chapman et al. 1972).[2] Python parodied the famous anthropological investigations of the Norwegian explorer Thor Heyerdahl, who re-created the journey of the *Kon-Tiki* raft across the Pacific Ocean to test a hypothesis that people from South America could have settled in Polynesia. In their sketch the comedians replace Heyerdahl with a 'Mr and Mrs Norris', who, clearly inspired by Heyerdahl, want to determine whether the people of Surbiton are related to the people of Hounslow (a similarly average suburb to the north of Surbiton). Mr Norris notes similar mock Tudor vernacular housing, shared 'lawnmower technology' and 'similar language' in the two places, and determines that the areas must have been linked through a historical movement of populations. Monty Python plays on the idea that suburbs look similar to each other, are distinctly unexotic and are not places of adventure (in comparison to Heyerdahl's journey). However, as Bourne (1996) explains, suburbia was once portrayed as the new ideal place to live (particularly in the inter-war period of the 1920s and 1930s, and again after World War II). Advertising enticed people to retreat from urban squalor to the suburbs with their balance of city and countryside living (Clapson 2003). It represented a reclamation of community, and a simpler life than the city. The suburbs offered clean air and spacious homes, without totally losing the link to the jobs and culture of the city (Bourne 1996:180). However, today the notion that the suburbs represent a utopian vision of post-war living has given way to a bleak dystopian discourse. As Rowan Moore (2016) reported in the *Observer* newspaper, market researchers claim that 'all these ideas we have about leafy suburbs have changed', drawing attention to the erosion of their architectural integrity: 'Family homes have been denatured. They have been made into mini apartment blocks and their gardens are torn up and turned into car parks.' The conclusion is that they 'are turning into dormitories – and not very nice dormitories at that' (Ben Page, chief executive of Ipsos Mori, quoted in Moore 2016). In the popular imagination the suburban dream has turned into a dystopian nightmare. Television programmes and films such as the US-based *American Beauty* (Mendes 1999) and *Desperate Housewives* (Cherry 2004–7), and the UK-based *The Good Life* (Esmonde and Larbey 1975), have portrayed suburbs as 'inauthentic consumption centres and conformity factories' (Muzzio and Halper 2002:543). *The Good Life* was set in Surbiton and featured a couple who desired a slower-paced self-sufficient life, only to be watched over by nosy and comically interfering neighbours. Despite such imagery many people still choose to live in such places. In Surbiton people told me that they never expected to end up living in a suburb, especially not Surbiton, but they have found living there a joyful, fun and pleasant experience. They have told me stories of community, finding a home and deep friendships and of finding a pride in where they live.

Some of my interlocutors told me about local history, whilst others knew nothing about it. However, most had a story to tell about Surbiton. People told me tales of friends, memories or events in the area. These stories were deeply tied to place; they were layered with sensorial memories. From the light at dusk to the sound of birds, or kicking autumn leaves in order to feel 'the passing of the seasons', to walking the long way to the train station via the park so that one could remember a Seething event that happened there, there were many reasons for liking Surbiton and suburban life.

My interlocutors repeatedly told me that Surbiton allowed a space for people to play, to mix with others and have fun, to make friends, and find a pace of life that suited them. They described this as a deeply suburban lifestyle. Many of my interlocutors described a feeling of enjoying the calm life of suburbia that cannot be easily quantified but relates to the ways in which people triangulate the co-ordinates of relations to other people, to place and to themselves in ways that are deeply tied to the affordances of suburbs. These affordances relate to the spacious and pleasant environment, neighbourly relations and a sense of localness, whereby people enjoyed remaining in the local area, using its facilities and building core relationships there. People used the local parks and public spaces for events to develop a familiarity with others and with the local landscape which helps cultivate this suburban feeling. Seethingers were deeply aware of the public image of the suburbs and Seething tales played with some of the ideas of suburban dystopia. At their core, Seething stories were about creating a utopian community whose members shared with and cared for each other. In the legend of Lefi Ganderson (see Box 1.1) the Villagers realised that they should have treated Lefi with love and eventually promised to be good to each other and to work hard to build community.

In Surbiton the sense of community is produced less through provincial historical societies or stuffy and restrictive residents' groups (as popular portraits of suburbs, such as *The Good Life*, may lead you to believe) and more through a shared love of place and a genuine desire to meet, hang out and build friendships locally. People want to know others in the local area and build relationships of trust and shared values. There was a strong desire to be proud of the local area in terms of its people and the life it enabled you to live. This sense of local pride is practised through such things as the Seething festivals. But before we get to the sardine festival, I will outline the emergence of the modern UK suburb, and give more specific detail on the history and architecture of Surbiton.

The historical emergence of the suburbs

There is a popular misconception that suburbs are, necessarily, the result of urban expansion from a centre, in particular as a result of rapid urban sprawl that began with the dawn of the industrial era. However, the outskirts of cities have always hosted commercial activities. This is particularly true in the UK, where cities have long had historical relations to surrounding settlements. This is in contrast to suburbs in places such as the USA and Australia, where they grew with the increased popularity of the motor car (and so are more sprawling) (McManus & Ethington 2007). As Peter Ackroyd notes, London's suburbs are 'as old as the city itself' (Ackroyd 2001:727). From medieval times 'dirty industries', such as tanneries, butchery and charcoal making, were located outside the city walls. This produced minor satellite settlements (Bourne 1996). Many of the places we know as suburbs today were, at one point, distinct villages apart from the city, prompting the old adage that London is 'a city of a thousand villages'. The city did not, as many believe, spread from the centre to swallow up these places. In a meticulous historical review, Harold James Dyos (1961) outlines how the built environments and transport infrastructure of such places have grown into each other, co-evolving with London's centre in a symbiotic social and economic relationship (see also Jackson 1987; McManus and Ethington 2007). By the sixteenth century, the dispersal of industry to the suburbs had become quite marked, with the suburbs taking on a definite character by the 1700s (Dyos 1961:34). By the 1800s, advancements in road building and transport saw the suburbanisation process accelerate, especially in

London (Bourne 1996:167). However, most people still walked to get around. It was not until the 1860s, with the development of rail and the removal of road tolls, that regular movement between different places started to occur on a large scale for many people. Cheaper rail fares, encouraged by government via the 1883 Cheap Trains Act, allowed people to 'escape the city' and 'delocalise', that is, be less tied to their local area, for both work and recreation (Clapson 2003:25). The economy and the infrastructure were not the only forces behind suburban expansion. Social and cultural factors, such as the idealisation of country life, were extremely influential. In the 1900s, this manifested in the garden city movement, which saw brand-new, predominantly suburban settlements that sought to balance the ideals of city and country living.

The Housing, Town Planning, &c. Act of 1919 saw an increase in the responsibility of local authorities to provide housing for their constituents. An estimated 700,000 homes were needed to replace slum housing and provide for those returning from war; the suburbs could support this expansion of provision. And so, when there was a huge housing boom in the inter-war period, this boom was particularly evident in the suburbs. Most growth occurred on the outskirts of London (Clapson 2003). The boom prompted architectural uniformity. Particular elements – such as pitched roofs and brick cavity walls – proliferated. The popular vernacular styles included mock Tudor and neo-Georgian. This uniformity has led to the suburbs being derided as a 'non-place urban realm' (Clapson 2003:159 following Webber 1964; see also Augé 1995) and 'everywhere, all alike' (Priestley [1934] 1984:22).

A reputation for characterless homogeneity grew and fuelled the reputation of suburbs as being nothing more than a dormitory for commuting workers. More recently the media have widely reported the so-called 'death of the high street' (see Duncan 2014), whereby locally owned, small-scale businesses fail, since they are unable to compete with supermarkets and online shopping. In 2011, the UK government commissioned a review of the future of the high streets that recognised that they were important to a sense of community and needed to be thought of as more than a place for shopping at chain stores (see Portas 2011). Hinchcliffe (2005:900) has argued that the traditional focus on the residential nature of suburbs has 'distorted our conception' of what they should and can be whilst Griffiths et al. add to Hinchcliffe to note that suburbs often conceal 'more variegated social activities' (Griffiths et al. 2008:1157), such as small trade, innovative and specialist industries, and flexible work and meeting spaces such as coffee shops and other places where hanging out can be encouraged.

The Seethingers were deeply aware of the (negative) popular image of suburbs and Surbiton's special place within such an imaginary, and were keen to counter it. They were also deeply keen on supporting small-scale businesses and encouraging people to shop and eat locally, to counter the decline of the suburban high street. The Community Brain was involved in many projects to encourage people to see the area as a centre of community. The CIC helped organise the 'Surbiton Food Festival' and a 'village fete', which were focused on increasing local business revenue; Seething events, in contrast, did not have such an explicit economic agenda, and focused on being silly.

The history of Surbiton

As well as being deeply aware of Surbiton's place in the cultural imaginary, locals thought a lot about its relation to Kingston, its historical big brother. The story of Surbiton is tied deeply to the history of Kingston. Surbiton sits just south of Kingston, an ancient market town. Both places are part of the regional local government borough of Kingston upon Thames. They both hug the River Thames on the south-west border of London next to the county of Surrey. Kingston derives its name from 'the King's manor' and is reputedly the site where several Saxon kings were crowned (Mills 2010). The symbol of the borough comprises three fish. This symbol can be found all over the borough on street furniture such as street signs, bins and bus stops, and on official council letterheads and above government buildings. The symbol was derived from one of the earliest known records of the town, in the Domesday Book of 1086. This book was commissioned by King William to assess the taxable assets across the land, and it recorded three fisheries in the Kingston area. Today, Kingston is a lively town with a busy shopping centre, a picturesque market square and a pleasant river walkway by the Thames called the Queen's Promenade where people fish, walk, and sometimes stop for a drink or to take in the view over the river.

If you were to walk south along that walkway you would find yourself in Surbiton after 15 minutes or so. The river path ends by ushering you from the river walk onto the busy Portsmouth Road, which runs parallel to the river but is separated from it by a sizeable disused water filtration site. This site was built in the early to mid-1800s and is separated from the road by some distinctive Victorian-era blue railings that are considerably rusty (see Figure 7.1). The material excavated when the filtration works was built was used for the promenade. Many of the nearby houses are small workers' cottages that housed people who worked on the site in the 1800s. The filter beds cover around six acres and once pumped clean water from the River Thames to the city of London; they are hugely important in the story of cholera and clean water, particularly during the epidemics of 1831, 1848–9, 1854 and 1867 (we will return to this in more detail in Chapter 7). The site is of huge importance to the local community. It has a unique history and ecology that relate to the history of clean water, epidemiology, and the protection of endangered species (particularly Daubenton's bat).

The Surbiton area both looks and feels much more residential than the buzzing urban centre of Kingston. Whilst it does not have a strong regional pull for shopping like Kingston, there is a traditional linear high street upon which one can find an uncontroversial mix of nationally known chain stores with a scattering of local independent shops and charity shops (see Figure 5.1) that serve the local area well. To my interlocutors Surbiton is noticeably pleasant (and I have to say that I agree).

Surbiton is not as old as Kingston, but it is not a new town. At the time of the Domesday Book, 1086, there was no record of Surbiton. Whilst there is no definitive record of the origins of the place name, Statham (1996:2) suggests that the name may be derived from 'south of the belltower', as there is also a Norbiton in the area. More likely, it may be related to 'bereton', denoting a grange in an outlying part of the

Figure 5.1   The Lefi Day Parade on Surbiton High Street. Author's own, 2015.

manor.[3] For many years, the area was farmland, mainly serving Kingston. By the 1800s maps showed an area largely uninhabited but for a Maple Farm. In 1801, the Inclosure (Consolidation) Act[4] was passed, accelerating the speed at which common lands, owned by all people, could be sold, and in 1806 an Inclosure Act was passed for 'lands in and around Kingston upon Thames and Imworth'. By 1825, much of the land in and around Surbiton Hill and Tolworth, to the east of present-day Surbiton, had been sold. Land in and around the current high street was still being used by Maple Farm, and the owner, Christopher Terry, had no intention of selling. Around the same time, a proposal was made to build a London to Portsmouth railway line. Initially, the route was to go through Kingston, but this plan was opposed by the gentlemen of Kingston, who feared it would interfere with their profitable coach trade. The Earl of Wimbledon opposed the railway line passing through his land. Consequently the 'Kingston-upon-Railway' station opened in 1836 around two miles from Kingston, on land that was then mainly farmland with only a scattering of residents. This new station fuelled a coaching trade between 'Kingston-upon-Railway' and Kingston. It would later become Surbiton station.

Upon the death of Terry in 1838, the land in and around the current high street was purchased by Thomas Pooley for £10,000. Pooley built grand townhouses on the land, and grew rich from this investment. His townhouses were often three storeys high and with classic yellow-brown London brick and distinctive large steps to the front doors and large windows (see Figure 5.2). The housing and road infrastructure introduced by Pooley still makes up most of Surbiton's housing stock and architectural character. Pooley had planned to build similar houses in the area directly east of the River Thames, at the western extremity of Surbiton close to the filter beds, but was unable to finish his building plans. Pooley was not a 'gentleman', an established member of the business class of Kingston. He, and his wealth, were much disliked by the Kingston elite. His funding for building was withdrawn as he lacked support from the wealthy lenders; he became bankrupt and eventually fled to France. The names Pooley gave to the roads were changed, and today there remains in the area little or no direct visible link to Pooley, such as street signs or commemorative plaques, other than the houses he built (Statham 1996). Pooley's unfinished project, which would have built houses on roads leading from Maple Lane to the river, was completed in the late 1800s by William Woods. Woods built large grand houses by the Kingston end of the land and smaller workers' houses by the Surbiton filter beds (Figure 5.3). These 'river roads', as they are known locally, form a metaphorical ladder from Surbiton's small cottages to the grand townhouses at the more

Figure 5.2 Thamas the giant parades down a typical Surbiton street with Pooley houses. Author's own, 2015.

Figure 5.3 River road houses. Author's own, 2015.

affluent and upper-class Kingston end. Between such roads, inter-war housing of the distinctive mock Tudor, pitched-roof style has, over the years, filled in the gaps in the master plans of Pooley and Woods, leading to varied housing styles, but overall, the area maintains a typically suburban feel with gardened family homes and spacious streets.

Today most of the Pooley and Woods houses remain. The evening sun shines across the river and down the river roads. The houses flow between Surbiton's commercial side by the rail station and the calmer, greener side by the river, and people flow down these streets as they leave the busy commuter station at rush hour. Surbiton locals pack the morning trains towards London and spill out of them in the evening. The area is excellent for commuting, as the train which leaves the now art deco station only takes 17 minutes to reach Waterloo in central London (although curiously it was 14 minutes when it was first built). As one moves from the station to the river, one moves through Pooley's townhouses before reaching Maple Road or, as the estate agents like to call it, Maple Village (it was never a village), with cafés, gastropubs and monthly farmers' markets. Large established trees line most streets. There is a scattering of small parks and green spaces, in addition to well-kept front gardens. The area has a generous number of small pubs which historically served the filter bed workers. Each pub has its own character, and a specific local role, from showing televised sports to being a place to eat, a centre of community activity or a venue for live music. The pubs support a lively social scene. Despite the number of social venues in the pleasant environment of Surbiton, many people felt more needed to be done to strengthen the sense of community in the area and established the Seething events so as to provide a suitable means to that end.

The state of Seething

In the introduction we outlined how the Seething events emerged from a series of meetings of like-minded people who wanted to encourage community togetherness in the area. We looked at how Seethingers describe these events as 'stupid', in that they lack sense, are for fun and aim to avoid the traditionalism, commitment or political affiliations of other community-based groups. This section outlines further the look and form of the events, in particular the Seething Freshwater Sardine Festival.

As outlined in Chapter 3, Seething events revolve around a moral story and are often written up as children's books. They often attach rich myths and histories to local landscapes. They represent and promote an ideal notion of community: a perfect village of people who value each other's time, company and difference (see Box 1.1). The Seething events are also future-orientated: they tell of a time past in order to work against negative aspects of contemporary life, in pursuit of a better future. However, there is also an emphasis on the process and labour needed to build community. The Community Brain stated:

> The objectives of the Company are to carry on activities which benefit the community, in particular anyone who believes they are outside of a perceived, meaningful community. This could be people isolated by culture, geography, poverty, disability or simply a lack of connection with the people around them.[5]

The organisers of the Seething events are aware of the pervading cultural imaginary of suburbs as dull, lifeless places. They do not reject this imaginary outright but play purposely within those imaginaries in order to challenge and change them. The events often use public space and involve parading and live music. They rupture the daily habits of suburban shoppers, dog walkers and commuters and insert, in the words of one interlocutor, 'a something else' into the public space. They give a different reason to gather, and prompt participants to use the suburb in a different way. The aforementioned 'stupidity' of the events is generated by playing with established tropes of suburban life and twisting them. This stupidity enables a conceptual crafting, by means of the redistribution of established normative suburban relations, aesthetics and habits. This stupidity is an ongoing process. The Seething events, whilst they follow a loose narrative, are far from prescribed. In fact, the core stories are malleable; as explained in Chapter 3, the Seethingers reject expertise to ensure that everyone can be included. As people socialise at the event they might be presented with Seething 'facts'. For example, someone might tell you that the area used to be home to a sardine cannery which exported sardines to London via the train line. This, it is rumoured by Seethingers, is why locals describe riding the train as being 'packed in like sardines'. Once presented with this 'fact' one can decide to ignore it and walk away, join in, or even embellish the story (see Chapter 3). Suburbs are thought of by the Seethingers as places for fun and improvisation and, as Harry – a regular Seethinger who chatted to me at his birthday drinks – said, 'Suburbs are places you can fail'. Fran interjected, as she heard me asking Harry why the Seething myths were important, 'Yes, failure doesn't matter because you can [get something wrong], then just embellish the legend that you were trying to illustrate by bringing in some already established characters and bringing them into the plot and thus adding to the legend.' Flexibility and doing things in a non-prescribed way extends to all Seething life: it is part of 'the state of mind'. Fran adds:

> The point is you can have a go at something that isn't your field or your day job or whatever and it's fine because there is nothing to lose from it. ... It's different to the local history society or something, because they've all got rules and it's all set up, there is a set way of doing things that's established and looked up to and if people don't meet those norms they are frowned on. You hear about it all the time – someone has upset the Surbiton Ladies' Association because they have put the cake ingredients in the wrong order or something.

I suggested to Fran that she could not take a substandard cake to the pub. Fran responded, 'I did! To the Clandestine Cake Club. I had a brick of a cake, I'd left it in the oven to cool when I went out, and when I came back it was solid, but I still took it to show I'd had a go.' In contrast to the cake in the ASP meetings, which could be eaten but not discussed, here we have cake that should be discussed, but not eaten. Both perform a social function of bonding people by aligning them with a common social project. The ASP's cake enables the maintenance of a vertical social organisation whilst the seething cake enables horizontal social organisation.

Planning an event

Whilst Seething events are full of improvisation, experimentation and flexibility, it does require significant time and energy to organise and execute them satisfactorily. All Seething events originate from an idea which gets bounced around until someone calls a meeting in the local pub to make the idea happen. Steve has been a central figure in Seething events and usually chairs the meetings, although, it must be noted, sometimes with a degree of reluctance. He wants the meetings to be open to everyone and has, on occasion, insisted that others chair the meetings. Despite this, in my time following the planning meetings, Steve was always central to steering meetings and had a skill for including everyone and listening to ideas.

The meetings would be advertised on social media (typically Facebook) as well as through flyers, posters and word of mouth. They were almost always held in the pub on a weekday evening. The pub allowed a degree of informality. Seethingers often gathered around a large table that had been temporarily assembled out of smaller tables that fitted together awkwardly. People sat around it, whilst some would sit on bar stools slightly further back. Some people stood away from the meeting, talking to others, but could be drawn in by specific requests and might well chip in. For example, if there was a discussion of how to run electricity to a park and there was a local electrician having a drink, then the table would call them over and get them involved. Zara, who almost always went to the meetings, told me they once tried having the meeting elsewhere, in a conscious effort to move away from the pub and drinking environments, but 'it didn't work, it just wasn't the same vibe'. There was an intuitive phenomenological awareness of the conditions needed for the right sort of meeting: the room, the atmosphere and the flow of bodies needed to be 'just right'. The landlords of the pub were committed Seethingers; they ran a charity bar at Seething events, reserved tables for meetings and gave over the pub garden to craft days so that Seething sculptures could be made. Historically, pubs in the UK have always provided a relaxed meeting space conducive to social mixing, and are considered key spaces for (resilient) communities (see Miller 2019).

Around 15 to 20 people would usually attend meetings, with one or two new faces each time. At the start, attendees would say their names and, if they liked, something about themselves by way of introduction. Seethingers were committed to getting to know others on a personal level, and people would make an effort to get to know newcomers. People would ask about other people's interests, hobbies and hopes. They were keen to discover what people might be able to contribute to Seething events. Meetings would not have agendas or minutes. They were usually initiated around an event that needed planning. People would talk about previous events – what went well, what didn't go so well. They often discussed how to get others involved. After a few years of the events, once they were firmly established in the local area, the Community Brain, the CIC that was set up by a small group of Seethingers to help gain funds and help other communities do similar things, started doing more extensive research in the community around feelings of inclusion and has focused events on harder-to-reach groups, such as younger people. The work of the Community Brain is often done very much in the background of the events and has virtually no noticeable presence at the Seething meetings and events in any official sense.

Being 'stupid' extended to the Seething meetings through parodies of professional and bureaucratic 'meeting language' that seemed out of place, such as 'theoretically we have the lino to make it work'. Play and invention were a way to have fun in solving practical problems; there was no set way of doing things, as long as they got done. Stupid suggestions

Figure 5.4 Suburban skiing. Author's own, 2014.

were taken seriously, and serious suggestions were, to a degree, considered a little boring. Any person who suggested how things could and should be done was then expected to make them happen. The moral responsibility fell on them alone. For example, during the planning of an event called 'suburban skiing', which sees people attach large blocks of ice to their feet (see Figure 5.4) and slide down a stretch of lino on the area's only (rather gentle) hill, there was an issue of how to get people from this morning event on the hill to the afternoon event of the King's Soup, in the nearby park. I, despite knowing better, joked that we should build a ski lift, to which Steve responded 'Great Jeeva, you're in charge of that then. A ski lift! Brilliant.' With the joke I had committed myself to the task and hence to others, to the event, to the community, to being 'stupid', and to Seething. Over the next month or so people asked how my plan was going, came up with ideas and suggested solutions. Eventually I made something that resembled a button-style ski lift by attaching old vinyl records to bamboo garden sticks. People would hold a stick between their legs, with the record serving as the button, and walk from one event to the other.

This 'can-do' attitude, of 'getting things done' and 'chipping in' with the 'spirit of inclusion', ran across the events. Local businesses were often invited to run small stalls to sell produce, crafts and food. A range of local musicians always performed at the events. On the day of the events many people would arrive early and stay late to help set up and pack down the stage, bunting and stalls and pick up litter. This was considered a key moment to meet new people, as well as to recruit people into the process of volunteering, as tidying up was an opportunity to tell people, one to one, how these events come about and what they aim to do. Seething events were largely held in spring or autumn and were usually attended by 200 to 500 people. There would be a wide range of people, but families and young children were especially well represented. A recent survey by the Community Brain CIC showed that most of the people who were involved in some way with the events were in full-time work or retired, and homeowners. Of the crowd of attendees, a quarter or more would 'chip in' to help with the delivery of the events in some way.

The Seething Freshwater Sardine Festival

The Sardine Festival marks the local relationship to the river and is usually held in the spring, at the beginning of May. The story of the 'last sardine', outlined in Chapter 3, tells a tale of a young child who, after talking to a fish about the ecological peril to the local waterways, persuades a disillusioned old man to come and help clean up the river. The tale is steeped in local landmarks, moral tales about looking after the environment, the inspiring perspectives of innocent children who have not been disheartened by the greed and individualism of modern life and, at the heart of it, the importance of community. Before the event, Seethingers circulate videos and stories on social media about the old sardine traditions. Old (but, apparently, recently rediscovered) 'archive footage' of the sardine industry is used to promote the date of the event.

People gather, many in fancy dress, on the banks of the Thames at the Surbiton end of the walkway from Kingston. Hundreds watch as a boat is rowed around the bend in the river to drop a fishing net. The Seething fishermen draw no fish, and the crowd groans. They then sing 'Seething sea shanties' from sheets given out by volunteers, led by local

Figure 5.5 Seethingers pulling 'Seething freshwater sardines' from the River Thames. Author's own, 2014.

musicians. The fishermen drop the net again but on the other side of the boat. To the joy and cheers of the onlooking crowd they pull a full catch of Seething 'freshwater sardines' (see Figure 5.5). The catch is rowed ashore and placed in an old blue cart. This is pulled through the streets of Surbiton by four people dressed as giant guinea pigs (nobody seems to know why guinea pigs) and the crowd follows (see Figure 5.6). Volunteers wearing high-visibility jackets line the parade to stop traffic and frantically run from the back of the parade to the front to keep everyone safe. People dress up as fish and other sea creatures. Many costumes are home-made with varying levels of skill and inspired by all things fishy, from fish-related dresses and hats to umbrellas made into jellyfish. Some people hand out things that they have made, such as a small felt fish badge, and there is a stock of props, or 'historical objects', that join every parade, including a giant can of 'freshwater sardines' and a banner of the ancient guild of Seething fishermen. When the crowd reaches the park the 'freshwater sardines' are 'cooked' and shared out, while the Villagers are entertained by local musicians. Drinks are served from a charity bar and the park is filled with the stalls of local food and craft businesses.

The book *The Last Sardines* (Hutchinson 2012) is read aloud from the stage and the tale is re-enacted by some of the Villagers in front of a crowd of onlookers, with small children sitting at the front (see Figure 5.7). At the end of the afternoon the whole community helps clean

Figure 5.6 The Seething Freshwater Sardine Parade. Author's own, 2014.

Figure 5.7 A reading of 'The tale of the last sardine'. Author's own, 2014.

the park and pack away borrowed tables, stages and sound equipment, and most head to the pub soon after. Whilst the event is officially over, the pub stays busy until closing time. Music continues here, and old and less old Seethingers share tales, recounting the events of the day. Sometimes you can hear people less familiar with the Seething tales stating their surprise that there was a sardine cannery in the area, or asking a Seethinger for more details about the history. It is at this point that Seething facts come to be productive in getting people to join in the creative mode of Seething semiotics. Whilst this was outlined broadly in Chapter 3, here we will look in more depth at the semiotic processes and manoeuvres involved in being stupid. It is these semiotic manoeuvres that form the detail of how community is crafted from the field.

The impact of the Festival: realigning fish

As well as being a link to ecology and the river, the focus on fish is a purposeful nod to the historical iconography of the local area, its three-fish crest. However, the local government's use of the fish as a symbol is rather more serious and official than the approach of the Seethingers. One Seethinger told me that after it used the three-fish symbol a local fish and chip shop was ordered to chisel one of the fish off its shop sign because the use of the symbol was not officially sanctioned. I never did determine if the anecdote was accurate or a Seething 'fact'. However, it demonstrates the contrast between the Seething use of the fish and the perceived approach of the council.

Tim, an active Seethinger, described how his relationship to the local area changed after his involvement in the Seething events. He drew attention to his sense of citizenship and ownership of place in particular. Tim had been one of the dozen or so Seethingers who had kept walking diaries for me as part of my research. I had asked a small group of people to keep a diary over the period of a week, three times a year. I asked them to note in it any thoughts and feelings about living in the area. I wanted the diaries to capture the more dreamy, unexpected or private thoughts about living in Surbiton that may not have been observed at Seething events, in formal interviews or in casual chats. I had conducted some walking interviews to try to develop a sense of people's relation to place when they were away from the carnival of the events. But the diaries opened a way to understanding people's individual relationship to place, away from community activity, in times of solitude. Tim wrote that he would leave his house each day for work or a leisure walk. He would notice the fish on street signs, litter bins and around the local area. For Tim the events had changed (or *obviated*, in a Wagnerian sense; see Chapter 2), the symbolic associations of the fish. The festival had the effect of realigning the indexed meaning (following Gell 1998) of the fish sign from one of government, officialdom and hierarchy to one of community, fun times and silliness. The fish was now an everyday reminder of community, togetherness and inclusion which gave Tim a sense of horizontal citizenship as opposed to the feelings of vertical citizenship he got from the council's use of the fish. Tim wrote to me in an email exchange about my writing on this issue.

> We look forward with our fish, whereas the reactionary conservative council look back – with a prominent fish in the 'coat of arms' that is more martial than social, we hope to recover what they believe has been lost [meaning togetherness, love and balance] ... This too is totally different from what the council believe is lost, the council is **civic-above-citizen** – ours is more inclusive and wants it to be **civic-for-the-citizen**. (Emphasis in original)

For Tim, the Seething events had helped him form a different relation to the area and changed his idea of his position as a citizen. To uncover the empirical detail of how the Seething Freshwater Sardine Festival enables these manoeuvres, I will use a semiotic analysis derived from anthropological work on ritual, humour and material culture to examine the productive aspects of being 'stupid'.

The semiotics of being stupid

The Seething Freshwater Sardine Festival, whilst stupid, can be thought of as a mode of ritual in terms of the semiotic manoeuvres it involves, how it enables Seethingers to change the relation between the fish symbol and its meaning, and so craft their sense of citizenship. As Rupert Stasch explains, ritual can be thought of as 'composed of densely crisscrossing indexical and iconic relations between its different internal elements and of densely crisscrossing indexical and iconic relations between the ritual spacetime and larger macrocosmic orders made present in that spacetime.' (2011:161). Stasch is referring to the ability of ritual forms to bring different elements of meaning and materials together in new and novel ways. This happens in a special ritual moment, that is to say, outside normal everyday time and space. Rituals can reconfigure the co-ordinates of relations between different meanings and symbols to forge new relations and associations. Similarly, the use of the fish symbol by the Seethingers transforms the index of the fish from 'civic above citizen' to 'civic for the citizen' through playing in the gap between meaning and materials by drawing on the wide range of semiotic associations the fish has in the local area.

As discussed in Chapter 2, Alfred Gell argues that the slashing of the Rokeby Venus is politically efficacious because the object attacked 'may objectify a whole series of relations in a single visible form' (1998:62). For Tim, the fish symbolised a particular mode of being governed, associations of hierarchy, officialdom, and power over the population. When placed in the context of a 'stupid' Seething event, the fish came to symbolise a less hierarchical and more community-oriented type of governance. Seethingers had obviated (Wagner 1981) the power of the official fish by 'supplanting a conventional semiotic relation with an innovative and self-contained relation' (Wagner 1981:31). Seethingers had recontextualised the fish, played with it, and animated it as an icon with new memories and associations. In doing this, they realigned the index of meaning.

The use of humour is crucial to the way Seethingers execute this manoeuvre. Marianna Keisalo uses Wagner's notions of semiotic convention and invention to analyse the ways in which comedians play with 'an element in the wrong place' (Keisalo 2014:42, citing Wagner 1981) to make abrupt shifts in semiotic perspective to achieve their performative aims of politically impactful humour (see also Keisalo 2018:119). In Seething their use of fish similarly puts an 'element in the wrong place' in order to create humour but also a realignment of citizenship. The philosopher of language J. L. Austin (1962) argued that a sign (in our case, the fish) can only have force and communicate meaning if it is recognisable. The iterability of the sign is essential to the performative act. In his 'speech act' theories Austin asserts that words, icons and signs are used not only to present information but also to carry out actions, and these actions are involved in the ongoing and dynamic relation between the icon, or sign, and its meaning. A performative utterance, then, uses a sign or icon in a dynamic way, which can change its meaning. However, prior knowledge of a sign's meaning is important. If one utters 'fish', another must know what it represents for it to have social force and meaning in a moment of use. For a performative utterance to have 'illocutionary force' – that is, for it to create meaning – a number of conditions must be met (Culler 1981:18). A key condition is 'an accepted conventional procedure having a certain conventional effect' (Austin 1962:14–15). Iterability of the sign, or recognisability, is central to the performative act; an utterance must be made within the context of a convention and a shared realm of signification. The Seethingers are aware of the fish's symbolism in the area. The political power of humour arises because failure is always immanent within the performance of the sign, that is, it can fail to align with a convention (Jeevendrampillai 2017:121). If the normative index of a sign must be reiterated to support conventional meaning, then when a sign is iterated in a non-normative way, as Butler argues, a 'radical rearticulation of the symbolic horizon' (Butler 1993:23) occurs. This is the essence of a joke. To stay with Butler's line of thought, the Seethingers 'queer' the normative context of the fish and carve new possibilities (see Halberstam 2011).

In her work on the semiotics of jokes, Shosanna Felman notes that the 'third feature common to analytic theory and Austinian theory, with respect to the transformation of the status of the referent, consists in the fact that referentiality – analytic or performative – can be reached and defined only through the dimension of failure on the basis of the *act* [and I would add the possibility] *of failing*' (2003:55; emphasis in original). It is this possibility of failure in the performative moment between linking meaning and material that makes jokes and new meanings possible. Applying this idea, we may say that the Seethingers' fish is funny because it doesn't quite align with the conventional use and meaning of the fish symbol in the area; indeed, it fails to align. But whereas Austin (1962) calls this failure a 'misfire', in Seething the uses of fish constitute purposeful performative failures. Felman writes that the 'act of *failing* thus leads, paradoxically, to an *excess* of utterance' which is 'constantly in excess over the *meaning* of the theoretical statement' (Felman 2003:80; emphasis in original). This excess is discharged through humour and carves room for new meaning. As Felman states, the 'act of failing thus opens up the space of referentiality – or of impossible reality – not because *something is missing*, but because *something else is done*, or because something else is said: the term "misfire" does not refer to an absence, but to the enactment of a difference' (2003:57). By playing with the symbol of the fish, the Seethingers create an excess, they overidentify with the symbol of the area. In creating an excess of the fish symbolism they detour the index and take it in another direction. In that moment when the symbol fails to align with its conventional meaning, they insert a new meaning, one of community, inclusion, crafting civic *for* citizen, rather than civic *above* citizen. This occurs through intimate and sensorial interactions with the fish in the Seething Sardine Festival, where the fish are crafted, worn, caught, paraded, cooked, shared, eaten and sung about. Being stupid differs from political comedy in that the performative misfire is not quite satire. The Seethingers do not work to fully reject systems of power or government. Rather, they reject overly hierarchical power and assert their place as active citizens and active agents of community.

The political force of being stupid

In her review of the use of humour in social movements, Kutz-Flamenbaum (2014) describes a binary of internal and external forms of political humour. Internal humour is important in the establishment of a collective identity and the development of a 'We-ness' as opposed to a 'them' (Bernstein 1997, cited in Kutz-Flamenbaum 2014:300). When presented with a story of Seething freshwater sardine history one is faced with a choice: do I question the 'fact' or do I play along? This choice serves to bring people into a community of people who perform a particular history in relation to the local area. External humour, Kutz-Flamenbaum argues, is directed at an audience beyond the immediate group enacting that humour, and is common in protests and political activism. This is clearly seen in political satire. Satire uses humour and irony, usually in the form of an exaggeration of a characteristic or style of the person being ridiculed. According to Angelique Haugerud (2010, 2013), who conducted ethnography amongst American activists and satirists, political satire 'can be a vital step in helping to destabilize political categories, reframe debates, introduce new ideas and norms, rewrite discourse, and build new political communities' (2010:126). Public use of political satire can shape and engage forms of moral citizenship through 'carnivalesque politics' (see Klumbytė 2014). Despite the stupid use of fish, Seethingers do not aim to satirise and undermine the local council and forms of local politics. Indeed, when campaigning directly, people switched their subject position from Seethingers to active citizens, and took up the official, serious language and practices associated with mainstream local politics. Within the events they may have destabilised political frames, but not so as to exclude them. They do it so that additional forms of sociality (distinctly local ones based on local networks of trust and familiarity) can emerge. They made efforts not to offend or exclude anyone from their Seething events, and kept these gatherings separate from more polemical political activity. The Seethingers use internal humour to cultivate the forms of social relations and social capital required to be a good local active citizen. The Seethingers do not use external humour to attack or critique the entirety of late liberal democracy; rather they attack only the assumed citizen position within traditional hierarchies of local governance in order to assert their notions of a more horizontal relation between the citizen and the state. They do this to insert the role of the community into the operations of civic governance.

Working on stand-up comedy in New York, Morten Nielsen asks when political jokes may lose their critical potency. He asks why it is hard to satirise Donald Trump effectively. Using Lévi-Strauss's work on Amerindian myths (in particular the article 'How myths die', 1974), Nielsen argues that, just as myths exhaust their transformative force when they turn into legends, political jokes lose their critical potency when they turn into mockery (Nielsen 2018:153). Nielsen outlines Lévi-Strauss's suggestion that 'myths reach a point of exhaustion when they cease to engender transformations. Myths die, we are told, when their internal system of variations is no longer capable of producing differences in other structures' (Nielsen 2018:175). Nielsen suggests that humour only works *within* a prevailing context. For Nielsen, a satire of Trump by liberal comedians fails because Trump, or rather his supporters, don't consider themselves part of the same social collective. In a similar way, Seething 'facts' only work within the prevailing context of asserting local political citizenship in Surbiton. They work as they are about and for themselves. In this sense the humour of Seething events enables localism; it enacts the kind of locally engaged, community-focused citizenship favoured by 'third way' neoliberal political democracies. The events destabilise traditional relations and hierarchies associated with traditional political life, and introduce horizontal political dynamics. Through humour, Seethingers craft room for themselves in local political life.

Nielsen, paraphrasing Max Gluckman (1963), asks whether political jokes lead to revolution or are merely an ineffective 'ritual of rebellion' (Nielsen 2018:177). One can ask the same of Seething 'stupidity'. Stupidity, as I argued above, is not the same as explicit jokes found in stand-up comedy. Stupidity has parallels with Boyer and Yurchak's discussion of stiob (2010). Stiob, a Russian word for which there is no direct English equivalent, relates to an ironic aesthetic which 'differed from sarcasm, cynicism, derision, or any of the more familiar genres of absurd humor' (Yurchak 2006:250). It involves a high degree of overidentification, to the degree that 'it was often impossible to tell whether this is a form of sincere support or subtle ridicule, or both' (Boyer & Yurchak 2010:185). Yurchak argues that stiob involves a performative 'shift' (2006:24), that is, a communicational turn away from constative (literal or semantic) meaning towards a performative meaning where predictable and repeatable forms of authoritative discourse, such as visual imagery, rhetorical structure and performative style, are mobilised to create excessive aesthetics. These styles could be performed in a form of parody, such as an article in a newspaper that used formulistic communist-party language to critique subcultures of rock music, written anonymously by one of the members of such a rock group. Boyer and Yurchak (2010) argue that such performances are increasingly visible in late liberal democracies, for example the US comedian Jon Stewart's *Daily Show* or the yes-men who parodied corporate rhetoric in their release of a fake apology from Dow Chemical for the Bhopal disaster. Such performances draw attention to the hyper-normalised conditions of social aesthetics and to the mechanisms and recursive formalisations that late liberalism has turned to in order to 'stabilize itself ideologically in much the same way that late socialism did' (Boyer & Yurchak 2010:211). Drawing attention to the hyper-normalised social aesthetics of an ideological mode of social organisation has a radical effect in that it can break the 'frame of perception' (Boyer & Yurchak 2010:212). Boyer and Yurchak lean on the work of Jacques Rancière (2010) to describe how such aesthetic play creates sensorial ruptures and 'redistributes the sensible', that is, it enables a perspective on things that once made sense in a way that renders them far less sensible.

Whilst overidentification with a social aesthetic may, in Boyer and Yurchak's example, aim to reveal the logics and tensions within the aesthetic practices of an ideological social order, that is, late socialism or late liberalism, the stupid acts of Seethingers should not be considered an ideological attack. The changing relation between the state and the citizen and the emergence of the localism paradigm requires collectives of citizens working as a recognisable community. Stupid events take inclusion and participation, and the idea of community, to be a universal good. They confirm the late liberal ideal of locally grounded participation. My interlocutor's explanation of the events as 'just an excuse to get together and be stupid' belies the ways in which the very act of getting together and the social relations it enables are in themselves a response to changing configurations of power.

After the events

In private conversations, Seethingers often told me how the events had altered their relationship to the community and the area. Hannah, a regular organiser and attendee of Seething events, explained that dancing, drinking and having fun in certain public spaces had changed her relationship to them. This was particularly true with regard to Claremont Gardens, where the Sardine Festival was held. She explained that she now walks a longer way to the bus stop just to go through it: 'Until that event, I hadn't walked through that park, now I walk through it every day ... it's one of my favourite places.' Walking through the park now stimulates pleasant memories and feelings. Animating spaces and changing people's relation to them had always been an aim of the Seething events. The first Lefi Day Parade started and ended in a privately owned timber yard. The community worked to convince the council that the events should happen in public spaces, and a few years later the Mayor of Kingston stated from the stage of the Sardine Festival, 'Claremont Gardens' moment has arrived ... It has been waiting to have its moment for around a hundred years and it has become a new home for Lefi.' A conscious effort had been made to build relationships, memories and positive associations with the underused spaces of the area.

In this way Seethingers are 'crafting affect' (Navaro-Yashin 2012). The term 'affect' relates to feelings or dispositions. It is often related to the work of Benedict Spinoza who, when discussing emotion, describes 'modifications of the body, whereby the active power of the said body is increased or diminished, aided or constrained, and also the ideas of such modifications' (Spinoza [1677] 2001: Part III, p. 2). It is this relation between emotions, feelings and bodily dispositions that is key. The term has been used by social theorists to describe the relation of one's body and subconscious to their environment. 'Affect' has been described by geographer Steve Pile (2013) as pre-emotional, pre-representation and/ or pre-expression. 'Affect' refers to the ability of any matter to affect the state of being, as Seigworth and Gregg (2010:2) say:

> Affect can be understood then as a gradient of bodily capacity – a supple incrementalism of ever-modulating force-relations – that rises and falls not only along various rhythms and modalities of encounter but also through the troughs and sieves of sensation and sensibility, an incrementalism that coincides with belonging to comportments of matter of virtually any and every sort.

Affect theorists have drawn attention to the ways in which the body is subtly affected by a wide range of forces, such as lighting, materiality, noise, rhythms, and habits of embodied experience of being in a place. In her analysis of life in Northern Cyprus, Yael Navaro-Yashin draws attention to how the landscape of ruination, abjection and crumbling infrastructure affects the Turkish-Cypriot experience of the everyday materiality of place, often at a subconscious level. Navaro-Yashin believes that material and imagination work together to produce a sense of being that comes simultaneously from the person and the environment. The materiality of the landscape is more than a setting for the production of social relations, emotional states and concepts; 'conceptual crafting emanates or emerges from the tangibilities of the field' (Navaro-Yashin 2012:11). In a similar, if less extreme, way, Seethingers are attentive to the ways in which the materiality of the suburb affects the experience of life in Surbiton. They make efforts to animate underused spaces and infuse them with positive memories. But they are doing more than crafting memories; they are crafting bodily feelings and dispositions to the area (which we consider more in later chapters).

In addition to the new affective and emotional states, Seethingers are producing new forms of social and economic relations. Rachael, another regular organiser, had recently been made redundant from her job and decided to become self-employed. She explained how the Seething community enabled her to feel 'supported' to try new things and 'discover I'm good at stuff', such as organising and running events. This gave her confidence in her professional life. She said: 'For me, getting involved in Seething is the first time I have felt like I belong, for the first time in my life! I have been able to be myself and become a part of that group.' Rachael had decided to stop working in central London in order to work locally, using the contacts and networks she had developed through Seething events. For her the suburb was not a dull commuter town but a place of hope and vibrancy. However, whilst explaining how much energy she needed to use her skills and time for Seething events, Rachael added that she needed to keep a 'balance' and aimed to find time to develop herself. The Seething events helped locals form community and bonds, but, as Rachael's comments remind us, this can be seen through the lens of the neoliberal trend to push the onus of responsibility for development onto individuals and community. Seethingers were aware that the Surbiton area was blessed with a large number of people with well-paid jobs, relatively large amounts of free time and appropriate professional skills to help put on the events. Such skills and resources are not evenly distributed across all communities but are rather a particular luxury of a largely middle-class area. Seethingers were always trying to consciously reflect on their community-building practices. As Harry told me over a drink in a pub one evening, 'Actually, I don't think we are that inclusive at all, and that's one thing that gets me, actually. I mean, how many meetings do we have that aren't in or don't end in the pub, and we have a particular sense of humour that takes some getting used to.' Rachael added, 'It's so open, people find it difficult to become involved.' The idea that one can try and fail in doing Seething, and the constant invention of 'facts', were crucial in finding new ways and styles through which people could be encouraged into this community-making process.

Conclusions: making life in the suburbs

This chapter has outlined how the Seething events serve to alter the ways in which people relate to the local area. Being stupid changes how people feel about the area both in an emotional, embodied way and through their approaches to work and citizenship. Seethingers perform their 'stupid' events in the context of the dystopian suburban imaginary of sleepy, lifeless places. These performances counter this imaginary, as well as the pervading spectre of the traditional hierarchical organisation of local governance. Being deeply aware of the negative image of suburbia, Seethingers seek to assert a form of suburban life that is future-focused and predicated on togetherness, meaning community members know, trust and spend time with each other. These ideals are typified in the Seething stories, but the stories also serve as a playful way of making new forms of suburban life.

When Seethingers obviate the meaning of the fish (shifting its meaning from 'civic-above-citizen' to 'civic-for-citizen'), they assert a form of politically qualified life. That is, returning to Agamben's (1998) notions of *bios* and *zoë* (see Chapter 2), these citizens have an active relationship to the area, and are able to craft conceptually their relation and response to symbols of civic authority, to the local landscape and to their feelings of citizenship.

Through playing with what Halberstam calls the 'grammar of possibility' (2011:2) the Seethingers' play allows them to assert alternative indexical relations to otherwise stable signifiers and, by doing so, creates new modes of association between Surbiton residents and the civic realm. The Seethingers assert a form of sovereignty here. As Antigone's love for her brother was unsupported by the current conditions of the symbolic (in Butler's 2000 reading; see Chapter 2), the Seethingers assert a form of life and modes of association that were otherwise unsupported by the symbolic. Through playing with the fish, the Seethingers test the threshold of its known symbolic meaning, and detour it, creating new associations and meanings. They carve out a role for themselves in the management of the icons of localism.

We will return to the concept of a politically qualified life more explicitly in Chapter 7, where we see locals engage in a political campaign in the area. Both there and here it is important to note that the Seethingers are not, however, engaging in a social project that is radically different from that of the mainstream contemporary UK. They do not, fundamentally, reject neoliberal ways of life, nor do they reject the local authority, systems of local governance or prevailing social ideologies. In fact, many Seethingers have worked for and with, and support, the council. Many Seethingers have what Gershon (2011) might call a reflexive neoliberal agency, in that they are skilled workers who care about being better workers (more employable, more efficient). The work of Seethingers is best thought of as a corrective to pervading everyday patterns, rhythms and relations of daily late liberal life, rather than a rejection of it. They work hard to assert values of community, localness and their sense of citizenship, which are at the core of the late liberal social project. Seethingers reject the idea that their events are directly political. They avoid potentially divisive contemporary issues, such as Brexit and protest movements like Extinction Rebellion. Whilst I learnt that individuals may have clear positions and opinions on such topics, the events are carefully stewarded to avoid association with political campaigns.

Seethingers play at the edge of prevailing ideological norms, symbolic orders and notions of citizenship through mechanisms of humour that are not quite jokes or satire but do involve overidentification (excess fish, mythical histories, etc.) with the everyday aesthetics of the suburb. Through their stupid events they emphasise values associated with community in the face of crushing neoliberal dystopias of lonely work life. They find new, local modes of work. They assert an engaged form of citizenship in terms of their relation to the civic realm, positioning themselves as rightful moral agents in the management of place, taking on responsibility for how people relate to the landscape and governance of the area in an emotional register. They play with historical symbols of political authority and notions of expertise, and assert their agency, and that of others, through invented stories. If we return to the ASP's map, hopefully it is now clear why the Seethingers needed to persist with the presentation of their Seething 'facts'. They needed to place Mount Seething on the map in order to assert their position as active agents of local citizenship. Whilst the map remained unused, the Seethingers did not ignore the ASP. Rather, they took an active role in trying to add their ideals and forms of life to the project via my ethnographic engagement. A lot of this work occurred in relation to my research. As already discussed, my attempt to engage with the community as part of the ASP prompted the formation of the Free University of Seething. Whilst the Seethingers may not have populated the Community Map, they did, through regular updates via the Free University lectures and the Facebook page, engage with questions such as 'Where is the boundary to Surbiton?' This continued engagement exemplifies the ways in which Seethingers work at the edge of a social project. It is imperative that they assert their values, but they do so in their own way. The next chapter looks at the work of the Free University of Seething in terms of their ongoing and productive relationship with the ASP and with my ethnographic practice. This ongoing relation demonstrates the productive capacity of working at the edge of social projects.

Notes

1. Marks & Spencer is a popular UK department store chain associated with comfort.
2. Series 3, episode 2, 'Mr and Mrs Brian Norris' Ford Popular', first broadcast 26 October 1972.
3. See 'Norbiton' and 'Surbiton' in the *Survey of English Place-Names*. https://epns.nottingham.ac.uk/search/p/%28placeName%3A%2ANorbiton%2A%29# (accessed 28 June 2021).
4. This archaic spelling is maintained in the names of such Acts.
5. http://thecommunitybrain.org/ (accessed 3 June 2014).

References

Ackroyd, Peter. 2001. *London: The Biography*. Random House.
Agamben, Giorgio. 1998. *Homo Sacer: Sovereign power and bare life* (trans. Daniel Heller-Roazen). Stanford, CA: Stanford University Press.
Augé, Marc. 1995. *Non-places: Introduction to an anthropology of supermodernity* (trans. John Howe). London: Verso.
Austin, J. L. 1962. *How to Do Things with Words*. Oxford: Oxford University Press.
Bourne, Larry S. 1996. 'Reinventing the suburbs: Old myths and new realities'. *Progress in Planning* 46, no. 3: 163–84. https://doi.org/10.1016/0305-9006(96)88868-4.
Boyer, Dominic and Alexei Yurchak. 2010. 'American stiob: Or, what late-socialist aesthetics of parody reveal about contemporary political culture in the West'. *Cultural Anthropology* 25, no. 2: 179–221. https://doi.org/10.1111/j.1548-1360.2010.01056.x.
Butler, Judith. 1993. *Bodies that Matter: On the discursive limits of 'sex'*. Abingdon: Routledge.
Butler, Judith. 2000. *Antigone's Claim: Kinship between life and death*. New York and Chichester: Columbia University Press.
Chapman, Graham, John Cleese, Eric Idle, Terry Jones, Michael Palin, Terry Gilliam. 1972. 'Mr and Mrs Brian Norris' Ford Popular'. *Monty Python's Flying Circus*, series 3, episode 2.
Cherry, Marc, producer. 2004–7. *Desperate Housewives*. Cherry Productions.
Clapson, Mark. 2003. *Suburban Century: Social change and urban growth in England and the USA*. Oxford: Berg.
Culler, Jonathan. 1981. 'Convention and meaning: Derrida and Austin'. *New Literary History* 13, no. 1: 15–30. https://doi.org/10.2307/468640.
Duncan, Emma. 2014. 'Death of the high street? Hurrah ...' *Observer*, 27 April. https://www.theguardian.com/commentisfree/2014/apr/27/dont-mourn-loss-of-high-street-turn-shops-into-houses (accessed 28 April 2021).
Dyos, Harold James. 1961. *Victorian Suburb: A study of the growth of Camberwell*. Leicester: Leicester University Press.

Esmonde, John and Bob Larbey. 1975. *The Good Life*. BBC. 4 April 1975–10 June 1978.
Felman, Shoshana. 2003. *The Scandal of the Speaking Body: Don Juan with J. L. Austin, or seduction in two languages* (trans. Catherine Porter). Stanford, CA: Stanford University Press.
Gell, Alfred. 1998. *Art and Agency: An anthropological theory*. Oxford: Clarendon Press.
Gershon, Ilana. 2011. 'Neoliberal agency.' *Current Anthropology* 52, no. 4: 537–55. https://doi.org/10.1086/660866.
Gluckman, Max. 1963. 'Rituals of rebellion in south-east Africa.' In Max Gluckman, *Order and Rebellion in Tribal Africa: Collected essays, with an autobiographical introduction*, pp. 110–36. London: Cohen & West.
Griffiths, Sam, Laura Vaughan, Mordechai Haklay and Catherine Emma Jones. 2008. 'The sustainable suburban high street: A review of themes and approaches.' *Geography Compass* 2, no. 4: 1155–88. https://doi.org/10.1111/j.1749-8198.2008.00117.x.
Halberstam, Judith. 2011. *The Queer Art of Failure*. Durham, NC: Duke University Press.
Haugerud, Angelique. 2010. 'Neoliberalism, satirical protest, and the 2004 U.S. presidential campaign.' In Carol J. Greenhouse, ed., *Ethnographies of Neoliberalism*, 112–27. Philadelphia: University of Pennsylvania Press.
Haugerud, Angelique. 2013. *No Billionaire Left Behind: Satirical activism in America*. Stanford, CA: Stanford University Press.
Hinchcliffe, Tanis. 2005. 'Review essay: Elusive suburbs, endless variation.' *Journal of Urban History* 31, no. 6: 899–906. https://doi.org/10.1177/0096144205276993.
Hutchinson, Robin. 2012. *The Last Sardines: A Seething legend*. [Surbiton]: Homage Publishing.
Jackson, Kenneth T. 1987. *Crabgrass Frontier: The suburbanization of the United States*. New York and Oxford: Oxford University Press.
Jeevendrampillai, David. 2017. 'Failure as constructive participation: Being stupid in the suburbs.' In Timothy Carroll, David Jeevendrampillai, Aaron Parkhurst and Julie Shackelford, eds, *The Material Culture of Failure: When things do wrong*, pp. 113–32. London and New York: Bloomsbury Academic.
Keisalo, Marianna. 2014. 'Forum: Anthropologies of humor. Introduction: Humor in its own right?' *Suomen Antropologi: Journal of the Finnish Anthropological Society* 39, no. 4: 40–4.
Keisalo, Marianna. 2018. 'Perspectives of (and on) a comedic self: A semiotics of subjectivity in stand-up comedy.' *Social Analysis* 62, no. 1: 116–35. https://doi.org/10.3167/sa.2018.620108.
Klumbytė, Neringa. 2014. 'Of power and laughter: Carnivalesque politics and moral citizenship in Lithuania.' *American Ethnologist* 41, no. 3: 473–90. https://doi.org/10.1111/amet.12088.
Kutz-Flamenbaum, Rachel V. 2014. 'Humor and social movements.' *Sociology compass* 8, no. 3: 294–304. https://doi.org/10.1111/soc4.12138.
Lévi-Strauss, Claude. 1974. 'How myths die' (trans. F. C. T. Moore). *New Literary History* 5, no. 2: 269–81. https://doi.org/10.2307/468396.
McClellan, Jim. 1999. 'Everything you think you know about suburbia is wrong.' *Big Issue*, 4 November.
McKie, David. 2004. 'Surbiton's sinful secrets.' *Guardian*, 19 August. https://www.theguardian.com/uk/2004/aug/19/britishidentity.comment (accessed 28 April 2021).
McManus, Ruth and Philip J. Ethington. 2007. 'Suburbs in transition: New approaches to suburban history.' *Urban History* 34, no. 2: 317–37. https://doi.org/10.1017/S096392680700466X.
Mendes, Sam, dir. 1999. *American Beauty*. DreamWorks Pictures.
Miller, Daniel. 2019. 'Of pubs and platforms.' *Journal of the Royal Anthropological Institute* 25, no. 4: 793–809. https://doi.org/10.1111/1467-9655.13132.
Mills, A. D. 2010. 'Kingston upon Thames'. In *A Dictionary of London Place Names*, 2nd edn. Oxford: Oxford University Press.
Moore, Rowan. 2016. 'With the Good Life over, how can suburbia regain its place in the sun?' *Observer*, 19 July. https://www.theguardian.com/cities/2016/jul/09/suburbs-architecture-stagnation (accessed 28 April 2021).
Muzzio, Douglas and Thomas Halper. 2002. 'Pleasantville? The suburb and its representation in American movies.' *Urban Affairs Review* 37, no. 4: 543–74. https://doi.org/10.1177/10780870222185469.
Navaro-Yashin, Yael. 2012. *The Make-Believe Space: Affective geography in a postwar polity*. Durham, NC, and London: Duke University Press.
Nielsen, Morten. 2013. 'Analogic asphalt: Suspended value conversions among young road workers in southern Mozambique.' *HAU: Journal of Ethnographic Theory* 3, no. 2: 79–96. https://doi.org/10.14318/hau3.2.006.

Nielsen, Morten. 2018. '"An army of comedy": Political jokes and tropic ambiguity in the Trump era.' In Jana Kopelent Rehak and Susanna Trnka, eds, *The Politics of Joking: Anthropological engagements*, pp. 168–78. Abingdon: Routledge.
Pile, Steve. 2013. *The Body and the City: Psychoanalysis, space and subjectivity*. Abingdon: Routledge.
Portas, Mary. 2011. 'The Portas review: An independent review into the future of our high streets.' Department for Business, Innovation and Skills, London.
Priestley. J. B. [1934] 1984. *English Journey*. Chicago, IL: Chicago University Press.
Rancière, Jacques. 2010. *Dissensus: On politics and aesthetics* (ed. and trans. Steven Corcoran). London and New York: Continuum.
Seigworth, Gregory J. and Melissa Gregg. 2010. 'An inventory of shimmers.' In Melissa Gregg and Gregory J. Seigworth, eds, *The Affect Theory Reader*, pp. 1–25. Durham, NC: Duke University Press.
Spinoza, Benedict de. [1677] 2001. *The Ethics. Part III: On the Origin and Nature of the Emotions* (trans R. H. M. Elwes 1887). http://www.gutenberg.org/files/3800/3800-h/3800-h.htm#chap03 (accessed 28 June 2021).
Stasch, Rupert. 2011. 'Ritual and oratory revisited: The semiotics of effective action.' *Annual Review of Anthropology* 40: 159–74. https://doi.org/10.1146/annurev-anthro-081309-145623.
Statham, Richard. 1996. *Surbiton Past*. Chichester: Phillimore.
Vaughan, Laura, Sam Griffiths, Mordechai (Muki) Haklay and Catherine (Kate) Emma Jones. 2009. 'Do the suburbs exist? Discovering complexity and specificity in suburban built form.' *Transactions of the Institute of British Geographers* 34, no. 4: 475–88. https://doi.org/10.1111/j.1475-5661.2009.00358.x.
Wagner, Roy. 1981. *The Invention of Culture*. 2nd edn. Chicago, IL: University of Chicago Press.
Webber, Melvin M. 1964. 'The urban place and the nonplace urban realm.' In Melvin M. Webber, John W. Dyckman, Donald L. Foley, Albert Z. Guttenberg, William L. C. Wheaton and Catherine Bauer Wurster, eds, *Explorations into Urban Structure*, pp. 79–153. Philadelphia: University of Pennsylvania Press.
Yurchak, Alexei. 2006. *Everything Was Forever, Until It Was No More: The last Soviet generation*. Princeton, NJ: Princeton University Press.

6
How to make a suburb. Part 2: the research activities of the Free University of Seething

When I approached Seethingers in order to conduct research on and with their community, they responded in a characteristically eccentric manner: they established the Free University of Seething (FUS) to host and facilitate these investigations. I had discussed my motivations and explained what the typical ethnographic research process involves. But I was also open about being unsure of the best approach to the research, and sought their thoughts, and their collaboration; the FUS was the response. During these initial conversations, the group had talked with me about what they saw as the prescriptive nature of 'official' knowledge (a direct response to the ASP's exclusion of the data they had submitted to the map). We were soon talking of public lectures, open universities, and involving everyone in my research, less as participants and more as collaborators. This chapter outlines the research of the Free University of Seething as a mode of curatorial anthropology. FUS stands as a space in which ethnographic relations and ways of knowing between interlocutor, academy and researcher emerge through play, disruption and experimentation in the field and in the academy.

The Free University of Seething

A couple of weeks after the idea was first floated, I had the honour of giving the inaugural (public) lecture at the newly founded Free University of Seething. I was joined by other speakers, Wendy and Steve, who spoke on local history and archaeology and on Seething myths respectively. The audience was made up of Seethingers but also of other locals, unfamiliar

Nolite comedere uvas non lautus

Figure 6.1 The Free University of Seething crest replete with cheese and Lefi heads. Courtesy of the Free University of Seething, 2014.

with Seething events, who had seen posters advertising the lecture. The event coincided with the creation of a new 'Free University of Seething' section of the Community Brain website, complete with an academic crest (see Figure 6.1) and an origin myth.

Box 6.1 The Free University of Seething

Long before the 'Open University' the people of Seething founded the Free University of Seething. Indeed, it is considered by many to be the oldest true university in the world. Built upon the foundations of Lefi's Law that 'all people good and true' should 'enjoy and prosper through knowledge freely given through love of learning of Seething'.

From 'all people' we get 'Universal' and from 'love of learning of Seething' we get 'learnseething' which became 'universalearnseething' which in its shortened form was spoken as 'universeethee', the origin of the modern pronunciation of 'university'. …

The Free University of Seething was closed as an institution in 1902 as a result of its then contentious work on global warming and the effects of overuse of the earth's resources. Subsequently much of this work has proved to be sadly correct although unfortunately the hypothesis that within 100 years 'man [sic] would have found a way to overcome greed and resolved a world where resource was shared according to need' … still defeats us.[1]

HOW TO MAKE A SUBURB. PART 2

Since the establishment of FUS and until at least the time of writing, there have been many lectures. They take place in the pub or in the Museum of Futures, an empty high street shop for which funding has been received to repurpose it into a community space. The topics have been varied and the lectures are organised by anyone who is inspired to hold a 'lecture series'. The have usually involved a local person talking about their field of expertise or professional interests, whether that be local history, health, hobbies, or cheese and wellbeing. This chapter will outline the FUS activities that related to my work and that of the ASP. It will consider how the FUS 'faculty' engaged with my research, the ASP, and the issues of finding data such as place boundaries. It will look at how the Seethingers became my research collaborators as FUS faculty members, engaging with and reinterpreting the research through FUS activities. The chapter outlines the ways in which Seethingers locate their community work on the edge of other social projects. Here, at the edge, they productively engage with and detour the aims of other, larger, perhaps more powerful social projects, such as the council's work (which seeks to maintain hierarchical, traditional authority) or that of the ASP (which aims to develop sanctioned forms of expertise, including through my PhD research). At the edge, they aim to detour the ways in which these larger projects understand and define the suburb. As seen in the previous chapter, Seething events have the effect of building community through playful, 'stupid' events. However, in this chapter, we will focus on the ways in which FUS activity can be seen as a form of collaborative research. Through this activity, the Seethingers took my brief and my anthropological approach and engaged with them in a sincere way, but also clearly asserted their own style and values in a way that emphasised their own understanding of suburban life. This allowed me and my colleagues in the ASP to reflect on the assumptions within the ASP research. It led me to reflect on my ethnographic practice in this specific context, but also on wider anthropological approaches. As well as prompting these methodological (and epistemological) reflections, my engagement with the FUS helped illuminate the productive processes and procedures involved in being local. The chapter focuses mainly on the walking tours that were formed as a response to the underused ASP Community Map and which, in many ways, paralleled the research of the ASP in its focus on walking, boundaries and points of interest. The chapter will conclude with a consideration of collaborative anthropological research.

Walking in the suburbs, landscapes of value

I spent a lot of time walking in Surbiton. I walked to make notes on the locations of businesses on the high street for the ASP. I walked in the processions of the Seething events. And I walked to get around the area. Upon learning of my interest in localism, community building and people's sense of relation to place, locals would often offer to show me their suburb with a walk. I started to do walking interviews with individuals, in which people would tell me how their experience of living in the suburb melded the built environment with their memories and experiences. I take the term 'meld' from the work of Bradley Garrett (2013), who, through his ethnography of urban explorers, asserts that when people interact with the built environment they play with constellations of self, city, power, citizenship, land rights, personhood, and other concepts that feed into one's sense of self. Thus one's subjectivity is deeply tied to the places in and through which one lives. In a less spectacular way my suburban interlocutors were also living through their experiences with place.

Tim had explained to me that he walked down certain streets in autumn in order to kick the leaves, and that he gained a sense of seasonality from doing so. Fay told me she would walk the long way round to pass her favourite trees and imagine stories of fairies living there. Louise told me that for her the coffee shop on Queen's Promenade marked the boundary between Surbiton and Kingston. There was no official boundary here, it was just a 'feeling'. I was interested in these stories and how they related to the work of the ASP. Space syntax analysis was based on walking the fastest or easiest route. There was no formula for measuring the route with the nicest leaves. I started to wonder if we could try to generate content for the Community Map through mapping walks.

There is much work on place making and walking. Michel de Certeau's book *The Practice of Everyday Life* (1984) dedicated a chapter to the practice of walking. Certeau asserts that individuals can employ 'tactics' such as walking to counter the 'strategies' of institutions, like urban planning organisations, to govern bodies in a particular way. That is, a walker can drift, dream and enter into an engagement with the city that may differ from the normative conception of what movement in the built environment is supposed to be like or for. I was interested in what locals were telling me about their drifting and walking in the area and how they were curating their relation to place. I was attentive to the ways in which people actively sought or avoided particular places because of the affective experiences that these places afforded. As Zara noted in the previous chapter, she once avoided Claremont Gardens, but after the Seething events she sought it out, because of the memories, experiences and affective atmospheres of that place. As Gillian Rose et al. (2010) have noted in their analysis of how people use the spaces of a shopping centre, rational subjects are able to deploy tactics – such as rhythm, pace and route, thinking and acting with the body – to manage affect, and so their relation to place.

Walking was a noticeable feature of many of my interviews. I started to think about people's relation to place as being more 'archi-textural' than architectural (invoking the philosopher Henri Lefebvre (1991:117–18)), whereby meaning arises more from the process of bodily interactions with the materiality of the suburb, its smells, sights and sounds, than from the mere utility or function of a location. In addition to the ethnography of the Seething events, walking interviews and diaries, I had done casual semi-structured interviews with locals in which I asked them to draw a map of 'their Surbiton' for me. Zara's map (see Figure 6.2) included a particularly prominent set of railings by the filter beds. She told me that she liked the railings, that the road wasn't very nice but that the rusted railings, with their flaky blue paint, had a Victorian charm and

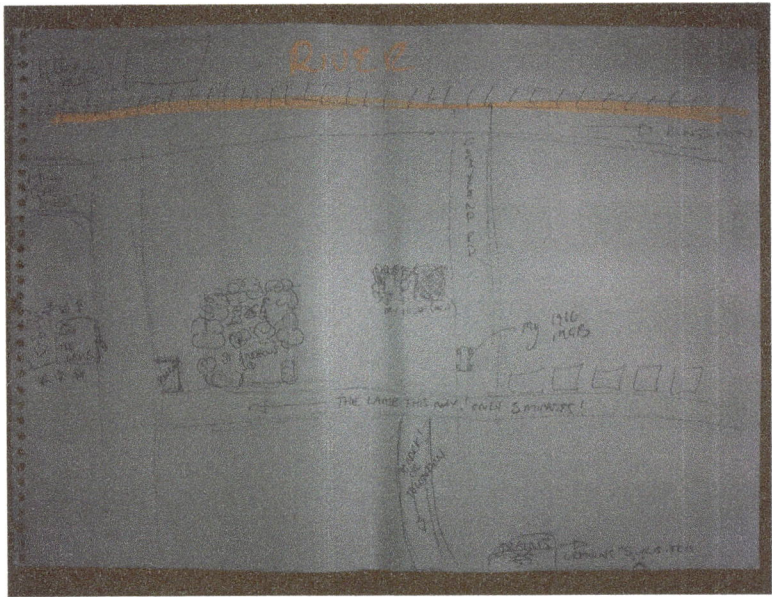

Figure 6.2 Zara's 'map of Surbiton' drawn during a drawing interview, 2012.

let her imagine what happened there when the beds were first built. Noticeably, Zara didn't draw a high street; she told me, 'It doesn't feel like the centre of Surbiton for me; it might be for non-locals and if I was giving people directions, but not for me.' Zara described other spaces in terms of their being more or less inviting, as being associated with memories of people or community activity. Others, such as Molly, who took me on a walk alongside her mother (as she was only four years old), told me that she had to go to see Fox City on each walk, and visit the sandpit, which was an ancient footprint of Thamas the giant. Benny had also noted the materiality of certain routes as he described taking certain streets to see certain house styles, depending on his mood.

As I learnt more about how locals thought about Surbiton in a sensuous, material way, I started to think about the places and values the ASP was foregrounding in its maps, that is, the high street, movement and integration. As Chris Tilley has said, walking, sensing and interacting with the landscape gives rise to novel forms of value. Things, such as railings, trees or leaves, become important in new ways. This 'kinaesthetic approach' (Tilley 2008) to landscape raises interesting questions about how to think about the value of place. The landscape theorist Tim Ingold notes that, as one moves through a landscape, 'things fall into and out of sight, as new vistas open up and others are closed off' (Ingold 2007:87). Through the maps, walking interviews and diaries, I was seeing how, as locals moved around the suburb, different aspects of the landscape would come to be more or less valued and tied to a sense of one's dwelling in the area, to one's local subjectivity.

We can think about the locals' movements in relation to how they value aspects of the landscape in ways that recall how commodity pathway diversion model theorists in anthropology have described notions of value (see Lambek 2013; Graeber 2001, 2013; Appadurai 1988; Kopytoff 1986). In her classic work *The Fame of Gawa* (1986), Nancy Munn outlines how Kula shells are imbued with value through the process of circulation between men on the Polynesian Trobriand Islands. As the shells move and circulate, they become imbued with value; the more they circulate, the more they are handled. This results in a deepening of the shells' red colour as it is affected by skin oils; the deeper the red, the more they are valued. However, in Surbiton, the objects of the landscape don't move; it is the people who move amongst them. With each pass of a street or a railing, habit, memory, rhythm and bodily familiarity are built up and people increasingly affiliate their subjectivity with place (we will see more of this in the following chapter).

Tim Edensor (2010) states that the concept of dwelling has been misunderstood as static. He argues that movement is a core aspect of dwelling, whether that be movement through place, having habits of passing places and seeing how they change, or moving in a particular rhythm or pace and feeling that through the body. In the building of community, walking together is a key mechanism through which people share their knowledge of place with others (see Hall 2009; Dobson 2011). As LaBelle notes, 'walking may be a site for a radical placement and displacement of self, fixing and unfixing self to urban structures, locational politics and cultural form, locking down as well as opening up to the full view of potential horizons' (2008:198). However, most anthropological work on walking has come from the phenomenological and psychogeographical traditions which have focused on one's internal rather than social experience. I was interested in how walking not only helped to meld one's sense of self to place but also crafted a sense of self to community and of community to place.

The Free University of Seething walks

At one of the regular ASP meetings, I gave an update on my walking interviews in Surbiton. A professor and co-investigator suggested I apply for an EPSRC inclusion award grant to fund walking tours. This would help develop the content for the Community Map, which had been underused. The application asked for around £10,000 to be used across three sites of the ASP's research. The application's supportive text read:

> With support from the *Inclusions* scheme we propose to recruit three 'Local Champions', one for each of our three suburban case studies – Surbiton, South Norwood and Loughton – for a unique collaboration between academic researchers and local community activists that focuses on suburban tour-guiding. Advised by our PhD students (under academic supervision) and trained by experienced walking tour guides, each Local Champion will devise and deliver (at least twice) their own walking tour in their local area and follow these up by leading a specialist community-mapping workshop (one for each suburb) organised through the *Adaptable Suburbs* project. As local history enthusiasts and community activists the Champions would be drawn from non-traditional research backgrounds. Our collaboration will innovate methodologically by developing and testing a web-based, community-orientated 'auto-ethnography', using the suburban walking tours as starting points. This approach will combine PPGIS with anthropological methods in new ways,

enabling our Champions to learn new skills and academics to develop existing techniques for gathering information on locality, living patterns and social networks in ways that differ from those offered by traditional academic methods.

Whilst I showed the grant application to the Seethingers, they were not involved in the writing process directly (I didn't want to promise money then not deliver it). However, once we received the award, I advertised on the Seething Facebook page that we had some money to organise the walks and called a meeting in the pub to invite collaboration. A small group of regular Seethingers turned up and formed a working group, which immediately rejected several aspects of the grant outline. In particular, they opposed the recruitment of professional guides; politely but firmly they told me they would rather see what walks local people could offer. The training budget for professional tour guides was rejected as an unnecessary and unSeething imposition of expertise. After a series of meetings, ideas for four walks emerged, all with very different styles and content. The details of the walks were not designed wholly in the context of meetings, but ideas that had been floating around casual conversations at Seething events would evolve into solid proposals in these meetings. Each walk would have a different working group to organise and plan it. The Free University of Seething would host the walks and award degrees to those who came along. Whilst we don't have the space to go through all the walks in detail, I will outline three of the walks briefly before giving a more detailed description of the final walk. This walk involved 'beating the bounds' and was the most popular of the four; 40 or 50 people participated, around twice the number for the other walks.

The first walk was the 'Canvas Walk'. The poster which advertised the walk described it as 'the anarchist tour guide's dream'. The idea for the walk was to meet at the pub at a set time and then decide, as a group, the first 'point of interest'. The term 'point of interest' was taken from the ASP's Community Map. The group would debate the first 'point of interest', decide what it should be and head there as a group. However, if there was disagreement about where the 'point of interest' should be, then people could head in a different direction. The only rule was that you needed to stay with someone with a camera. Six small handheld cameras were distributed to the group at the start of the walk and were used to record the route. As the walk progressed people split into smaller and smaller subgroups. The Canvas Walk was inspired by a combination of factors. Firstly, the walk aimed to assert Seething principles. There was no leader, no pre-planned route and no 'right way'. Linear walking was out; drifting, playing and wandering were in. In this way the Seethingers asserted a form of horizontal decision making, rejecting the idea that any one person can lead and reflecting the ethics of the research event emerging from the field. The walk was inspired by conversations about the Situationists, the avant-garde revolutionaries of mid-twentieth-century France who would use walking in what they called a *détournement*. This idea was based on rejecting purposeful and routine walking in order to detour, wander, *dérive* and meander through city streets, allowing new associations and relations to emerge. Much has been written on this mode of unplanned walking (see Benjamin 1999; de Certeau 1984; Debord and Wolman [1956] 2006), and in the build-up to the walk Seethingers talked about this literature, as well as more recent, London-based literature on walking, such as the work of regular newspaper columnist and psychogeographer Will Self (2012) and popular writer Rebecca Solnit (2001) (both had paid particular attention to London's suburbs). People met back at the pub at a pre-agreed time (a couple of hours after departure). Each group then marked their route on a large paper map of the area. People debated the 'points of interest' over a selection of sandwiches and drinks. The initial plan was for the videos and the route map to be uploaded to the ASP's map. However, this did not happen, because of the inability of the ASP's Community Map to display lines. After some difficulties in trying to adapt the Community Map, the Seethingers decided to host the digital map on a different website and link to it through their own FUS section of the Seething website.[2]

The second walk was called 'Fact & Fiction'[3] and was advertised as 'a walk around Surbiton that draws together local history and folk tales with no delineation between the two'. It indicated that it was 'up to those who walk to decide what they wish to believe as "truth"' – reflecting the contingency of truth and knowledge in research practice. This walk was led by Steve, along a pre-planned route with pre-planned stopping points. However, the walk was open to others to interject with either Seething or non-Seething 'facts'. This walk played with the forms of parafiction and Seething facts that have been outlined in earlier chapters of this book. The walks went some way to assert the whole series of walks as particularly Seething-like. Many people who came on the walks would go away and research 'facts' that sounded made up, but had a strong base in improbable local histories, such as the fact that Surbiton was once home to a sprint cycling world record holder, John Jack Kean, who also played an important role in the development of the modern bicycle.

The third walk, called the 'River Roads Walk', drew attention to the roads that linked the west side of the suburb by the filter beds and the

River Thames to Maple Road in the middle of the neighbourhood. As mentioned in the previous chapter, the river roads had a distinctive character that set them apart from the main area of Surbiton. The inspiration for the walk came from information Seethingers had uncovered in the local archives as they worked with me in researching the history of the area, as part of the grant. For this walk we set the meeting point to be a local coffee shop. As with every walk, new people came along. The walks were advertised in local businesses through posters and flyers and even received a write-up in the local newspaper. Seethingers made efforts to greet new people and make introductions. Hannah, who had helped make the posters and artworks for the walks, greeted newcomer Dom. He asked Hannah, 'Are you a Free University of Seething student?' Hannah explained that she was, and that she was involved in organising the walks. She then explained that at the end of the walk everyone on the walk was to receive a 'Master's in Walking' from FUS. Dom asked, slightly confused, 'So, erm ... it's not a proper university, then?' Hannah explained that it was not an accredited university, to which Dom responded, 'Well, who are the students?' Hannah said that everyone was a student, just as everyone was a teacher. She explained that the walks emerged from the links to my research project and to the grant. She tried to explain the wider Seething events and the forms and style they took, before turning to me (after apparently confusing Dom) and joking, 'You must be loving this – data, data!' The walk took the group up and down a selection of the river roads. At various points actors from a local theatre group, who had helped research the walks, would enact imagined historical scenes from the various characters we discovered in the archival research. They included a Victorian-era philanthropist, a merchant, and a ghost from local folklore. Again, all this was filmed and placed online.[4]

The last of the four-walk series was called 'Beating the Bounds'.[5] The next section takes a deeper look at how this walk came about and was performed. I do this to demonstrate the collaborative, parafictional and stupid nature of the event. An examination of the detail of this event will highlight the ways in which Seethingers were careful to assert their relation to place on their terms. It will also show that they always aimed to work on the edge of larger, conventional social projects, using their language and authority. This walk, more than the others, spoke back very directly to the ASP's needs. It was concerned with boundary lines as well as points of interest, and with the relationship between mapping and walking. Crucially, though, this walk demonstrates how these apparently common, overlapping concerns are understood very differently by the social projects that share them.

Beating the bounds

Whilst researching the historical boundary lines of one of the other ASP field sites, South Norwood, I had come across a description of an old English custom that I previously knew very little about. Beating the bounds, or 'going a-ganging' as it was otherwise known, is the practice of walking the boundaries of a place in order to reinforce and pass on the knowledge of where they are. Before places were marked as set territories through the practice of mapping, places had more fluid boundaries that were negotiated with neighbours regularly. In order to determine a local parish boundary (a parish being a territory that is under the care of the church via the priest), a group of commoners (usually men and boys) would walk the area, led by the parish priest, officials of the church and elders. They would share knowledge of the boundary lines and pray for their protection and for them to be blessed and healthy. The procession acted as a way to pass knowledge of the boundary lines down through the generations, enabling liability and accountability for governance and for taxes owed to the local church by the area.[6]

In order to instil the memory of the exact locations of the boundaries, 'pains' would be taken upon the significant boundary markers. Historically, taking pains literally meant creating pain in order to create a memory. During the walks, boys could be whipped or violently bumped against boundary stones, thrown into ditches or knocked against trees to make them remember the markers of the boundaries. Later, 'taking of pains' evolved into the act of young boys carrying a length of willow or birch with which they would beat boundary markers such as stone walls, trees and other features of the landscape. In years to come the boys' memories, often aided by the memory of pain, would be the testament and memory of where boundaries lay. Further, the priest would often recite Psalms 103 and 104 and say such sentences as 'Cursed is he who transgresseth the bounds or doles of his neighbour', and hymns would be sung (Tate 1946:73–4).

This ritual demonstrates that a firm folk memory of boundaries was understood to be an effective way to prevent encroachment and changes to the boundaries from neighbouring parishes or manors. Whilst the religious purpose of blessing the harvest through perambulation was prohibited by Elizabeth I in 1559 as England became increasingly Protestant, these processions continued in order to maintain boundaries (Houseman 1998). Today, such boundary-defining practices are obsolete, since formal mapping and legal orders hold boundaries static (though they are still based on the old parish system). However, some boroughs, such as Tower Hamlets in London, and some Oxbridge colleges, still practise the tradition of beating the bounds for the preservation of heritage.

'Perambulation' is defined as 'a walk to define the bounds of a legal area',[7] and perambulations were commonly practised by landowners to define the boundaries of their manors. Whilst differing slightly from the parish 'beating the bounds' in terms of ritual and religious purpose, these perambulations of private lands appear to have had a similar function in terms of defining boundaries; they also decreased as the use of cartography and legal charters increased (see Hewitt 2010).

In *The Phoenix Suburb*, the local historian Alan Warwick sets out how South Norwood sits across the boundaries of three London boroughs (Croydon, Bromley and Lambeth) because of a quirk in the history of perambulations in the area (1972:11–18). In the late 1700s, perambulation was being phased out. Its authority was overruled once an area had been officially mapped, and boundaries fixed. According to Warwick, at the time the first maps of South Norwood were being made, the priest responsible for conducting the perambulation was particularly elderly and unable to climb a rocky slope marking the furthest extent of South Norwood in the direction of Lambeth. Because of this, the boundary was marked closer to South Norwood than had been understood since 1540. Since this incomplete perambulation coincided with the introduction of official maps, this boundary became established as *the* boundary. Today the area remains in an ill-fitting alignment of borough boundaries which can be traced to the bodily movements of an elderly priest and his inability to climb a hill at a historical moment when the boundary became fixed through government mapping. In the light of this, a walk in the area evokes history as embodied memory. Warwick states, 'Tracing that broken dotted line along Church Road and down Fox Hill, it is almost as though one can follow the reluctant footprints of Revd. Richard Finch' (1972:14).

Michael Houseman's (1998) 'Painful places', an academic anthropological text on the subject of boundary rituals, compares a number of traditions that demonstrate how the relationship between bodies and land is often forged in ritual experiences. Houseman compares the English custom of beating of the bounds with the gisaro ceremonies of the Kaluli of Papua New Guinea, which link people to the surrounding landscape through dance, and with the initiation rites of the Australian Aranda, which involve pain rituals. All of these rituals trouble the ontological distinction of body and land as separate things. Houseman explains how ritual, pain and place are intimately wound together and how memory is created through painful acts specifically associated with boundary markers. He states in relation to beating the bounds:

> Thus, the 'impressing of memory', as the local idiom would have it, consists in bringing about a certain mindfulness of territory, not indirectly, by means of an abstract conceptualization of the perambulated land, but directly, by means of a certain intimate physical encounter with it. This intent is clearly expressed, for example, in a recurrent feature of processioning in which the victim's head is placed in direct contact with the terrain being perambulated: 'at each halting point, one of the visitants is bumped smartly against the boundary-stone, or placed head downwards against it'.
>
> (Houseman 1998:450–1)

I had come to think about the ways in which local people thought about the boundaries of Surbiton today. I wondered to what degree the official boundaries of place made sense to the daily experience of living in Surbiton and to what degree a more corporeal, felt relation to boundaries was at work.

Ask a stupid question

As I was sitting on a bench in the pub garden with eight other people one Friday evening, most of whom knew about or were involved in my research in some way, the conversation turned to the boundary between Surbiton and Kingston. Earlier that week I, alongside Andy – a Seethinger who was very interested in local history – had spent a significant amount of time looking for evidence of the historic boundary lines of Surbiton in the local studies archives. Andy and I had found various official maps of voting districts, postcodes and local authority boundaries. Andy had found some interesting newspaper cuttings about boundaries and some 'really old' maps of the area. Around this time, I had also been asking people about their own idea of the boundary line between Surbiton and Kingston in my walking and map-drawing interviews. I decided to ask the people at the pub if Seething had a boundary. My question caused some controversy. I had already anticipated the answer, but I wanted to know if the table considered Seething a 'Surbiton thing'. Anton responded immediately with a big smile, 'Seething has no boundary … I mean, how can you put a boundary around love?' As multiple conversations broke out, Andy and I told Anton about the 'beating of the bounds' and of the work of Houseman on pain rituals. Anton got really excited and said loudly, 'Let's do that here!', to which I responded, 'Let's not!', thinking that re-enacting pain rituals would not pass any form of research ethics.

Anton turned to the table and demanded attention from the group, then drunkenly recited a version of the English ritual of beating the bounds, mixing in rehashed versions of the pain rituals we had talked about from other places. Anton's tale made little sense to most at the table, but the revelation of the old beating the bounds rituals was met with energy and enthusiasm that transformed into the idea that the bounds needed to be beaten as a Seething event. People started to look on their smartphones to see if the 'bounds' were ever 'beaten' around Surbiton. Suggestions of re-creating pain rituals made people laugh and the idea of doing the walk became more and more appealing. People reiterated that Seething should be understood as unbounded (recalling Anton's romantic idea of unbounded love). The question of how to beat the bounds of a place that has 'no boundaries' raised a problem. If Seething is for everyone then how can it be bound to a geographical area? The table quickly decided that as long as it was a Free University of Seething event, the bounds of Surbiton could be beaten in the 'spirit of Seething'. And so the actual bounds of Surbiton ceased to be the focus of the event; rather, getting together, learning, being a little silly and going on a walk were to be the focus.

The event

The walk occurred on a cold, but crisp and sunny, Sunday in January. The day was split into two halves, with a workshop in the morning and the walk in the afternoon. This was the longest of the four walks and the best attended. We had booked a local restaurant for the workshop, but as the event approached the restaurant stopped returning my calls and I found it difficult to establish any line of communication. Rachael told me she had walked past it and seen that it looked closed. I told Leon, the pub landlord and key community member, that I was worried. He knew a lot of people in the area and was well respected by the business community. Leon put me at ease, saying, 'Leave it to me, Jeeva, I'll make sure he opens that place for you.' And three days later he called me to let me know it was all back on. The way in which this issue was resolved showed me the importance of local connections, trust and familiarity in doing local business.

The event started with coffee, a presentation of the history of the beating the bounds tradition and an outline of what Alan and I had found on the history of the boundaries of Surbiton. Below is a summary of the historical content we delivered to the group from the archival research.

Surbiton and Kingston boundary histories

In the past, the area of Kingston extended over a considerable area and had considerable influence in the county of Surrey. The Domesday Book of 1086 recorded Kingston as part of the personal estate of the king and not held by a subordinate. It had three fisheries, of which two paid taxes to the king and one did not (today these fisheries are remembered in the emblem of Kingston Council). Whilst it was geographically within the county of Surrey, Kingston achieved administrative independence from King John (1199–1216) and successfully became a borough in 1481, which gave it a degree of administrative independence. Surrey was divided into areas called hundreds, administrative units with their own courts which exercised civil and criminal jurisdiction (McCormack 1988).

The hundreds of Kingston were similar to the present-day administrative boundary extending south to Long Ditton. However, at the time the boundaries of the boroughs were not clearly defined, and even as late as 1837 it was reported that there was 'some confusion' over the boundaries of the borough, exemplified by the land dispute between two of Kingston's manors, the Manor of Imworth (also named Imbercourt), and the Manor of Weston.[8] This confusion arose from the need for government to record and manage stable boundaries through the process of state mapping, as opposed to the localised practices of settling boundary disputes through walking or perambulation which were dominant until that time. The earliest records of the boundaries of the above manors were not pictorial, but descriptions of walks – 'Turn right at the tree and walk one hundred paces' – and so on. The need to eliminate confusion aided the rise of a universal, stable and scientifically replicable map, made to the standards of objective science (see Hewitt 2010; Daston & Galison 1992; Chapter 4).

In 1964, Queen Elizabeth II granted the current charter, forming the new London Borough of Royal Kingston, uniting three former boroughs of Kingston: Malden, Coombe and Surbiton.[9] This new borough included the whole of 'Kingston and Surbiton' parliamentary constituency, created in 1997. The number of parliamentary seats covering the boroughs of Kingston upon Thames and Richmond upon Thames constituency was reduced from four to three, the Surbiton constituency being lost and subsumed into Kingston.[10] The constituency has seen many amendments, most recently changes to the northern boundary edge to reflect ward changes.

Controversies

Such changes caused much displeasure to those locals whose homes fell into newly defined wards. The new boundaries affected not only people's postcodes but also their social position, local reputations and property values. A sense of local identity was at stake. In 1988 the local newspaper, the *Surrey Comet*, carried the dramatic headline, 'Kingston stunned by news it may vanish'. According to councillors at the time who were quoted in the newspaper article, of whom Steve, today a prominent Seethinger, was one, the problem was that Kingston 'hadn't done a good job of promoting itself', or of showing that it was an able and historically important area. He stated that 'it would be a disgrace' if the historic Royal Borough of Kingston vanished (*Surrey Comet*, 25 March 1988). More confusion occurred, concerning the use of postcodes, on the publication of an article in the *Surrey Comet* (see Figure 6.3) on 5 July 2005 which asked if Kingston was in Surrey or not. The article points to the 1965 boundary changes and quotes a White Paper from 1974: 'The new county boundaries are for administrative areas and will not alter the traditional boundaries of counties, nor is it intended that the loyalties of people living in them will change.'[11] Seven days later, the *Surrey Comet* reported that the council had decided not to drop 'Surrey' from its address, even though the Royal Mail had dropped it from the Kingston address three decades previously. Local historians encouraged people to add their local area to their address in order that 'years of history not be wiped out' (*Surrey Comet*, 25 March 1988:1). In the end the borough of Kingston was not dissolved into other areas.

Going further back in time, current borders in the area can be seen to originate with the Parliamentary Boundaries Act 1832: 'An act to settle and describe the Divisions of Counties, and the Limits of Cities and Boroughs …'.[12] The act served to force a settlement between the manors of Imworth and Weston, whose residents contested territory in the local regions of Long Ditton and Thames Ditton by perambulating the lands. After a written agreement, signed and sealed, between the lords of the manors of Imworth and Weston, such perambulations were deemed unnecessary. This was the only mention of perambulating or beating the

Figure 6.3 Cuttings from the *Surrey Comet*: 25 March 1988, 'Kingston stunned by news it may vanish'; 5 July 2005, 'So are we in Surrey or not?' by Yvonne Gordon; 12 July 2005, 'Defiant council decides to fly the flag for Surrey' by Yvonne Gordon. With thanks to the Kingston Local Studies Archive.

bounds within Kingston and Surbiton that the Free University could find. However, it shows that in however limited a capacity or with how scant a record, the act and practice of walking *had* been an important official means of determining the boundaries of place in Kingston and Surbiton.

Discussions at the event focused on the attention-grabbing idea of 'Kingston vanishing' and the boundary between Surbiton and Kingston. When boundary lines change, the index of what counts as local changes with them. Here a direct link between the official practices of mapping place and the sense of local belonging is evident. The consensus at the event was that if the boundary change had gone ahead and Kingston had 'vanished' – which in the end it did not – it would not have meant the loss of 'years of history' but rather a loss of a sense of local sovereignty for the area. Thus this move would have had a real impact on the sense and definition of the local. Such controversies reminded me of the work of anthropologists such as Howard Morphy (1993), whose work, particularly on colonial Australia, has focused on how practices of surveying, mapping and recording place create the 'frame' through which landscapes come to be understood as a distinct entity. This framing has very real consequences for the politics of place. Throughout the fieldwork period I heard many comments about the difference between Surbiton and its neighbour, Kingston, about what type of person lived in what area, the sorts of bins and lampposts they had and how they marked the different areas: it appeared boundaries still matter.

Dots and lines

After the lecture, the group split into groups of five or six people and spent 30 minutes discussing and drawing the personal boundary markers of 'their' Surbiton on large paper maps (see Figure 6.4). People selected places from their everyday journeys, including schools, playgrounds, parks and pleasant places to walk, such as the riverbank. Many road choices ran counter to those highlighted by the ASP's assessment of route choice, which was unable to account for the personal and affective quality of these spaces, such as a pleasant or quiet feel. The corporeal and sensorial – in terms of noise, atmosphere and pleasantness – were clear factors. Each group presented its map to the rest of the room and a master map was drawn from the common and recurring boundary points. The whole group debated and came to a consensus on a series of landmarks that marked the boundaries of Surbiton, including a former children's home and an army training centre.

Figure 6.4 Seethingers marking the boundaries of Surbiton. Photograph by Tangle photography, 2013.

Figure 6.5 Beating the boundary stone. Photograph by Tangle photography, 2013.

The group elected to include an actual boundary stone on an old wall at the side of a building (see Figure 6.5). Alan became aware of this stone through the archival records. The wall was once part of the Surbiton House estate, which covered a substantial area of present-day Surbiton. Around 1850 Alexander Raphael sold the estate to a William Woods, a local developer, who built many of the river roads we know today in Surbiton (Statham 1996). The stone was interesting as an intersection of the old pre-suburban Surbiton and its current boundaries. Because of time limits, the large number of children taking part, and the cold, we only walked half the route. Instead of 'taking pains', we had decided to mark these boundaries with small rituals which had a characteristically Seething nature. Some of these had been planned before the day of the event with the assumption that key landmarks like the river would emerge as boundaries (which it did). Our final destination was the pub, where sandwiches and hot chocolate waited for us.

Walking the line

The walk was led by Alan, who guided with the master map. Each person held a willow cane in the tradition of beating the bounds (see Figure 6.6).

Figure 6.6 Seethingers about to beat the bounds. Photograph by Tangle photography, 2013.

At boundary points the rituals, songs and dances were performed. At some points people formed a circle with the willow sticks and danced around in folk style, changing direction and then finishing the song. Passers-by were seemingly bemused by the event, as it interrupted the normal daily rhythms of suburban life. Cars were made to slow; most people smiled at us or asked what was happening. We received one shout of 'Shut up' from a window, which we did for a moment as we passed. The group spontaneously knocked their sticks along fences and signs. At various points, the children led the adults on the route and told people what to do.

Upon reaching the boundary stone of Surbiton House, which was set in a discreet wall, Alan read aloud, 'This wall marks the boundary and belongs to Surbiton House, May the nineteenth 1863,' and then playfully suggested that the wear and tear on the boundary stone is 'clearly' evidence of the stone having previously been beaten. Alan then told some Seething 'facts', suggesting that the hooks in the wall were once used to tie naughty children to. The children in the group smiled whilst trying to decipher if Alan was telling the truth or not. The group walked on and passed other markers, where they performed more dances, read local history or told personal stories. Upon reaching the river path, Molly, Louise's child, was asked where we were. She replied 'Kingston', then changed her mind and said 'Surbiton', confirming that we must be on the boundary. We walked towards Surbiton and performed sardine-based rituals marking the sardine-fishing site. The group danced around, 'ritually' beat Anton around the face with a felt sardine and pretended to fish the river with their sticks.

Wallis then walked the group through the sardine salsa dance at the site where Seething sardines are fished during the Seething Freshwater Sardine Festival. Wallis had worked on the dance with a local dancer, and filmed an instructional video which she placed on social media so that people could learn the dance before the walk. The walk and a link to the dance received numerous write-ups in the local press (see Box 6.2).

Box 6.2

Residents are invited on a 'once in a lifetime' exploration to the ends of the town, with the so-called Free University of Seething.

Made-up traditions, including goat-boy Lefi Ganderson, are at the heart of their community projects, attracting hundreds of people over the years.

The activities include a revival of the 'Beating of the Bounds', an ancient practice of walking the boundaries of a parish before the existence of maps, to reinforce the community.

Residents can learn the arcane Sardine Salsa for the event.

Rachael, from the Free University of Seething, said: 'It will be a once in a lifetime experience. The "Beating of the Bounds" is a tradition that ended before Surbiton was actually created.

'There will be a breakfast and rituals for the community to decide where the boundaries are, and everyone will be given a hand-out on which they can make notes.'

The event is led by a UCL student who is studying Surbiton as a community.

Rachael said: 'The idea of the walks came from him, but the people of Seething made them more interesting, in their own way.'

Hausmeister 2013 (the name has been changed)

After leaving the riverside the group moved down the Portsmouth Road alongside the filter beds (see Figure 6.7). As we walked, Wallis gave an extended explanation, in the style of a TV presenter, of the importance of the filter beds to the local area and declared that she learnt all this through her studies at FUS.

> This is very important to the area of Surbiton. It is basically why we have a pub here, which to us is the most important communal area.

Figure 6.7 Seethingers beating the bounds by the filter beds. Photograph by Tangle photography, 2013.

> The filter beds was where clean water was filtered and pumped into London and the correlation of the water being pumped from above the tidal area of the Thames and people not suffering from cholera, er, was ... the link was made by John Snow back in 18-something, the link was made ... It was pumped directly from these filter beds and as a result a big industry built up, which is why we have the pub and other distinctive Victorian buildings in the area.

On arriving back at the pub, people performed one last dance in the rear garden before getting a drink and mingling whilst Fay drew up the master's certificates. A Free University of Seething degree was presented to all students who had completed any of the walks, including myself. A larger graduation ceremony was held as part of the annual Seething Parade, for which gowns and robes were made. People received their awards later in the year, in full gown, at the Lefi festival after the procession (see Figure 6.8).

After the walks

The walks were originally intended to revive interest in the ASP's Community Map. However, the Seethingers asserted their way of doing things. The walks, based on parafacts, were rather different to how they were envisioned in the funding application. The friction between the ASP and Seething ways of doing things became manifest once again after

Figure 6.8 Free University of Seething graduation. Author's own, 2014.

the walks had been executed, and it became clear that they would not resolve the fundamental problems associated with the long-neglected Community Map.

We had good recordings of all the walks, in terms of video footage and maps of where people walked and the points of interest, ready to use. Back at UCL I met with Rick, the ASP research assistant. Within our inclusion grant he was employed as our technician to help load the walks to the map. Rick explained that, in addition to the technical difficulties of adding lines to the map, there was still an unwillingness to use Seething stories. He explained: 'Flo doesn't want Mapping for Change[13] branding associated with Seething … We could build a new mini-site which is the same as the one we have, just for Seething, and we can strip it of any Mapping for Change branding'. However, another ASP co-investigator ruled this out, stating that Rick would have to spend too much time building this interface and his expertise and time should be placed elsewhere in the ASP.

Rick and I talked further with a few of the core Seething group about how to use the map. Leon and Steve thought through some ideas, which included using different technologies, such as augmented reality or geolocated data, but over time it became apparent that we lacked the time, skills and motivation to pursue this. Rick explained that he had no more time to work on the walks, whilst another ASP team member said they 'didn't realise the degree to which anthropologists have spent time in the field with participants' and that they could not focus on the walks any more.

For the Seethingers the value of the walks was to be found in the fact that they brought people together and crafted community, relations to place and moments of knowledge exchange. The archiving of the walks was less important; as Leon noted, 'If it doesn't happen, it doesn't happen', whilst Steve said of the general frictions with the ASP, 'This is a bit miserable'. The dialogue between UCL and Seethingers started to get in the way of the fun of the walks, but Seethingers made great efforts to ensure that I felt positive and good about what we did; Steve told me, 'I'm really excited by all this, by the way. ... I'm not giving that away, but I am.' Finally, after four months of learning to code, with some major help from Rick, I had built a fully independent map from basic Google code with embedded YouTube videos. It was eventually hosted by the Seething community web site. Most Seethingers didn't seem overly concerned with the online map of the walks but talked about the walks for months after. The ASP's Community Map remained empty.

Collaboration and curation

The description of the walks presented above shows the processes through which the Seethingers entered the research process as collaborators. They challenged the power relations and forms of authority associated with the Community Map, ethnographic research and knowledge production by making institutionally funded activity 'stupid'. In this way they didn't walk away from interaction with academic research but played on the edges, or limits, of the semiotic and performative authority of the university and the expert. They seized opportunities, and resources, to craft community in a novel, creative way. They entered the ethnographic practice as co-curators of moments of knowledge exchange, when new ways of being in the world, new ways of relating to others, could be thought through in practice. The chapter has shown that walking not only melds the individual with the built environment but can also create opportunities to meld with the environment as a community. After the walks the community talked of how nice it was to get to know new people, new places, and old places in new ways. Examinations of walking have also productively challenged the ASP's assumptions about movement, that is, that people would walk the fastest or simplest route. This chapter has revealed alternative ways of moving in the built environment, and the diverse ways people find value in movement and the built environment.

After the account of their activities in the previous chapter, it might seem obvious that the Seethingers would take this approach to the ethnographic research. However, this chapter emphasises that it is also important that the ethnographer is open to new forms of doing research. As Rafael Schacter (2020) argues, anthropological engagement must go beyond a medium through which one represents a distant 'other'. Writing in the context of museology, Schacter discusses collaborative curatorial processes through which knowledge is produced and which enable new modes of research. Viewed in this way, 'Curation becomes a model in which the anthropologist engages in experimental, speculative, long-term processes wherein we can speak together with our interlocutors, mediating not controlling their own ways of seeing' (Schacter 2020:202). I argue that the walks described in this chapter constitute a form of collaborative curation. Through them, the Seethingers discover which aspects of the built environment and suburban lived experience they wish to emphasise. The collaboratively curated FUS activities enabled modes of seeing that allowed me and the wider ASP project to understand the way in which people engaged with the suburb. This 'opening up' was prompted by the involvement of interlocutors in the development of the research method, its execution, and the dissemination of the data gathered. This form of collaborative ethnographic practice is political. It aims to take others seriously on their own terms. As outlined in Chapter 2, anthropology has a long-standing ambition to find ever more equitable modes of representing and talking about other people. But, as Schacter notes, a more equitable mode of ethnographic practice has to emerge through open-ended processes of engagement. Anthropology must be open to new forms of interruption and disruption (O'Neill 2012; Flynn 2019).

Here I want to think of FUS as a form of anthropology in itself, that is, less as data which needs to be represented through writing and more as a way of exploring relations of difference, modes of sociality and ways of being human in the moment of data and knowledge generation itself. Within anthropology there has long been attention to modes of representation. As Adolfo Estalella and Tomás Sánchez Criado (2018) have demonstrated, there is an increasing body of work that advocates a collaborative form of anthropology, in the ways outlined above. For them, the collaboration of interlocutors in fieldwork processes is collaboration mode one. Co-writing the outputs of research is collaboration mode two. They describe collaboration mode three as the co-production of data, which prompts new modes of knowing. Crucially, they argue that this is not an end in itself. Rather, it is the starting point for further research. In Chapter 4, I argued that data can be understood as a phenomenon. That is, data is more than a representation of the world. Rather, the generation of data contributes to world-making, as data collectors bring things into relation in new and productive ways. The activity of the FUS constitutes novel forms of data generation. It has brought people, ideas and the materiality of place into novel relations.

Hannah Knox (2021) has taken a similar approach in her work on anthropology as a 'hack'. Her work focuses on people who use sensors and measuring devices to gather data that will help them become more climate-friendly. Knox uses the concept of the 'hack' to explore people's relationship with data beyond representation. She asks how people interact with data not only to gather information (say, to understand how much energy is being used), but also to engage fundamentally in relations with the world around us in new and otherwise inconceivable ways (to think about energy, and one's relations to it, in new ways). Data, then, is more than representative; it can generate new modes of relationality. The 'hack' goes beyond experimental design; it is speculative and generative of seeing the world in other ways. Knox extends this analysis to think through anthropological representation and asks how ethnography as practice could be less a starting point for representation and more a mode through which to experiment and play with collaborators in order to see the world differently.

With this in mind, the FUS can be understood as more than a spoof university. In doing fieldwork through FUS I was committed to working with Seethingers not only to represent their world but also to generate new modes of relationality to the world around us and to the practice of anthropology through play. This commitment included new modes of relating to anthropological description.

Towards the end of my PhD research process, I was invited to fill a small number of display cabinets in UCL's anthropology department with items from Seething. I took this invitation back to a few Seethingers, who decided that we should involve the community in the process. I explained that the department had a rich history of material culture and an extensive collection of objects from around the world, which we could add to. The Seethingers wanted to know more about material culture, anthropology and the exhibition. They wanted to know how anthropologists could go about thinking through social relations through objects, and in particular they wanted to know how they would be thought about. So we decided to apply for another small grant to fund an exchange between FUS and UCL.

Around 30 Seethingers travelled to the department. They were given a brief introductory lecture on material culture and then a tour of the material culture room, with the help of Nikki Lan Xiao, a UCL master's student at the time, Delphine Mercier, the collections manager, and Dr Timothy Carroll, an expert in the field. Certain objects were brought out of storage to demonstrate key moments in anthropological thinking, or significant ways in which social relations can work through material culture.

As the day progressed, the Seethingers considered which Seething items could represent their community. They also considered which Seething objects were similar to the items they had seen in the collection. Wallis responded to the Kula valuables[14] and described the pride she felt when people wore the Seething jewellery she made; she could, over time, see that Seething was more and more popular as people wore it. She asked if she could display the Seething jewellery alongside the Mwali armbands and Soulava necklaces that circulate within the Kula exchange system in the Trobriand Islands. The aim was not to find a direct equivalence between the objects, but to show how objects may have similar aesthetic properties yet perform different social functions, or, conversely, how objects may perform similar social functions whilst having different aesthetic properties.

The exhibition also displayed a tin of Seething freshwater sardines alongside an Ibibio fish trap from Nigeria.[15] Within the Ibibio society, fishing is the main source of wealth. Here, community wealth is gathered and redistributed. Some pairings were talked about, but eventually not displayed alongside each other in order to maintain respect. Seethingers were aware of their 'stupid' approach to community building and were careful not to draw an equivalence between it and the practices of others, with reference to cultural sensitivity. This was the case when Seethingers encountered a 'figurine of a single person, with decorative carvings on the face ... from Oceania/New Zealand'. This ancestral figure could be considered similar to the figure of Lefi in terms of its size, the fact that it was a figure of a single being and in that it performed a role of linking current generations to ancestors in some way. However, Seethingers decided not to draw an equivalence as they thought it inappropriate to draw a link between their 'stupid' stories of Lefi and this figure which was much revered and respected. Box 6.3 shows a text from the sardine tin which was displayed alongside the fish trap (which had its own text).

> **Box 6.3** Freshwater sardine tin
>
> Seething, being by a river, was the location of ancient freshwater sardine fisheries, the basis of the economic prosperity of the village. In later times the suburban location of the fisheries meant that sardines were packed onto trains and sent into London, hence the phrase 'packed in like sardines', which is often heard on the train line today. Unfortunately, latter-day pollution of the Thames killed off the fish and the fishing industry, leaving the area to reinvent itself once again. The sardines are remembered in the annual Seething Freshwater Sardine Festival, at which people give thanks for the river and remember their relationship with and responsibility to the local ecologies.

Whilst all the objects were selected for the specific parallels they offered, some links were clearer than others, and the text accompanying the exhibition was written in such a way as to leave room for the reader to trace their own connections between the items on display. The most explicit dualism manifested in the introductory texts, which set the tone for the reader. Rather than one authoritative introduction to the display, two texts were displayed side by side. One described the exhibition from the perspective of the Seething Villagers and adopted the logo and language of the Free University of Seething. The other described the exhibition from the perspective of UCL anthropology and had UCL branding. The texts purposely mirrored each other in structure. The content of each paragraph was roughly the same. However, the style and emphasis were different between the UCL and FUS texts, despite the subject matter being almost identical (see Box 6.4 for an illustration of the contrast).

The parallel texts offered different ways into the exhibition, showing the multiple perspectives through which the objects could be viewed. The overlapping perspectives aimed to draw attention to the contingency of anthropological knowledge and the possible gaps between ethnographer and ethnographed. They aimed to place the viewer in a position of learning about 'local' life less through a direct representation of 'life in Seething' and more through having to recognise and navigate the differing perspectives. The viewer was placed on the edge between the perspectives in order to bring their attention to the productive aspects of that edge.

The exhibition invited multiple readings of the display, as viewers were invited to compare items and ask questions about them. They were invited to see the differences and similarities between the objects, and the multiple ways they can be seen or understood. This invitation to the

> **Box 6.4**
>
> *UCL text*
>
> Founded on common anthropological themes of communitas, co-presence and participation, Seething arose out of a group of community enthusiasts in Surbiton, South West London. In 2009, the community began to craft a mythical corpus integrating local history, the suburban landscape, and creative etymologies in a highly participatory programme of merry-making and good cheer known only in 'yesteryear'. The Seething Villagers host over ten major events a year, each retelling legends of ancient Seething. These legends, festivals, and community events work to re-enchant the suburban space, engendering the kinds of sociality and mutuality of a close community.
>
> *FUS text*
>
> Founded on familiar social desires for togetherness and inclusion, Seething emanates from a community in Surbiton, South West suburban London. In 2009 Surbiton experienced a social renaissance through the re-discovery of the ancient Village of Seething. Seethingers spearhead an alternative programme of participatory engagement and merry-making, of a kind usually told of only in civic archive and folk tale. The community hosts over ten major events a year based around the recovered 'new' legends of Seething. With the aim of re-enchanting the suburb, these stories are reminiscent of classic folk tales and myths told around the world.

viewer shifts the dynamic of the exhibition from one of display, a didactic mode of delivering knowledge from the curators to the viewers, to one that invites interpretation and play. The exhibition invited the viewer not only to think through Seething life, but also to contemplate how common modes of display and representation of others have been structured through historical power relations (see Boast 2011) by engaging in Seething modes of play. Exhibition-goers then have to curate their own relation to the show and to their understanding of Seething and UCL.

James Clifford developed Mary Louise Pratt's conception of the museum as a 'contact zone' that constituted a 'space of colonial encounters, the space in which peoples geographically and historically separated come into contact with each other and establish ongoing relations' (Pratt 1991:6–7, quoted in Clifford 1997:192). For Clifford, the idea of the contact zone emphasises the interactive and performative encounter whereby the collection becomes an 'ongoing historical, political, moral *relationship* – a power-charged set of exchanges' (Clifford 1997:192). The concept worked well within a new museology influenced by postmodernism (Boast 2011:59), in which objectifying modes of display were challenged and the performative aspects of material culture, whereby objects are animated within an ongoing context of social networks and relations, came to the fore. However, the concept has also been critically analysed by authors such as Boast (2011), who note that the museum is still the dominant place where budgets, and forms of display and encounter, are worked out for such objects. Boast argues that the museum as 'contact zone' continues to be informed by unequal power relations.

By presenting multiple narratives, incorporating Seething facts and inviting viewers to enter a Seething 'state of mind', the Seethingers played with the power dynamics of the museum. The exhibition played with notions of authority, voice, perspective and the positions of the curated and the curator. The FUS claimed an equivalent status with UCL and co-opted its authority and style in presenting objects within the exhibition. In doing so, it drew attention to the typical political (im)balances of the contact zone. Such a critical engagement is possible because Seethingers are deeply aware of how museums operate, curate and display. Surbiton is less than an hour from UCL and many Seethingers regularly visit museums and galleries in central London. Many have worked with such institutions and have attended London's universities. In Surbiton the Seethingers later secured funding for a 'Museum of Futures'. This space, in a disused shop, hosted talks, events and workshops. Here, as in the exhibition, the emphasis was on process, on encounter and on disruption to normal patterns and habits of thought (cf. Flynn 2019; Walsh 2016).

The display at UCL was done *with* rather than *about* Seethingers. Here, ethnography was open to interruption. It offered informants-as-curators the opportunity to communicate their social projects in new ways. The Seethingers also came to the department to talk about being the subject of my ethnography in a conversation called 'ethnographer meets ethnographed'. They demanded that my PhD examination should occur through FUS, where I presented my work to a gathering of 40 people in the Museum of Futures, at which Seethingers listened to the thesis outline, then, after some discussion, awarded me a PhD. My UCL examiners were offered fellowships at FUS by the Seethingers at the end of my 'other' viva at UCL.

Conclusions

Whilst the above has outlined the playful and 'stupid' ways in which Seethingers, through the Free University of Seething, asserted agency in my research, there is a serious point to the form and action of Seethingers. In playing with the dominant forms, semiotic structures and styles of research, the Seethingers sought to obviate the traditional dynamics of researcher and researched. They asserted their version of what life in the suburbs is like. They used the dominant narratives, not only of suburban life, as outlined in the previous chapter, but of university life, of expertise and of the semiotics of representing others in both anthropology and museum collections.

The Seethingers' engagement with academically funded and situated activities (the walks, the exhibition, the map) constitute ways of actively inserting themselves into the curation of the ways in which their suburban life is narrated. This can be read as a form of neoliberal personhood (see Gershon 2011), whereby one takes responsibility for the way in which one's life is defined. Being a Seethinger is an act of making *bios* from *zoë*, of making visible a citizenship that counts. This takes work. Whilst the ASP's map remained empty, the work of asserting a presence, of building community resilience, and of playing on the edge of a larger, potentially more powerful social project had been done. However, as we will see in the next chapter, being a Seethinger (with its associated practices of linguistic play and stupidity) doesn't always work. Sometimes one needs to speak in the language of authority, as the locals did when they were objecting to an application to build on the site of the filter beds.

Notes

1. seethingwells.org/University_of_Seething.html (accessed 19.May 2021).
2. https://www.youtube.com/watch?v=0mnz2cEOCJs&list=PLdJTq-WxKY6qxP8x3AgdQS MjGHCfj6dGr (accessed 28 April 2021).
3. See https://www.arcgis.com/apps/MapTour/index.html?appid=b500acbffb024de396196c0 7fb53aff3 (accessed 28 April 2021).
4. https://youtu.be/eVg3df0cQpY (accessed 28 April 2021).
5. https://www.youtube.com/playlist?list=PLdJTq-WxKY6q3somfPDkGdxWkEZDyc1ef (accessed 28 April 2021).
6. http://en.wikipedia.org/wiki/Beating_the_bounds (accessed 28 April 2021).
7. http://en.wikipedia.org/wiki/Perambulation (accessed 28 April 2021).
8. Reports from Commissioners on Corporation of Kingston-upon-Thames 1836. Surrey 2892. Kingston Local Studies Archive.
9. GB Historical GIS / University of Portsmouth. Kingston and Surbiton BCon through time | Boundaries of Constituency, *A Vision of Britain through Time*. Surbiton: http://www.visionofbritain.org.uk/place/1025; Kingston upon Thames: http://www.visionofbritain.org.uk/place/706 (both accessed 29 June 2021).

10 http://www.tudorconservatives.com/#/boundary-changes/4555352876 (accessed 3 January 2013).
11 Kingston Local Studies Archive file on boundaries compiled in 1988 by Anne McCormack. Consulted 2 February 2012.
12 Kingston Local Studies Archive file on boundaries compiled in 1988 by Anne McCormack. Consulted 2 February 2012.
13 The UCL-based company that designed the map.
14 Catalogue numbers J.0060, J.0061, J.0063, J.0064. http://ethcat.museums.ucl.ac.uk/search.aspx (accessed 29 April 2021).
15 Catalogue number C.0010. http://ethcat.museums.ucl.ac.uk/detail.aspx?parentpriref= (accessed 29 April.2021).

References

Appadurai, Arjun, ed. 1988. *The Social Life of Things: Commodities in cultural perspective*. Cambridge: Cambridge University Press.
Benjamin, Walter. 1999. *The Arcades Project* (trans. Howard Eiland and Kevin McLaughlin). Cambridge, MA: Belknap Press of Harvard University Press.
Boast, Robin. 2011. 'Neocolonial collaboration: Museum as contact zone revisited.' *Museum Anthropology* 34, no. 1: 56–70. https://doi.org/10.1111/j.1548-1379.2010.01107.x.
Brand, J. 1870. *Observations of Popular Antiquities*. Newcastle upon Tyne: T. Saint.
Certeau, Michel de. 1984. *The Practice of Everyday Life* (trans. Steven F. Randall). Berkeley: University of California Press.
Clifford, James. *Routes: Travel and translation in the late twentieth century*. Cambridge, MA: Harvard University Press, 1997.
Daston, Lorraine and Peter Galison. 1992. 'The image of objectivity.' *Representations* 40 (Autumn): 81–128. https://doi.org/10.2307/2928741.
Debord, Guy and Gil J. Wolman. [1956] 2006. 'A user's guide to détournement.' In *The Situationist International Anthology*, revised and expanded edn (ed. and trans. Ken Knabb). Berkeley, CA: Bureau of Public Secrets.
Dobson, Stephen. 2011. 'Sustaining place through community walking initiatives.' *Journal of Cultural Heritage Management and Sustainable Development* 1, no. 2: 109–21. https://doi.org/10.1108/20441261111171675.
Edensor, T. 2010. 'Walking in rhythms: Place, regulation, style and the flow of experience.' *Visual Studies* 25, no. 1: 69–79. https://doi.org/10.1080/14725861003606902.
Estalella, Adolfo and Tomás Sánchez Criado, eds. 2018. *Experimental Collaborations: Ethnography through fieldwork devices*. New York and Oxford: Berghahn.
Flynn, Alex. 2019. 'The curator, the anthropologist: "Presentialism" and open-ended enquiry in process.' In Roger Sansi, ed., *The Anthropologist as Curator*, pp. 173–93. Abingdon: Routledge.
Garrett, Bradley L. 2013. *Explore Everything: Place-hacking the city*. London: Verso.
Gershon, Ilana. 2011.'Neoliberal agency.' *Current Anthropology* 52, no. 4: 537–55. https://doi.org/10.1086/660866.
Graeber, David. 2001. *Toward an Anthropological Theory of Value: The false coin of our own dreams*. New York: Palgrave.
Graeber, David. 2013. 'It is value that brings universes into being.' *HAU: Journal of Ethnographic Theory* 3, no. 2: 219–43. https://doi.org/10.14318/hau3.2.012.
Hall, Tom. 2009. 'Footwork: Moving and knowing in local space(s).' *Qualitative Research* 9, no. 5: 571–85. https://doi.org/10.1177/1468794109343626.
Hausmeister, Hana. 2013. 'Learn Surbiton's sardine salsa dance for "beating the bounds" walk this weekend.' *Surrey Comet*, 12 January.
Hewitt, Rachel. 2010. *Map of a Nation: A biography of the Ordnance Survey*. London: Granta.
Houseman, Michael. 1998. 'Painful places: Ritual encounters with one's homelands.' *Journal of the Royal Anthropological Institute* 4, no. 3: 447–67. https://doi.org/10.2307/3034156.
Ingold, Tim. 2007. *Lines: A brief history*. Abingdon: Routledge.
Knox, Hannah. 2021. 'Hacking anthropology.' *Journal of the Royal Anthropological Institute* 27, no. 51: 108–26. https://doi.org/10.1111/1467-9655.13483.

Kopytoff, Igor. 1986. 'The cultural biography of things: Commoditization as a process.' In Arjun Appadurai, ed., *The Social Life of Things: Commodities in cultural perspective*, pp. 64–91. Cambridge: Cambridge University Press.

LaBelle, Brandon. 2008. 'Pump up the bass: Rhythm, cars, and auditory scaffolding.' *The Senses and Society* 3, no. 2: 187–203. https://doi.org/10.2752/174589308X306420.

Lambek, Michael. 2013. 'The value of (performative) acts.' *HAU: Journal of Ethnographic Theory* 3, no. 2: 141–60. https://doi.org/10.14318/hau3.2.009.

Lefebvre, Henri. 1991. *The Production of Space*. Oxford: Blackwell.

McCormack, Anne. 1988. 'Kingston upon Thames: Ancient town & borough, manor & hundred.' Kingston Local Studies Archive (consulted 18 July 2013).

Morphy, Howard. 1993. 'Colonialism, history and the construction of place: The politics of landscape in Northern Australia.' In Barbara Bender, ed., *Landscape: Politics and perspectives*, pp. 205–43. Oxford: Berg.

Munn, Nancy D. 1986. *The Fame of Gawa: A symbolic study of value transformation in a Massim (Papua New Guinea) society*. Durham, NC: Duke University Press.

O'Neill, Paul. 2012. *The Culture of Curating and the Curating of Culture(s)*. Cambridge, MA: MIT Press.

Pratt, Mary Louise. 1991. *Imperial Eyes: Travel writing and transculturation*. New York: Routledge.

Rose, Gillian, Monica Degen and Begum Basdas. 2010. 'More on "big things": Building events and feelings.' *Transactions of the Institute of British Geographers* 35, no. 3: 334–49. https://doi.org/10.1111/j.1475-5661.2010.00388.x.

Schacter, Rafael. 2020. 'A curatorial methodology for anthropology.' In Timothy Carroll, Antonia Walford and Shireen Walton, eds, *Lineages and Advancements in Material Culture Studies: Perspectives from UCL anthropology*, pp. 190–204. Abingdon: Routledge.

Self, Will. 2012. 'Walking is political.' *Guardian*, 30 March. https://www.theguardian.com/books/2012/mar/30/will-self-walking-cities-foot (accessed 29 April 2021).

Solnit, Rebecca. 2001. *Wanderlust: A history of walking*. New York: Penguin Books.

Statham, Richard. 1996. *Surbiton Past*. Chichester: Phillimore.

Tate, W. E. 1946. *The Parish Chest: A study of the records of parochial administration in England*. Cambridge: Cambridge University Press.

Tilley, Christopher. 2008. *Body and Image: Explorations in landscape phenomenology 2*. Walnut Creek, CA: Left Coast Press.

Walsh, Victoria. 2016. 'Redistributing knowledge and practice in the art museum.' *Stedelijk Studies (Between the Discursive and Immersive)* 4, no. 4: 1–16.

Warwick, Alan. 1972. *The Phoenix Suburb: A South London social history*. Richmond: Blue Boar Press.

7
Citizenship in the suburbs: shit and the story of the filter beds

In this chapter we will look at the ways in which the work of being a good local citizen comes to matter. We will examine some of the hidden and unspoken aspects of the effects of the labour of late liberal citizenship. In particular, we will look at the ways in which locals feel this labour through their bodies. Whilst the previous chapter considered the phenomenological engagement of people with the local landscape through walking, this chapter will consider the ways in which the labour of citizenship is somatised in the body. The chapter thinks through the local body in three ways. Firstly, as already described, there is the *experience* of the local body-self. This is the phenomenological sense of the body as lived experience in terms of both the emotional and affective spectrum of experience and the more medicalised notions of health and wellbeing, illness and pain. Secondly, there is the local body as a *social* body: the body functions as a symbol for relationships amongst nature, society and culture. Thirdly, the local body will be considered as 'an artefact of social and political control' (Scheper-Hughes & Lock 1987:6). This analysis takes a Foucauldian approach, referring to the 'regulation, surveillance, and control of bodies' (Scheper-Hughes & Lock 1987:7).

Various interlocutors described the effect the campaign to save the filter beds had on their mental and physical health. In engaging with these effects, this chapter reveals the mostly unseen aspects (and costs) of 'being local'. People talked in very corporeal terms about the (negative) effects of activism. They talked of fears that they would be 'ripped apart', that there 'was too much of themselves involved', and reported that they felt sick during council meetings, and that they had developed issues with their guts. The chapter not only discusses the activism associated with the filter beds as an example of a local, community-based, political campaign, but goes on to outline the historical relation between the materiality of the built environment and the body. The chapter emphasises the dynamic performative nature of citizenship by focusing on the labour of the late liberal citizen. Moving beyond overly static notions of the subject as constrained by an external power, this chapter looks at how the locals work to maintain a form of politically qualified life, that is to say, the life of a politically effective agent who is able to argue that the suburb should be a certain way. The making and shaping of political efficacy is, I argue, the making of what Agamben (1998) would call making *bios* from *zoë*. I examine how locals feel this work with their entire bodies, and how they consider that such labour is a necessary aspect of being local despite its negative effects.

The community and the filter beds

The filter beds cover an area of around six acres that hugs the bend in the River Thames along the western side of the suburb (see Figure 7.1). Built in the mid-1800s, their innovative water-filtration technology pumped clean water to central London, during a period in which London suffered a series of cholera epidemics (1831, 1848–9, 1854, 1867). Dr John Snow famously mapped the incidences of cholera and discovered the source of the disease to be a water pump in Soho, central London, in what is widely

Figure 7.1 The filter beds. Author's own, 2015.

regarded as one of the first practices of epidemiological mapping. His work proved that the disease was waterborne (contrary to the popular belief that it was airborne), and linked it to water that was polluted with faecal matter. Dr Snow's mapping traced clean water back to the Surbiton filter beds, which were effective in removing dirt and bacteria. Thus the filter beds became the blueprint for water-filtration systems around the world. The history of the filter beds, and their importance in the history of epidemiology and clean water, were largely unknown in the local community until the Community Brain worked with people at Kingston University, and many local volunteers, on research funded by a National Lottery Heritage Fund grant. Since then, the community has held walking tours, put on plays in the old pumping house re-enacting the history of John Snow and cholera, and designed plans to transform the site into an ecological park with a visitor centre.

Community pride

Steve said he started to think about the site's history whilst out walking by the filter beds. The site had not been used since the mid-1970s and is largely hidden from everyday view, owing to its sunken location behind a brick wall wedged between a busy road and the River Thames. Steve visited the local history archives and was astonished at the site's links to the story of cholera and clean water. Steve played a key role in getting the grant to study the site further. At a public meeting in which findings from the heritage project were presented to a local audience, he explained that the site had become important for him and for Surbiton's public image:

> The site now ... it's so easy to rush past and look at it and think it's tatty. For many years I did that, stop [and] look at it through the blue railings. It is fundamentally a site of international importance: this is not just us saying this any more, it's the Wellcome Trust saying this, it's UCL, it's the Heritage Lottery Fund. This has been a neglected story! ... Eighty per cent plus of the play [audience] didn't know the story. One of the comments was, 'It makes me feel proud to live in Surbiton', because that's actually a big part of this. We don't want to be known as Margo and Jerry from *The Good Life*, we want to be known as the place that gave clean water to the world. ... This is not just a piece of history, it's alive today, it's massively massively important in our lives. ... This isn't the end of the project, this is the beginning, allowing others to get interested and involved in it.

Throughout the public meetings for the heritage project, and in the meetings arranged to discuss the objection to the planning application, local activists and heritage researchers talked about the site's importance in terms of its global history, the stories that it allows people to tell, and the way in which Surbiton residents could play an active role in telling the story of clean water. For the locals, engaging with the site was not only about local history, but also a way to ensure Surbiton could position itself as a meaningful and prominent part of the story of clean water and urban ecology, which was a global story. For locals, preserving this site would preserve a story that held important moral weight for future generations. Benny, a local-heritage researcher, explained at a heritage meeting:

> One of the big issues we are going to face in the future is water. … In Surbiton we have a site that celebrates water past, present and future, a place where we can go – yeah, we're proud we're part of the past, but we are trying to solve the problems of the future as well – once they [the filter beds] go, that is it, and I for one fear that in twenty years' time people will look at it and say 'and you were the ones responsible for giving away that heritage'. This is a story that resonates: you can hear the voices of Simpson and Snow but you can take that forward and see how they were tackling the problems of the future.

The community had ambitions to turn the area into an ecology park and visitor centre. They talked of celebrating and preserving the example of great Victorian engineering, of taking the story into schools and using the site as a key local resource. Steve and Benny were heavily involved in sharing the story of the filter beds (through the play, public talks and walking tours, which got good local press coverage) and became well known in the local area.

Zara, a keen Seethinger, explained the significance of the beds to me during an interview. I had met Zara in a quiet bar to ask her about her relationship to the local area in general. I had asked her, as I had asked others, to draw a map of 'her Surbiton' for me. She drew her house in the centre, the pub, and along the top edge the railings of the filter beds. It was noticeable that she did not include the high street and that she took some time to mark the filter bed railings, which were one of the few detailed features on the map. When I asked her about that part of the drawings, she said,

> The filter beds, this was an afterthought, it's been a big part of what I've done here but it's a little out of my hands here. I was involved

with performance in the coal shed [a historic building that once held coal for the water pumps, located on what is now a university campus]; since then it's become a political objection to a planning application, which is not an area I know that much about, but it's not my thing. It's important, but I'm not involved – nothing's stopping me getting involved – you pick your battles.

Some months later Zara expressed her concern about the prospect of losing the filter beds. Whilst she did not have the time to be involved in the campaign to save them, she still cared deeply. Zara sat next to me during the council's planning meeting. Amidst discussions of 'special circumstances' and 'Metropolitan Open Land' from the officials at the front of the room, Zara took my notebook, which I was busy scribbling in, from me and wrote 'I'M WORRIED' in big letters. I stopped writing and we went outside into the cold winter air to take a break from the long intense meeting. Zara, who had recently given up smoking, smoked a cigarette and we had a quick walk. 'I'm really scared they're going to allow it, I'm not sure I can handle that,' she said, looking tense and anxious.

Zara's feelings were mirrored through much of the local community. The Heritage Grant-funded research brought stories of the site 'to life' and increased awareness of its history in the local community. It had the potential, in the words of Tim, to 'put Surbiton on the map'. In addition to its infrastructural history, the site is of ecological importance, owing to the fact that it is one of the few areas of open still water in London. It is home to a rare bat species, Daubenton's bat. The bats have been anthropomorphised into the singular 'Benton the Bat', who has his own blog and website.[1] Benton has been made into a large puppet who joins the annual Lefi Parade alongside volunteers who hand out leaflets about his website (see Figure 7.2).

Whilst the Seething events and festivals, as outlined in Chapter 6, were purposely apolitical, they did serve 'soft' political ends; they brought people together in a way that built local networks of trust and familiarity. People got to know each other's skills and interests. People would then know who to turn to if they had a need, for example if they needed someone to build a website for a community campaign against a development. Efforts were made to steer clear of divisive local politics at Seething events. Whilst many Seethingers did get involved in the campaign to save the filter beds, they did so as locals, not as Seethingers. There was no use of stupid stories at campaign events and there was little or no discussion of the campaign at Seething events. At the most there was some advertising of the heritage project, but on the whole the Seething events and the campaign

Figure 7.2 Benton the Bat in the Lefi Parade. Author's own, 2014.

existed as separate phenomena in the social landscape. However, it is clear that Seething events allowed politically useful skills to be pooled, deepened a sense of local pride and gave people an increased sense of responsibility to the local area. This meant that when the campaign started, locals were willing and able to mobilise.

As the community was learning about the history of the filter beds during the heritage project, a company called Lake Properties submitted a planning application to build luxury homes on the filter beds (they had acquired the site some years earlier). The community quickly formed the Friends of Seething Wells Association (FoSWA), a CIC that would spearhead the opposition to Lake's plans. Tim, a key researcher on the community project, took the lead role in FoSWA. This involved organising meetings, keeping records, setting up a special business bank account for the CIC, fundraising, involving a wider public, getting local MPs on side, courting the press, and setting up and maintaining websites. Tim was by no means alone, but he was a pivotal figurehead for the group, and the scale of the work was significant. Eventually, FoSWA was given permission to speak at the council planning meeting. Its authority to do so was as a CIC, a recognised local interest group. Tim gave five minutes of evidence on behalf of the community on why the application should be refused and appeared clear and articulate to myself and others sitting in the public gallery.

Tim was widely congratulated by the community for his efforts and his articulate and clear arguments. He was seen as a vital part of the campaign against the filter beds. He was proud of the work he had done but was visibly tired, stressed as well as relieved when the campaign wound down.

The local body

A few months after the hearing and subsequent celebration I sat with Tim, watching the early spring sun dip behind the rusty blue railings of the old water filtration across the road from the pub. We met for an overdue catch-up on a lazy Sunday. During my fieldwork I met Tim regularly, often two or three times a week. However, in the build-up to the planning decision, we met less than once a month. Tim cancelled meetings and seemed relatively distant and unengaged. At the pub Tim apologised for his cancellations and told me that, as he looked back, he knew he was not 'in the best place' and that the stress and strain of being a key spokesperson for the community had affected him physically and mentally. He explained that his marriage was under strain because of the amount of time he was spending in community meetings, that he felt he carried responsibility for the community, and that he felt he was drinking too much. The stress had somatised in his guts, he had developed irritable bowels, and during the council meeting itself Tim had to run to the toilet numerous times between giving testimony. The irony was not lost on him that in the act of saving a site to which clean water was traced during the cholera epidemics of the 1850s, he had himself developed diarrhoea. In his struggle to preserve a historical landmark in the development of the modern city, one that was pivotal in the management of bodily fluids, Tim's body felt the strain.

Tim was not alone in this. Others had discreetly told me of the physical and mental effects of community activism. Again, the conversations came after many months of my doing fieldwork. People were careful not to be seen as complaining and aimed to put forward a positive disposition towards community work, but the effects were clear. Benny, a professional heritage expert who lived in the area and was a regular participant in Seething events, had become heavily involved in the objection process. Benny had led the research side of the Heritage grant and had become intimately familiar with the filter bed site. Benny spoke alongside Tim at the council meeting in his capacity as a heritage expert. However, in the summer before the council meeting, at the same pub where I met Tim, again overlooking the shimmering filter beds, Benny had explained to me that he had been careful not to get too involved in FoSWA. He said he needed to move away from the objection process for his own good, describing the difficulty in viscerally corporeal terms:

B: It's a funny one … I just had to move away from it all really. I just don't know, you know, I don't know what I would do if it doesn't work.
Me: What? If they win?
B: Yeah. … If [the developers] win, I'm not sure what I'll do, I'm not sure I can take that, I'm so involved, too much, it would tear me apart, to be honest – I've got so much of me in there – to see it just built on and all that lost, I'm not sure I could take it, to be honest. I have to be careful; I'm trying not to give too much of myself.

He was feeling the emotional strain and trying to manage it. This is something that Steve had told me he had also struggled to do. Steve was not only a key figure in the Seething festivals but was also well respected in the local community. He had initially kept his distance from the FoSWA campaign, as he and his political views are well known in the area and he feared his presence could have been 'divisive'. However, as the objection moved forward Steve played a vital role, using his experience and contacts to increase attendance at local meetings, drawing in other local organisations and businesses and getting local politicians to voice their oppositions to the plans.

At the council meeting itself Steve was waiting nervously outside the main hall, moving from person to person, thanking them for coming. With a smile and a hug, I asked how he was feeling. 'Sick', he replied with a sharp and serious demeanour before walking off to greet someone else with a smile. Throughout the meeting Steve, wearing a dark shirt, stood by the door, bit his nails and occasionally cried. Steve suffers from bipolar disorder and wears dark shirts when unwell and brightly coloured shirts whilst well, so that those who know him are aware and may be able to offer support. Steve had been wearing dark shirts for months before the meeting decision and later told me that the whole process had made him particularly unwell. Steve viscerally felt the responsibility of ensuring the filter beds were protected; he discussed with me many times the possibility that if these filter beds and their histories were lost, future generations might ask 'Where were you?'

Tim's guts, Steve's nerves, illness and low mood and Benny's expressions of being 'torn apart' and having 'so much of me in there' speak to the corporeal and emotional aspects of active citizenship. These corporeal anxieties were often hidden, suppressed or considered irrational in relation to the official processes of forming a community objection. The filter beds were known through a form of embodied knowledge. They were felt emotionally and through a sensual connection to their smells, sights and sounds. These relations were developed over time and in conjunction with the stories of the beds' histories and through the processes of community work which tie people to each other and to place. People often talked of their joy at seeing the filter beds, the green trees and plants that grow on the site and the sunsets that would skim off the water. This embodied knowledge was in stark contrast to the more bureaucratic ways of knowing the site as seen in the council meeting.

Bodily expertise

Just as the ASP members aimed to discipline their bodies in relation to the suburb in order to produce cool and rational assessments of place (see Chapter 4), so too did the FoSWA campaigners. Six months before the council meeting, in the rare glory of the British sun, Tim was leading a small group of around 20 interested locals in a heritage walk, publicised in the local press, along the side of the filter bed site to help raise awareness of the site. Tim described himself as wearing his 'heritage hat' and made an effort to remove any polemical and divisive language from the tour. Tim was well known in the area for his work with FoSWA but aimed to keep the tour, organised as part of the Borough's heritage programme, focused on the site's history rather than its present-day uncertainties. However, at the end of the tour, several of the tour group stayed to ask Tim about the campaign. This challenged Tim's aim to avoid controversy. Tim asserted that he aimed simply to deliver 'the story of the site', to let it 'speak for itself' and not 'cloud it with politics'. At the end of the walk Tim and I visited a local pub to talk about how the tour went. He asked me, 'Was I neutral enough?' Tim was trying to present a cool, rational account of the site, embodying what Dominic Boyer (2005) would describe as 'the corporeality of expertise', whilst trying to hide his emotions in relation to the site.

This tension between the rational and official and the embodied, affective and emotional aspects of knowing place came to be felt again at the council planning meeting. Here, Tim had to work to communicate corporeal, felt and emotional knowledge in a calm and rational manner; he was required to switch to using the bureaucratic language of a town planning meeting. Whilst Tim appeared to be calm, he admitted he was sweating profusely throughout the meeting, and that in the months before and after it his stress had manifested in irritable bowels, or, in his words, 'deep in my guts'. During the meeting itself he needed multiple visits to the bathroom. 'I was shitting profusely, I felt dizzy and almost blacked out. I thought I was having a stroke,' Tim said. As he apologised for cancelling meetings, he explained that he didn't really want 'the anthropologist' to see him struggling, or to show the negative aspects of his local activism. Tim was clearly trying to present a vision of community, and his participation in local life, that 'worked'. He did not want to moan or appear to complain. He made it clear to me that if the objection happened again (which it was threatening to do through an appeal) he would do it all again. For Tim these effects are for him a necessary and worthwhile aspect of being a citizen. Tim explained it in such terms, in particular with regard to his changing relationship with his son. 'I saw protecting the filter beds as looking after the child of tomorrow, but that meant I didn't look after the child of today [referring to his son] quite as I would like.' Tim had regrets about not seeing his son as much as he would have liked, but rationalised his actions as still being about kin in that his work would protect the local area and its rare ecology for future generations.

A number of my interlocutors expressed to me how the community work affected their health; they usually did so discreetly, and after I had grown to know them on a personal level. The effects on health demonstrate how their embodied experiences are tied to the local environment, and their relationship with it. Moreover, they manage the way these effects manifest in their body, and are able to hide aspects of emotion, distress or ill health in order to appear as calm, rational and active citizens. This particular dynamic is particular to late liberal citizenship, because such citizenship imposes moral and ethical obligations. However, the relationship between the state, governance and the body is historical, and it is important to lay out these histories in order to contextualise the position of the late liberal citizen.

The body and the city

As urban theorists such as Elizabeth Grosz have argued, the rise of scientific rationalism produced a Cartesian-like split not only between the body and mind, but also between the body and the city. The post-Enlightenment position understands that '[h]umans *make* cities' (Grosz 1998:45) with a rational mind. This presumes a one-way relation between the subjectivity of the rational human as the maker and the passive city. For Grosz, this underplays the degree to which the city makes the person, including their corporeal self. In our case, it would underplay the way the fabric of the suburban everyday affects the local suburban person.

The body and the city have long been linked through metaphor and analogy. Richard Sennett (1996) asserts that the urban plans of second-century Rome were based on idealisations of the body. He sets out how the centre was understood as the heart, the parks as the lungs, the roads as the arteries, and the sewers as the guts. The metaphor of the city as body serves as justification for forms of 'ideal' government and organisation through a process of naturalisation. The city becomes a parallel of the human body in that it is a natural form of organisation whose functions must be for the good of each organ and primarily for the good of the whole. The parallel between the body and social order saw its clearest formations in the seventeenth century 'when liberal political philosophers justified their various allegiances (the divine right of kings, for Hobbes; parliamentary representation, for Locke; direct representation, for Rousseau, etc.) through the metaphor of the body-politic' (Grosz 1998:45). For Grosz, 'The question is not simply how to distinguish life-enhancing from life-denying environments, but to examine how different cities, different sociocultural environments actively produce the bodies of their inhabitants as particular and distinctive types of bodies, as bodies with particular physiologies, affective lives, and concrete behaviors' (Grosz 1998:48). It is with reference to these ideas about the materiality of urban space that I describe the local, and its connection with particular physiologies, social values and behaviours in late liberalism.

Others working in the field of urban planning theory have theorised the connections between mind, body and city; my work draws on and continues this line of thought. The influential theorist Lewis Mumford stated that cities were a fact of nature, a part of man's natural expression in that 'Mind takes form in the city; and in turn, urban forms condition mind' (1938:5). This psychological link was taken further by Steve Pile, who has outlined how the body and the city interact in a complex kind of psychological grid (1996:177). Pile draws heavily from historians Stallybrass and White to describe how control, purification and disciplining of the city are mirrored in the body.

> [T]he reformation of the senses *produced*, as a necessary corollary, new thresholds of shame, embarrassment and disgust. And in the nineteenth century, those thresholds were articulated above all through specific *contents*, the slum, the sewer, the nomad, the savage, the rat – which, in turn, remapped the body.
> (Stallybrass and White 1986:148, quoted in Pile 1996:177)

The relation of the city to one's body both physically and conceptually is excellently outlined in Dominique Laporte's book *History of Shit* (2002). Drawing on Foucault, Freud and Descartes, amongst others, he outlines how the development of sanitation techniques in Europe affected notions of the modern self. For Laporte, the moving of shit to the private realm was synonymous with the founding of the modern family and bourgeois subjectivity. Laporte argues, 'Until the very eve of clinical medicine, it was maintained that shit had the potential to be unquestionably good' (2002:36) owing to its fertile qualities. However, the rise of the private family unit and an individual sense of self saw shit and its urban cesspools washed away and relegated to the private realm (2002:32). Shit, Laporte argues, was increasingly associated with sin (2002:36). Shit, then, must be collected, and it is, in huge volumes, by the state. Laporte argues that this produces a binding dialectic between the state and the individual. For Laporte the history of the management of shit by the state and the physiological movements of the body and our attitudes towards them are deeply entwined. Our relation to our bodies, both psychologically and physiologically, cannot be separated from historical shifts in the role of the state in managing bodies, and their excretions, through infrastructure. Laporte notes that as prevailing social attitudes towards our shit changed, so too did our relation to the built environment. As well as installing sewer systems, the state provided a cleansing infrastructure that cleared domestic furnishings, streets, public squares and the urban public realm of shit and dirt. As shit became increasingly separated from the domestic and public realm, so it became abject. Laporte argues that one's revulsion at the smell of shit is a particularly modern one that has developed alongside modern medicine, urban planning and the governance of the city and the body.

The rise in urban planning

In his 1989 book *French Modern* Paul Rabinow outlined the new forms of governance that emerged in nineteenth-century France alongside cholera epidemics. These led to changes in how city authorities managed the built environment, prompting infrastructural development, particularly relating to sewerage. Using a strongly Foucauldian approach, Rabinow argued that modern France, in terms of the state formation in relation to its population, emerged through the development of infrastructure and administration. Rabinow traced how, with the rise of scientific rationalism and bureaucratic administration, society became an object to be managed whilst the state simultaneously emerged as the prime unit of social organisation and an administrative force. The management of human waste was vital in this regard, shaping state–citizen relations. His approach leans heavily on the concept of biopolitics, which can be understood as a political rationality which takes the administration of life and populations as its subject in order to 'ensure, sustain, and multiply life, to put this life in order' (Foucault 1978:138). These changes in the relations between state, infrastructure and the body, via shit in this case, illuminate the biopolitical manoeuvres that give rise to new forms of relations and subjectivities.

Rabinow's story of the rise of state bureaucracy and control over a population of bodies through the urban infrastructure and management of waste in France is almost perfectly mirrored in the story of the filter beds in Surbiton and London's water. In the mid-1800s London had insufficient infrastructure to manage the bodily waste of the city's population, which had increased rapidly from one million around 1800 to 6.7 million one hundred years later. The bad air, or 'evil odour', and its associations with successive epidemics of dysentery, typhoid and cholera, saw pressure mount for solutions to the 'great stink'. In 1848 the City Sewers Act initiated widespread infrastructural development of water systems, but the problem was huge. In 1858, the 'hideous stench of human excrement rising from the River Thames ... finally got too much for Britain's politicians' (Mann 2016), and new works were commissioned. Joseph Bazalgette, the chief engineer of the Metropolitan Board of Works, built the 82 miles of new sewers and subterranean boulevards that make up the basis of London's sewage system today (George 2008). These sewers have been described as 'one of history's most life-enhancing advancements in urban planning' which 'laid the foundation for modern London' (Mann 2016). Before Bazalgette's sewer, London as it is understood today was divided into different administrations. The Old City, the Metropolitan Regions and the Square Mile all had different city commissioners, infrastructural plans and approaches (if they had any at all) for managing waste, people, buildings and so on. The problem of managing waste led to the unification of the administrations and to the modern form of urban governance in London.

The Surbiton filter beds were, at the time, a new form of water filtration system developed by an engineer called James Simpson. The beds were large because great quantities of water needed to be pumped to central London. Their scale makes them a prominent feature of the suburban landscape. In addition, they had a considerable influence on the early forms of housing in Surbiton (as has been mentioned, cottages built for workers comprise a notable part of the housing in the area). The beds used a new form of filtration to remove waste and impurities from water, the effectiveness of which marked them out from previous systems. Whilst cholera was first thought to be miasmic, Dr John Snow's mapping of the outbreaks led to the discovery that it was transmitted by bacteria that thrived in sewage-contaminated water. Owing to the filter beds' ability to remove dirt from the water they became the standard filtration system for much of the world. The locals often cite the moment Dr John Snow traced the clean water to the Surbiton filter beds as the first element of modern epidemiology. The global importance of these beds in this story put Surbiton 'on the map'. Steve stated to a public meeting:

> We've got something on our doorstep that people in Surbiton should feel incredibly proud about, the story of epidemiology and the beginnings of public health. ... This is a story that gives a real sense of pride and purpose.

This feeling towards the filter beds was prompted by pride in the contribution their suburb had made to the health of the larger city, and to a worldwide health movement. The filter beds tied them to the social body of the city at one scale and the world at another. Protecting the site, then, was also a form of protecting the locals' sense of relation to other populations in the city and across the world through the shared values implicit in the provision of clean water by the state via such infrastructures.

My interlocutors do not reject the idea of city-level governance of the built environment. Their respect for the filter beds reflects their respect for centrally managed infrastructure. Rather, the planning meeting was seen as one of the mechanisms through which a city and its population are managed. Whilst organising the campaign was stressful, and had negative effects on health and lifestyle, this work was seen as worthwhile. They became better citizens by interacting with the process of town planning. They enacted and embodied the ideal form of the late liberal citizen consistent with localism (see Chapter 3) and ideological shifts that assign moral responsibility for the built environment to the community and the self-motivated, self-skilled neoliberal subject.

The locals worked hard to translate their personal feelings (their pride in the history and ecological importance of the filter beds, and their phenomenologically informed intimate relations with them) into the language of state planning and local governance. Consequently, the two key social projects I have discussed in this book, ASP and the Seethingers, coincide at the planning meeting. They manifest here as the state and the engaged local. The distinct modes of knowing and relating to the materiality of the suburb come to matter in this context, as different groups work to assert the value of place and how such landscapes should be protected or developed in the future. Whilst the Seething events were understood as distinct from local political action, the efforts to develop strong community networks, and the forms of skill sharing, emotional support and shared values that they engender, came to matter in this political forum.

Citizenship and the city

As Laporte explained, the management of shit and the provision of clean water play a central part in modern notions not only of the city, but also of the self in terms of one's relation to the state, citizenship and bodily waste. Over recent years there has been increased attention to infrastructure in anthropology (Star 1999; Larkin 2013; Venkatesan et al. 2018).

Brian Larkin describes infrastructures as 'built networks that facilitate the flow of goods, people, or ideas and allow for their exchange over space' (2013:328). Larkin, building on the work of Walter Benjamin (1999), asserts that infrastructures can give rise to the 'collective fantasy of society' (Larkin 2013:329) and can allow particular notions of the city and citizenship to cohere around material assemblages. Susan Star notes that analysis of water and sewerage has been key in the increasing attention to infrastructure within the social sciences. She writes: 'Study a city and neglect its sewers and power supplies (as many have), and you miss essential aspects of distributional justice and planning power' (Star 1999:379). Following Larkin and Star, we can see how the filter beds aided the formation of London as a coherent socio-material entity towards which its citizen feels an obligation.

The link between city infrastructure and citizenship is outlined in Nikhil Anand's (2011) ethnography of water access in Mumbai. Anand outlines how citizenship is tied to access to water when the supply is scarce and sporadic, as it is in Mumbai. Whilst municipal engineers account for supply problems (and possible solutions) in technical terms, Anand's interlocutors demonstrate their understanding that 'phatic labour' (the work that goes into the establishment and maintenance of the social connections and channels of political influence through which they make claims to access water) generates real, effective solutions. What he terms 'hydraulic citizenship' is 'born out of diverse articulations between the technologies of politics (enabled by laws, politicians, and patrons) and the politics of technology (enabled by plumbing, pipes, and pumps)' (Anand 2011:545). Anand reveals the wider logics of citizenship at play here; he states that 'hydraulic citizenship is not just experienced as a unilinear extension of the biopolitical state. Rather, it is an iterative process that needs repetition, renewal work, and revalidation.' Anand's interlocutors needed to work constantly to manage their social networks and claims to material technologies. Thus they were able to influence the flows of water and access to sanitation.

In a similar vein, Brenda Chalfin (2014) notes that residents of Tema in Ghana fight to gain access to public toilets. Discussing Laporte's Foucauldian approach, she draws attention to the state governance of populations manifest through the everyday management and self-regulation of one's body. She does so to highlight the ways in which the relationship between the self-regulating citizen and the overarching apparatus of the modern state has been naturalised (Chalfin 2014:93). Chalfin explicitly equates 'the right to urban life' with the right to shit or, rather, to defecate in a particular way, that is, in a way that has become naturalised as synonymous with being a modern citizen who benefits from state infrastructure. For Chalfin, access to public toilets constitutes access to an infrastructural provision of the modern state. To be able to access a toilet is to be able to access state infrastructure, and so is to be classed as a valid citizen. She argues that those who are denied access to infrastructure, like public toilets, are denied the opportunity to be a modern citizen subject. They are, in her words, left in a 'zone of abandonment'. In Surbiton no one occupies such a zone of abandonment (certainly not in terms of toilet access); however, there is the spectre of abandonment. The community activists feel a responsibility to the community and to future generations to protect the filter beds and all that they symbolise. They must constantly work in order to maintain the status of the filter beds. They see this as their duty as citizens.

In *French Modern* Rabinow (1989) describes how urban expertise served as a technology of biopolitical power. Such expertise manifested in the emergence of a managerial class of town planners and new forms of municipal governance. Whilst this analysis illuminated the historical contingency of power, commentators have levelled criticism at the way it puts the state in a position of supreme authority, as a 'super-coordinator' of the processes and institutions of governance (Sharma & Gupta 2006:9). This produced a faulty analysis in which the dynamic between power and the formation of the modern subject is abstracted from the material processes on the ground. In particular, the role the individual plays in negotiating subjectification within dynamics of power has been overlooked. As Nikolas Rose (1996) has said, non-state institutions, communities and individuals play active roles in the mundane process of governance. Such processes have become increasingly important, and within the UK context the increasing 'de-statization of government' (Rose 1996:56) can be seen in such processes as the Localism Act 2011 (Department for Communities and Local Government 2010), which aimed to increase decision-making powers for communities and individuals. Whilst the overriding accompanying narrative from government has been one of increasing inclusion and participation in democracy, this chapter shows how such procedures manifest as a negative *burden* of action on local communities and particular individuals. Partaking in the urban planning process as a 'local' is, I argue, an act of performing biolegitimacy (following Fassin 2009). Fassin states that biolegitimacy, the forms and types of biological life which are considered valid by the state, gives the foundation to 'biological citizenship' (2009:51). This citizenship is a subject position afforded to a person upon proof of their alignment with institutional power and the prevailing social contract of the population.

Fassin examines the case of a Kenyan man who, after living in France under permanent threat of exclusion, was legally allowed to stay upon being diagnosed with AIDS. The irony is found in the man's statement, 'It is the disease which kills me that has become my reason for living now' (Fassin 2009:51). Biolegitimacy, states Fassin, links the matter of living, the biological, with the meaning of politics. Hence, a focus on biolegitimacy rather than biopower 'emphasize[s] the construction of the meaning and values of life instead of the exercise of forces and strategies to control it' (2009:52). Fassin aims to move the politicised body beyond governmentality and thus to move the focus of study 'from the "rules of the game" to its stakes' (2009:52). In cases like Surbiton, the stakes are the future of the suburb as a valuable place with a distinct and important character. The stakes are one's own sense of belonging, the sense of place one leaves to the next generation, and – because a local's sense of place is so deeply tied to their body – their health and wellbeing.

The site that Tim and others were trying to save was intimately tied to their sense of self and to the values they held dear, such as ecological and historical value. Because of this, protection of the site was also a way of protecting themselves and the forms of social relations they wished to enact via the urban landscape into the future. To lose it, they argued, would be to lose part of themselves. Therefore the stakes were high. The practice of performing local citizenship is a necessary part of performing one's biolegitimacy. Such biolegitimacy must be performed constantly in order for social legitimacy to be maintained. This chapter is therefore less a discussion of forms of biopower in terms of the way in which human conduct is governed than a description of how local citizenship is performed by individuals to assert their legitimacy and efficacy within particular mechanisms of governance (here, urban planning procedures). Locals work hard to translate their personal and local conceptions of the value of the built environment into the processes of urban planning. The body, the built environment, one's sense of self and one's citizenship are deeply connected. Through the practice of being local, of performing one's citizenship, the body somatises the stress and strain of having to maintain a form of biolegitimacy.

Making local forms of life

Here I want to return to the work of Giorgio Agamben on forms of life and death, and in particular my contention that the making of a local is a process by which a politically qualified life is made (see Chapter 2). Writing in the context of the political and philosophical discussions that followed from the atrocities of World War II, Agamben was, to some degree, responding to Hannah Arendt's and Foucault's studies of totalitarianism and biopolitics. In his attempts to understand how it came to be that people could become subjects killable by the state, Agamben argued that contemporary parliamentary democracies had transformed into totalitarian entities. This journey is possible because of the changing figure of the sovereign. Agamben (1998, 2005) draws on Carl Schmitt's ([1932] 1996) notion of the sovereign as the one who has the power to decide the 'state of exception' from law. Whilst the sovereign could easily be imagined as a monarch deciding law, Agamben argues that the power of the sovereign no longer resides in the monarch but, through the auspices of a representative democracy, in the state. Following Foucault, Agamben describes how the state had, with the rise of scientific rationalism, bureaucracy and power, turned democracies into regimes of biopolitical management (Agamben 1998:122).

In late liberalism, the ability to perform as an active citizen maintains *bios* and prevents *zoë*. Use of appropriate language is key to this performance. The locals in Surbiton transform their personal, affective relations to the filter beds into the official language of a planning process which enables them to maintain themselves as part of the demos, that is, the politically active population involved in the process of deciding the conditions of law. Specifically, they inhabit the position of the citizens who decide what can legally be built and what can't. The locals are constantly on a threshold of *zoë* and must labour to make *bios*, living out Agamben's conjecture (1998:9) that

> modern democracy presents itself from the beginning as a vindication and liberation of zoë, and that it is constantly trying to transform its own bare life into a way of life and to find, so to speak, the *bios* of *zoë*.

As part of the process of the democracy, the figure of 'the local' is both threatened with exclusion, and the arbiter of exclusion; the local sits precariously on the threshold of exclusion (its preferred form of living is in danger of being denied), and simultaneously this local performs a political role to maintain its influence over exclusions. According to Agamben, the citizen must engage with the state in order not to be subject to it:

> The fact that in this process the 'subject' is, as has been noted, transformed into a 'citizen' means that birth – which is to say, bare natural life as such – here for the first time becomes (thanks to a transformation whose biopolitical consequences we are only beginning to discern today) the immediate bearer of sovereignty. …
> It is not possible to understand the 'national' and biopolitical development and vocation of the modern state in the nineteenth and twentieth centuries if one forgets that what lies at its basis is not man as a free and conscious political subject but, above all, man's bare life, the simple birth that as such is, in the passage from subject to citizen, invested with the principle of sovereignty.
> (Agamben 1998:128)

The locals are constantly performing this 'passage from subject to citizen'. This performance emerges from the conditions of late liberalism, whereby one needs to sculpt oneself into an active and effective agent of politics. Locals engage with the languages and mechanisms of different social projects as they move between being a Seethinger, with the embodied and emotional relations to place, and being a local, talking in a formal way in council meetings. They perform 'the local' on the threshold between citizen and bare life, both subject to, and constantly responding to, the processes and infrastructures of the biopolitical regulation of late liberalism. They do this to protect and realise potential futures for their neighbourhood. This future is under constant threat from neoliberal market forces, such as those that motivate the building of luxury apartments. These forces threaten a future premised on particular arrangements of the local built environment (particularly, here, preserved filter beds). Locals are not only trying to maintain themselves as included in political life, *bios*; they are also seeking to influence the nature of *bios*, that is, what particular values that form of life maintains. They do not reject late liberal citizenship but aim to sculpt it in a particular way.

My use of Agamben's terms *bios* and *zoë* adapts his original use of the terms. Here I follow the work of Schinkel and Van den Berg (2011), who deploy a similar use of the terms in their analysis of the urban policy practice of 'intervention teams' in Rotterdam. Schinkel and Van den Berg note that these specialised combined teams of police, social work and immigration intervene in areas of perceived urban decline. They argue that government by exception, meaning the exclusion from citizen rights of certain persons, has gradually become routine within democratic government (Schinkel & Van den Berg 2011:1912; Agamben 2005:16). However, they emphasise that the biopolitical positioning of bodies is a kind of performance, in a way that recalls Anand's attention to the 'iterative process'. In their case, exception from rights is delineated by city officials who take 'advantage of the blurriness of their mandate, rhetorically overpower citizens and enter their homes' (Schinkel & Van den Berg 2011:1921). They develop their perspective from the work of Aihwa Ong, whose position they summarise well, stating: 'As Aihwa Ong has argued, Agamben's "rigid binary opposition" between bare life and the rights-bearing life would miss 'the rich complexity' of reality and "seems to preclude the possibility of non-rights mediation or complex distinctions that can buttress claims for moral protection and legitimacy"' (Schinkel & Van den Berg 2011:1915, citing Ong 2006:23). Examination of the practice of biopolitics, in the rich complexities of realities of lived experiences, yields rich, nuanced ethnographic detail. We may discover the precise conditions by which the conditions of citizenship are laid out, how it is desired, performed and laboured for and, in turn, the effect that such labour has on subjectivities and the body.

In Surbiton the locals understand the processes through which the built environment is either protected or developed, and they understand their role. To enhance their agency within this process, they seek to form a 'resilient community'. Here, the forms and mechanisms of exclusion and inclusion are incredibly subtle. We must follow the cue of Chalfin, who makes use of Agamben in a way that 'avoids extremes' (2014:99) so that she can understand the complex ethnographic detail of the situation she studies. Chalfin examines how infrastructure produces a '"public" as social formation, realm of interaction, and collective consciousness'; further, she asks how 'these iterations of "publicness" augment, reject, or replace state authority' (2014:106). In a similar way we can ask how sewerage infrastructures produced publics of the city of London, citizens of an urban area. These citizens then work to be politically effective in the management and running of the city infrastructure. Work such as Chalfin's demonstrates how Agamben's ideas can usefully bridge a perceived gap, within the Foucauldian approach, between governmentality and biopolitics. As Schinkel and Van den Berg assert, 'The link between neoliberal governmentality and biopolitics that Foucault first highlighted in his 1978–1979 lectures at the Collège de France (Foucault 2004) can thus be illustrated by bringing Agamben's link between biopolitics and sovereign power to bear [on] urban policy practices' (Schinkel & Van den Berg 2011:1933). By adding a consideration of sovereignty and citizenship to the analysis of governmentality (see also Donzelot and Gordon 2009) we are able to illuminate the processes through which people subjectivise and work within the forces of governance. Further, we are able to see the effects of this work of subjectification on the body of the local.

I draw on Agamben to think through the forms of subjectivities and publics constituted through the process of being an active 'local' citizen. It would be remiss of me to apply Agamben's terms of absolute exclusion to describe the ethnographic situation outlined in this chapter. However, there is purchase in thinking through *how* the threshold of a politically qualified life is delimited. Whilst the power to exclude originates in a particularly aggressive form of state authority in both Chalfin (2014) and Schinkel and Van den Berg (2011), it comes from a more subtle force in the case study we have seen in Surbiton. Here the threat of exclusion comes from the structures of late liberalism, which demand an active citizen. If the locals do not cultivate an active citizenship, they risk being subsumed by the overarching neoliberal forces, which would bring about a suburban dystopia of selfishness, greed and the loss of important community spaces. I argue that the Surbiton community activists had come to feel the moral weight of their responsibility regarding the management of the built environment and the protection of the filter bed site for future generations. The location of this form of moral responsibility is one that is particularly neoliberal in the Gershonian (see Gershon 2011, 2016) sense, in that it puts the onus on the individual to cultivate social capital. The community activists are responsible for maintaining themselves as politically qualified persons through their actions as active citizens. If they do not, they risk losing the valuable forms of urban environment and associated socio-political landscapes to normalised capital developments, such as the impending building of luxury flats.

Thus the state does not so much exclude in a direct way, but rather sets the terms by which citizens must maintain themselves over the threshold of a politically qualified life and embody the responsibility for maintenance of the moral good. This responsibility is one that is actively taken up by the community activists. It becomes a huge part of their life, friendships and moral landscapes, but it is also one which is felt emotionally, corporeally in the guts, as it causes stresses and strains. It produces not only a local political or social subject but localness in terms of the forms of places and bodies that become materially manifest.

Conclusions

This chapter has shown how a local subjectivity and bodily disposition emerges through the conditions of late liberal citizenship. It has outlined the historical emergence of the late liberal citizen, with its particular constellation of relations to the state, material infrastructures and the body. It has drawn attention to how this works in a phenomenological sense, that is, in the ways locals feel the local landscape through moving through it, sensing it and caring deeply about it – so much so that they feel it deep in their guts. In order to protect aspects of the local built environment they must mobilise themselves and their community into politically efficacious local citizens. The local is made through the long history of infrastructures, which involve the biopolitical management of bodies, but further through their labour in responding to the demands made of them as late liberal citizens as they strive to make *bios* from *zoë*. This takes work, and shapes not only the forms of local subjectivities of late liberalism but also their bodily dispositions. These aspects are often concealed, because dysfunctional guts, depression and anxiety are considered worthwhile side effects of the labour needed to be a good citizen.

This chapter, as well as the ones preceding it, have also outlined the degree to which 'making the local' requires labour in addition to campaigning. Locals must develop networks of skills and establish shared values and trust. In Surbiton these manifest as stupid events. These events cultivate the kind of community required by the late liberal preoccupation with localism and participation. It was not lost on my interlocutors that they lived in an affluent, largely middle-class suburb. They recognised that they had a certain privilege to be able to cultivate community in such ways. They would often remark on the fact that certain people in the community had skills that made community action easier. These skills and other resources (including time) allowed this community to mobilise and enact their citizenship, even if that came at a certain cost.

Note

1   http://bentonbat.blogspot.co.uk/ (accessed 29 April 2021).

References

Agamben, Giorgio. 1998. *Homo Sacer: Sovereign power and bare life* (trans. Daniel Heller-Roazen). Stanford, CA: Stanford University Press.
Agamben, Giorgio. 2005. *State of Exception* (trans. Kevin Attell). Chicago, IL: University of Chicago Press.
Anand, Nikhil. 2011. 'Pressure: The politechnics of water supply in Mumbai.' *Cultural Anthropology* 26, no. 4: 542–64. https://doi.org/10.1111/j.1548-1360.2011.01111.x.
Benjamin, Walter. 1999. *The Arcades Project* (trans. Howard Eiland and Kevin McLaughlin). Cambridge, MA: Belknap Press of Harvard University Press.
Boyer, Dominic. 2005. 'The corporeality of expertise.' *Ethnos* 70, no. 2: 243–66. https://doi.org/10.1080/00141840500141345.
Chalfin, Brenda. 2014. 'Public things, excremental politics, and the infrastructure of bare life in Ghana's city of Tema.' *American Ethnologist* 41, no. 1: 92–109. https://doi.org/10.1111/amet.12062.
Department for Communities and Local Government. 2010. 'Decentralisation and the Localism Bill: An essential guide.' London: Crown Copyright. [The Localism Act (2011).]
Donzelot, Jacques and Colin Gordon. 'Governing liberal societies: The Foucault effect in the English-speaking world.' 2009. In Michael A. Peters, A. C. Besley, Mark Olssen, Susanne Maurer and Susanne Weber, eds, *Governmentality Studies in Education*, pp. 3–15. Rotterdam: Sense.
Fassin, Didier. 2009. 'Another politics of life is possible.' *Theory, Culture & Society* 26, no. 5: 44–60. https://doi.org/10.1177%2F0263276409106349.
Foucault, Michel. 1978. *The History of Sexuality. Volume 1: The Will to Knowledge* (trans. Robert Hurley). London: Penguin Books.
Foucault, Michel. 2004. *Naissance de la Biopolitique: Cours au Collège de France, 1978–1979* [The birth of biopolitics. Lectures at the Collège de France 1978–1979]. Paris: Gallimard/Seuil.
George, Rose. 2008. *The Big Necessity: Adventures in the world of human waste*. London: Portobello Books.
Gershon, Ilana. 2011. 'Neoliberal agency.' *Current Anthropology* 52, no. 4: 537–55. https://doi.org/10.1086/660866.
Gershon, Ilana. 2016. '"I'm not a businessman, I'm a business, man": Typing the neoliberal self into a branded existence.' *HAU: Journal of Ethnographic Theory* 6, no. 3: 223–46. https://doi.org/10.14318/hau6.3.017.
Grosz, Elizabeth. 1998. 'Bodies-cities.' In Heidi Nast and Steve Pile, eds, *Places through the Body*, pp. 42–51. Abingdon: Routledge.
Laporte, Dominique. 2002. *History of Shit* (trans. Nadia Benabid and Rodolphe el-Khoury). Cambridge, MA: MIT Press.
Larkin, Brian. 2013. 'The politics and poetics of infrastructure.' *Annual Review of Anthropology* 42: 327–43. https://doi.org/10.1146/annurev-anthro-092412-155522.
Mann, E. 2016. 'Story of cities #14: London's Great Stink heralds a wonder of the industrial world.' *Guardian*, 4 April 2016. www.theguardian.com/ cities/2016/apr/04/story-cities-14-london-great-stink-river-thames-joseph-bazalgette-sewage-system (accessed 30 April 2021).
Mumford, Lewis. 1938. *The Culture of Cities*. New York: Harcourt, Brace.
Ong, Aihwa. 2006. *Neoliberalism as Exception: Mutations in citizenship and sovereignty*. Durham, NC: Duke University Press.
Pile, Steve. 1996. *The Body and the City: Psychoanalysis, space and subjectivity*. Abingdon: Routledge.

Rabinow, Paul. 1989. *French Modern: Norms and forms of the social environment*. Chicago, IL: University of Chicago Press.

Rose, Nikolas. 1996. 'Governing "advanced" liberal democracies'. In Andrew Barry, Thomas Osborne and Nikolas Rose, eds, *Foucault and Political Reason: Liberalism, neo-liberalism and rationalities of government*, pp. 37–64. Chicago, IL: University of Chicago Press.

Scheper-Hughes, Nancy and Margaret M. Lock. 1987. 'The mindful body: A prolegomenon to future work in medical anthropology.' *Medical Anthropology Quarterly* n.s. 1, no. 1: 6–41. https://doi.org/10.1525/maq.1987.1.1.02a00020.

Schinkel, Willem and Marguerite Van den Berg. 2011. 'City of exception: The Dutch revanchist city and the urban *homo sacer*.' *Antipode* 43, no. 5: 1911–38. https://doi.org/10.1111/j.1467-8330.2010.00831.x.

Schmitt, Carl. [1932] 1996. *The Concept of the Political* (trans. Matthias Konzen and John P. McCormick; notes by Leo Strauss). Chicago, IL: University of Chicago Press.

Sennett, Richard. 1996. *Flesh and Stone: The body and the city in Western civilization*. New York: W.W. Norton.

Sharma, Aradhana and Akhil Gupta, eds. 2006. *The Anthropology of the State: A reader*. Blackwell Publishing.

Stallybrass, Peter and Allon White. 1986. *The Politics and Poetics of Transgression*. London: Methuen.

Star, Susan Leigh. 1999. 'The ethnography of infrastructure.' *American Behavioral Scientist* 43, no. 3: 377–91. https://doi.org/10.1177/00027649921955326.

Venkatesan, Soumhya, Laura Bear, Penny Harvey, Sian Lazar, Laura M. Rival and AbdouMaliq Simone. 2018. 'Attention to infrastructure offers a welcome reconfiguration of anthropological approaches to the political.' *Critique of Anthropology* 38, no. 1: 3–52. https://doi.org/10.1177/0308275X16683023.

8
Conclusion

I opened this book by discussing the idea that Surbiton is, in the words of a proud local, 'a community that works'. I have argued that it 'works' not only in the sense that it functions successfully, but also in the sense that it *labours* to be 'resilient'. Late liberal subjectivities emerge out of such labour. Throughout this book I have examined what kinds of labour *make the local*.

The local subject comes into being within a constellation of ideals and values associated with democracy, inclusion and participation. A good local citizen is constituted through the everyday activities that produce a form of politically qualified life in late liberalism. This can be arranging a community event, campaigning, or walking with others to tell them about how important a place is. These activities are given orientation and shape by the need to communicate value to others, such as the local council. We see the locals strive to translate and communicate their values into required registers. The need to resolve aporia between different epistemologies, different modes of knowing, motivates the practices of the good local citizen.

The late liberal subject strives to achieve their idea of 'the good life'. Through that process they constantly reflect on how to be 'a subject of a certain qualitative kind' (Faubion 2012:72): they aim to be a good citizen, a good expert or a good councillor, extending their own ideals, but also working to alter the overarching normative conditions of social life. That is to say, the locals presented here were not only trying to create community in order to foster 'resilience' to the perceived pressures of neoliberalism on social life but were also – through developing social networks and mobilising political power – trying to sculpt a place for their ideals and in the everyday practices and procedures of everyday modern life and its governance. They shopped locally, they interacted and engaged with the local council, and they made efforts to develop local community.

I have outlined how the Seething community use parafictions (Lambert-Beatty 2009) and techniques of being 'stupid' to build social networks and community resilience to the perceived threats of neoliberalism. These threats loom in the form of work pressures, increased individualism and the development of the built environment for short-term profit, all at the expense of long-term quality of life. This community activity produced a form of vibrant suburban life, local pride and neighbourliness which was seen as necessary for the development of the moral responsibility of individuals and communities for political action both directly (through such things as the planning objection) and less directly (through the development of a local sensibility). I have outlined the context of the emergence of this local subjectivity, and recent governmental agendas of localism, within the shifting ideological forces of neoliberalism, with its emphasis on self-responsibility and organisation. I argue that neoliberal logic is consistent with and *prompts* the practice of being local in the Gershonion sense. Just as Gershon (2011, 2016) describes how the neoliberal worker must sculpt themselves, so too must the members of the community sculpt themselves into good locals who must self-organise and 'skill up' in order to produce the forms of social networks needed to make resilient communities.

In Surbiton I have, I hope sympathetically, outlined how a community has responded to the challenges of being local. This response is seen in the work of the Community Brain CIC, in FoSWA, and in a strong 'local' attitude through which people emphasise and prioritise localness and neighbourliness in their social life, their work and their consumption habits. This engagement, however, as the community recognised, takes a lot of work, skills, time and resources. The community understood that they were well placed to respond to such challenges and, through the Community Brain, aimed to help other communities by working with them. Their privilege extended to having the means to enact the forms of local politics that late liberalism demands. They were also invested in the forms of social life and structures of governance of late liberalism. Most of the people here had good jobs, homes and nice lifestyles. The suburb is relatively affluent and a pleasant place to live; this was a good place to be. Their efforts to make a politically qualified life, *bios*, did not require a radical departure from the prevailing ideology of late liberalism; they were not proposing a radical 'world otherwise'. Rather, they wanted a seat at the table to articulate their values and ways of life within late liberalism. Their labour was one of cohering a community that would be able to translate their values into the language of late liberal governance, into council meetings where they would be heard as part of the political process of governance which they are themselves invested in. The active/activist local citizen works to assert a politically qualified form of life rather than to reject the overarching ideological mode of social organisation wholesale.

In consistently and tirelessly performing a particular kind of role in order to attain and maintain social efficacy, the late liberal subject maintains their citizenship within this ideological order. This public demonstration of their valid ethical substance allows them to propose a version of life worth living, within (and not counter to) the prevailing modes of social organisation.

The work of being a citizen is about commensuration. That is, in order to communicate the value of the suburb to others, locals needed to work to translate their affection for the local area into a common matrix of understanding with other groups, such as the council. But this work of commensuration, which comes about through a desire to include, is also about exclusion. When it comes to the filter beds, the community and the property developer read and understand the filter beds very differently; there are two versions of the filter beds (with different meanings and values), and these versions are incommensurate. The council must adjudicate but can only do so by recognising and understanding each version of the filter beds (local heritage site or valuable real estate). But ultimately, the flats either get built or they don't. Furthermore, certain types of knowledge and ways of relating to the filter beds will be privileged above others, according to the hegemonic social project (in this case the state in the form of the local council), which attempts to establish the mode of universal judgement over what life should be and therefore the value of sites such as the filter beds.

There were also times when incommensurability was productive. In the case of the ASP's Community Map the Seethingers found it productive not to find common ground so that they could maintain the mechanisms of their 'stupid' stories at the local scale. The ASP used this moment to defer the map's ability to increase democratic participation in planning situations by creating a platform for communication (an ideal speech situation), into a future in which such issues would be resolved through technical advancements. In this case the social projects were able to ignore each other, and needed to do so in order to maintain the coherence of their own project. But they met again, in a different form, as state and citizen in the planning meeting.

Here the ideal of inclusion encounters a material impasse. All points of view, all versions of what should happen to the filter bed site, cannot be accommodated. One of the aims of this book is to draw attention to the detail of the process of exclusion and how this is implicit within the ideal of inclusion. My key analytical position has not been to locate the reader at the centre of a particular social project but rather to draw attention to the edge of social projects, that is to say, the place at which work must be done to translate one way of knowing into another register. Being local, mapping place, being expert and being a politically active citizen are deeply corporeal embodied experiences. The work required by late liberalism, within which one must labour to find a seat at the table, sculpts not only one's subjectivity but also one's experiences and forms of the body; being a local has material and corporeal effects – or, as is often the case, costs. But these costs are seen as a necessity and worthwhile, and this labour is undertaken in order to maintain one's politically qualified life within a social order with which my interlocutors on the whole identify.

By locating my analysis at the edge of social projects, where inclusions and exclusions are worked out, I have aimed, through a focus on the material, to detail the everyday work and constitutive exclusions of late liberal citizenship. Rather than remain focused on the ontology of a material – for example, how it is that 'powder is power' (see Chapter 2) – I am more interested in what such material allows one to do. That is, how does a perspective on the material world allow particular forms of life to be lived? From this point of view the question is not only how is 'powder power' but who has the powder and what does this allow them to do, or what do the filter beds allow the locals to do that luxury flats don't? How are these perspectives brought into the spaces through which the world is or is not curated?

I am interested in a form of anthropology that asks how forms of life are opened up, but also how they are closed down. How are some ways of living excluded even in the process of inclusion? But, further, we can ask what happens when the social project is so different that the subject does not necessarily want to get a seat at the table, but wants to destroy the table, or be somewhere else altogether. That is to say, what about radical difference or even forms of life that are unable, or unwilling, to be accommodated by the normative social order?

By way of conclusion, I want to return us to Seething, a community that aims to include all, to demonstrate the dynamic of the constitutive exclusion. That is the necessary exclusion of any social project, which, as we saw in Chapter 2, seeks a form of universality (see Laclau & Mouffe 1985). Towards the end of the time of my fieldwork, a new Seething legend was being written. It sought to correct a problem with the original Seething tale of Lefi Ganderson (see Box 1.1). This Seething legend describes an ancient village of dystopian selfishness and greed before they learnt their valuable lesson from little Lefi the goat boy and his selfless acts. This pre-Lefi community, which represents the worst version of contemporary life, excluded Lefi for being different, as he was half boy, half goat. He was the constative exclusion required to realise and maintain this version of Seething. Only the children took Lefi food and played with him; they did so because they were pre-social: they had not yet learnt to exclude, judge and be selfish. Ultimately, the excluded Lefi was the one to save the village from Thamas Deeton, the giant who terrorised the village. When Thamas left, the villagers were grateful to Lefi, and regretted how cruelly they had treated him in the past. They went to find him but could not. However, they do now celebrate him each year to remember his kindness and to remember to be kind to others and include all, no matter how different. It is not easy to include the other when the identity of the community has hitherto been defined by the exclusion of this other. Inclusion of the previously excluded takes a special kind of continued effort. Lefi Day represents this work, done repeatedly and in spectacular fashion. Whilst Lefi has been welcomed, the giant is now banished. Seething has welcomed one other, the previously excluded Lefi, but in doing so it has necessarily excluded another, the giant Thamas.

That Thamas was excluded was unnoticed and unremarked upon, until it suddenly became visible and problematic during the annual Lefi Day Parade in about 2011, in a manner remarkably similar to the Lefi tale itself. During this particular version of the festival a huge puppet of Thamas led the parade attached to a Segway machine, a two-wheeled motorised transporter (see Figure 1.2). Leon, who was inside the giant puppet and driving the Segway, took great delight in rushing up to cars and passing shoppers and other users of the Surbiton streets. He would force people to slow down, stop and notice the Seethingers. People took pictures and asked, 'What is going on?' Behind the giant, a tail of around 500 people walked carrying puppets, giant cheeses, bats and all manner of Seething-related items. As usual, newcomers were invited to participate. People would quickly get up to speed with the basis of the story and it was clear that Thamas was the baddie of the tale. People in the parade would boo Thamas loudly when he turned to face them.

But this presented a problem. When the story of Lefi Ganderson was first penned and turned into a children's book it carried, on the front page, a dedication to Molly, the then new-born daughter of an influential Seethinger who had done much for the community. Molly was now five years old. She had grown up with the Seething stories being read to her at night and in school, and had always been part of the festivals and parades. Molly was my youngest interlocutor. I had done a walking interview with her mother, who explained her Surbiton to me. Molly asked to do her own walking interview, which we did. She drew me a map of her Surbiton and told me, 'Thamas is my friend', as she pointed to a sandpit in the local park and explained that this was a footprint that Thamas had left when he was banished. Molly was still Thamas's friend despite being told by the adults that Thamas was bad. It was not surprising that Molly became upset when people booed at Thamas during the parade. She asked her parents to make the adults stop being nasty to Thamas.

Here the child, innocent of social norms, was telling the community to accept the excluded other, Thamas, just as the children in the Lefi tale had told the adults to accept Lefi. But this time the child was not in a Seething tale but in a modern Seething event. The story of Molly's distress spread around the Seethingers in the pub after the event. People agreed that Molly was right: they had been nasty to Thamas, and this was very un-Seething. They had judged him, been mean, and excluded him. Molly's distress had made this ethical relation of the Seethingers to Thamas present and visible and had drawn attention to a problem. If inclusion was one of the central ideals of Seething, then how could they possibly exclude Thamas? That night in the pub people speculated why he might be so bad-tempered, telling stories of what might have happened to him. Over the following few weeks a new story was penned. As usual, a thread ran on Facebook outlining the basics of the new story. Steve took it upon himself to pen a version of Thamas's tale, and a meeting was called in the pub at which the story was read aloud. People discussed the new story in small groups and fed back corrections and more 'historical detail' to Steve, who wrote up a second draft. After a second meeting, a final version was made.

Eventually it was decided or discovered that Thamas was not really evil but, rather, misunderstood. The new story explained that Thamas was one of four brothers. When they were younger, they used to enjoy family meals together for which their parents would make a special pie. With the left-over mix the giants would make little pocket-sized treats. They called these 'past eats', which today are known as pasties. However, as the brothers got older there was a family feud and the brothers left to live on mountains in the four corners of the UK. Today we see evidence of this through the local foods and mountains of places like St Michael's Mount in Cornwall, where it is no coincidence that you can get the famous Cornish pasty. The Seethingers wrote that it was because Thamas was from a broken home, his parents treated him badly and his brothers left him that he was angry. The Seethingers penned the story and had a new event to make pasties in order to remember Thamas.

The new story was written shortly after the London riots of 2011, during which people looted shops and burnt houses and cars. The trigger was clear: the shooting of a young black man, Mark Duggan, by the police and the way his family were treated in the aftermath. At the time there was much public conversation about the riots, why they happened, what should be done. Views ranged from conservative arguments for strong policing to liberal arguments for an examination of the role played by poverty and the ways in which young people may feel excluded from mainstream society (Ball et al. 2019 have subsequently drawn attention to the role that police racism, class disadvantage and political, social and economic geographies played in the spread and location of the riots). In Surbiton, or at least amongst my interlocutors, there were a range of views, but mostly people were asking why this had happened, and how to resolve the exclusion they suspected as a principal cause. A few Seethingers noted that 'like the kids in the riot', Thamas felt he didn't belong. They compared his behaviour in their new version of the story to the violent outbursts of the rioters. This comparison aligned the violent outbursts of both Thamas and the rioters as the expression of what Slavoj Žižek (2012) would describe as a 'symbolic deadlock', in which something manifests in behaviour that cannot be put into words. In his documentary film *The Pervert's Guide to Ideology*, Žižek argues that the most shocking thing for the then Prime Minister of the UK, David Cameron, and the press (according to their rhetoric) was not the street battles and burning of things but that people were taking things without paying for them. Žižek argues that poverty and lack of opportunity, the standard liberal explanation, do not adequately explain the riots. He says that to some degree Cameron was right: there was no ideological justification here, no world otherwise being presented. Rather, there is a deadlock as people are unable to enact the subject position demanded of them by the prevailing ideology of a consumer society, and so we should not be surprised at riots as a form of protest. Here I am not trying to advance Žižek's reading; rather I want to draw attention to the ways in which the Seethingers made an analogy between Thamas and the rioters as subjects who were unable, yet desired, to enact what was expected of them as they lacked the resources to partake in society. Here I do not wish to conclude with a rumination on the riots of 2011; I'll leave that for others. However, I do wish to think through the dynamics of inclusion.

In thinking through the attempts of Seethingers to include both Lefi and Thamas I want to make some observations. Firstly, both Lefi and Thamas served as the constative exclusions, that is the exclusion against which a society could define itself as something they were not, until, that is, the exclusion became unignorable and needed to be dealt with as a form of ethical problem. That is, their presence no longer served as the thing that a social project was not, but through their very presence (or rather an excess of being present) Lefi and Thamas demanded a rethinking of the universal basis of the ethical position of the social project of Seething (namely the ideal of inclusion). That is to say, how can a social world that claims to include possibly exclude? Secondly, whilst the solution to this was to recognise the good of Lefi and the troubles of Thamas, neither Lefi nor Thamas was actually included in the world of Seething. Lefi was, as the tale tells, nowhere to be found, and Thamas, whilst the story was given a prequel, is still dead at the end of the Lefi tale.

The story is still one about Seethingers, from a Seething perspective. We could ask what Seething would be like if it were run according to the values, lifeworlds and everyday practices of goat boys or giants. What would living amongst others really be like, and would Seething even be recognisable? Lefi and Thamas are not included but rather remain on the threshold of a *bios*; they still need to demonstrate their utility and qualities to Seethingers. They are unable to bring about radical difference but are able to alter, a little, what Seething is, to the degree that Seething as a social project is able to maintain its universality and coherence, in particular through its ideals of inclusion. Further, we know little about Thamas's parents: there has been little discussion of them in Seething. There has been no Molly moment where they have been recognised as unfairly excluded, empathised with, and brought in.

For my concluding point I want to think through how we might really get to know what the ontological worldviews of Lefi and Thamas, and to some degree that of his parents, are. Or rather, I want to ask if that is really what we wish to achieve. Returning to the notion of collaboration (Chapter 7), we can question what our anthropological task of understanding difference is here. Is it to understand who the other is, what it means to be them? Or is it to collaborate to see how the world might change if we think it through and enact being in the world together? I opened this book by talking about the ASP's Community Map and my role, as a hired anthropologist, in populating the map with stories in order to gain an understanding of what life in the suburbs is like for the people that live there. To this day the map remains unpopulated and unused. However, this was instructive of a gap between two different social projects that both had their own reasons for not making the map work. As an anthropologist I hope to have given you a sense of what life is like for the people of the suburb but, further, to have led you through this in a way that is open to failures, gaps and disruptions to what ethnography can be.

In focusing my analysis on the edge of social projects, where different ways of knowing the world meet, I focus on how tensions around understanding and representing difference make the world. I argue for a form of anthropology that is open to disruption, surprise and collaboration in order to see what other worlds might come next. I have argued that if, as Ghassan Hage (2013) asserts, anthropology is a series of first contacts, then, as well as embarking on a project of describing the other, we can see the ethnographic moment of contact as opening up a new space for collaboration. It is here, at the point of contact with others, that data is generated. Ethnography, and other forms of knowledge exchange about others, do more than represent; they bring about a world through enabling new forms of relation and relating.

References

Ball, Roger, Clifford Stott, John Drury, Fergus Neville, Stephen Reicher and Sanjeedah Choudhury. 2019. 'Who controls the city?' *City* 23, no. 4–5: 483–504. https://doi.org/10.1080/13604813.2019.1685283.

Faubion, James D. 2012. 'Foucault and the genealogy of ethics.' In Didier Fassin, ed., *A Companion to Moral Anthropology*, pp. 67–84. Chichester: Wiley-Blackwell.

Gershon, Ilana. 2011. 'Neoliberal agency.' *Current Anthropology* 52, no. 4: 537–55. https://doi.org/10.1086/660866.

Gershon, Ilana. 2016. '"I'm not a businessman, I'm a business, man": Typing the neoliberal self into a branded existence.' *HAU: Journal of Ethnographic Theory* 6, no. 3: 223–46. https://doi.org/10.14318/hau6.3.017.

Hage, Ghassan. 2013. 'Critical anthropology as a permanent state of first contact.' Talk delivered to the American Anthropological Association, 25 November 2013. http://culanth.org/fieldsights/critical-anthropology-as-a-permanent-state-of-first-contact (accessed 23 April 2021).

Laclau, Ernesto and Chantal Mouffe. 1985. *Hegemony and Socialist Strategy: Towards a radical democratic politics*. London: Verso.

Lambert-Beatty, Carrie. 2009. 'Make-believe: Parafiction and plausibility.' *October* 129 (Summer): 51–84.

Žižek, Slavoj. 2012. *The Pervert's Guide to Ideology* (dir. Sophie Fiennes). British Film Institute/Channel Four Television Corporation.

Afterword, by an anonymous interlocutor

This afterword is written by a Seethinger/local who, after reading a draft copy of this manuscript, was invited to respond to it. There was no distinct brief other than to write about the work from their perspective. The piece has been written anonymously and minimally edited.

What on earth did I think I was doing?

My story of ethnographic moments in the suburbs began 10 years ago. Then I would have said proudly that I'd been a medieval historian, that I had worked in the public sector for 20 years, and that I was doing my best at life. But I was working too long and hard and my mental wellbeing was medically managed. I began to seek change that would offer a more meaningful return for my efforts, that might also help me be well. I wanted to be contributing to something I chose to care about, not just because it was my job. I wanted to be cared about and cared for, learning, making things and, importantly, making a difference.

I am just the kind of white, middle-class, broadly skilled professional so aptly described as typical of the suburban residents from where this study found its informants. I was an archetype of the 'neoliberal' endeavour, living for a decade but neither working nor engaging with the community in my south-west London suburb, serving perceptions it was little more than a commuters' dormitory town.

Regularly returning late from work, I'd taken to decompressing with last orders at the pub that I'd recently discovered and that I quickly came to call my local. That's where it all started. I found myself amidst like-minded folk who made merry and made myths. I started participating in some of the shenanigans – telling any who asked that I was a civil servant who had been a medieval historian, that I was a happy and confident creative person who knew why he wanted to participate and make a difference. And that soon I'd have more time to make way for my efforts when I changed what I did for work. I had enquired after the hanging policy for the art on the walls, picked up a signed *Legend of Lefi Ganderson* book from its author, and started writing. I also started hearing a weird soup of emerging stories about filter beds, talcum mines, bats, clean water and cholera.

'Our hearts will leap with happiness when we help others.' 'Fact!'

'As the Surbiton filter beds site had been disused for more than 20 years, it had become a haven for wildlife as the largest area of standing open water in the borough – 76 species of bird and 11 species of bat had been known to visit, feed, breed and roost there. It is metropolitan open land, equivalent to green belt, and formed part of a conservation area. It has numerous protections – the most designated area of the Thames.'

'Twenty-nine fed you and me.' 'Fact!'

'Mapping for Change is not keen on the idea of putting ... false histories on the map.'

'People who engage with community activity are much prouder of where they live, happier with their neighbourhood, feel more included and enjoy more support for their wellbeing from those around them. Those who attend the community events or actively participate in projects feel more confident that they can make a difference to the area in which they live. They are more likely to contribute their time, energy and skills to help shape the future for themselves and the lives of those around them.'

'The Seething Festival and its community procession stopped in 1921 and the legend of Lefi Ganderson was last told in 1927.' 'Fact!'

'The Friends of Seething Wells are hysterical, destructive NIMBYs living in cloud cuckoo land, forced to lie and mislead.'

'There is no mountain in Seething any more.' 'Fact!'

No sooner had I chosen to stop commuting to full-time work than a poster appeared at this same local pub. It changed everything. The Surbiton's Hidden Heritage project, which investigated the history and impact of the local Victorian waterworks filter beds, embraced my enthusiasm and enriched my experience of being local. I was part of a motley team of volunteers piecing together a fabulous story from records, books, photos, drawings and maps. We researched, drank and laughed together. We cared about each other. We learned how the Seething Wells filter beds helped slay 'King Cholera'. We wrote articles and built a website about it. We gave presentations, talked at local schools and led local tours.

As the project had emerged mid-Seething season, I was, by now, in parades as often as I was in the archives. I was socialising with an inclusive and companionable cohort that resembled a community Venn diagram – which the study of making the local helps us understand as apolitical 'Seething villagers' on one side and more politically engaged 'locals' on the other. With some I shared my participation in all things as others looked on. With some I'd come to share time separately, in other places away from the fray. It worked.

As Seething shared some of the same space if not quite the same 'history' as Surbiton – and was regarded as a state 'of mind' as much as 'of geography' – I often felt as if I was simultaneously located in and working on behalf of two distinctly different places. As I found myself increasingly performing more than one part in both those places, my work on 'local' matters became ever more complex, albeit for much of the time no less comfortable.

I grew mighty proud of Seething Wells [the original name of the filter bed site] and felt part of the community around it. The waterworks site didn't just have a past, it had a potential future in community hands – as a public open space, for wildlife, leisure and learning. And what a community there was to make the most of it!

I felt like I knew exactly what I was doing, and why I accepted the invitation to help the Friends of Seething Wells campaign at a time when the owners of the filter beds site had applied for permission to build luxury housing, a marina, a restaurant and parking. They described it as an 'enabling development' for the wildlife reserve they proposed. Unquestionably inappropriate, their development plan would have to demonstrate 'very special circumstances', where the benefits it would bring would clearly outweigh any harm. Our research made clear the extent of that harm, and this became the heart of a community campaign featuring newsletters, packed public meetings, councillor briefings and local paper and radio interviews.

More than a thousand residents objected, and our representations at the council meeting contributed to the unanimous decision to refuse the application. I was contributing to something I chose to care about, playing my part as a welcome member of a community that cared for me and that worked together to make a difference. Not just for us, now, but for everyone and the future.

I needed no more permission to step forward when the community sought an advocate to represent it when the property developer appealed the decision. Previous campaigning had been bruising. We had been publicly vilified by the developer as hysterical and destructive liars, self-interestedly denying the local community a wonderful opportunity. I'm proud that over the week of a public hearing our genuine concern, well-researched thinking and business-like soberness of language exposed the fallacy in the picture of us that had been painted.

It worked. But it was hard work. We rehearsed arguments and evidence, fielding specialists across all subjects. But, however highly regarded, we were competing for respect with the developer's expensive veteran team, who glossed over inconvenient facts and disparaged our experience. These decisions felt too important to depend in such large part on the self-confidence, tenacity and resilience of community representatives. The willingness of community volunteers to contribute to discussions and agree the benefits of any development could be harvested so much earlier, long before the planning process gets adversarial – by when it is heavily weighted in favour of the better-resourced developers.

It was vital the community voice was heard at this stage of the democratic process. We earned the congratulations of the community and the respect and recognition of the professionals in the room. It was heartening to hear the planning authority's QC castigate the developers in his closing statement at the inquiry:

> It is both patronising and contrary to the whole spirit of the importance now attached to local views, for the appellant to try and argue that the claimed benefits for the local community override the clear harm, in circumstances where the local community have reached a clear view to the contrary by a significant majority.

I sense my experience of the ethnographic moments that illuminate this study was inevitably more complicated than it was for others. I was, as a result, more than comfortable with the idea of being an anonymous composite whose experiences are conflated. That's how many would have in any case regarded me. I was the Community Brain's 'Keeper of Knowledge', advocating with stakeholders; I was reassigned a nickname coined in school days and I paraded in Victorian garb as Sir Beeton; I was 'the engineer' of a Heritage Open Days website; I became the 'Friends of

Seething Wells' spokesperson that the developers vilified for misleading locals for 'our own ends'; I was, according to *The Planner* magazine, the 'accidental advocate' from the appeal. I was disparaged as slanderous by the site owner's QC and I was called on to justify my suggestion that their evidence had been selective at best and intended to misrepresent. I'd gifted artwork to the local pub, and devised poetry I would exhibit and perform at the Museum of Futures, which I helped found. It was a place where we could say, 'Something wonderful is about to happen'.

I understood that I was vested with my right to labour by the community that I felt I was labouring for, in the variety of its manifestations. And, like the ethnographer, in doing things *for* the community and the place and future we all shared, I knew I could only do it *with* them.

I was, perhaps distinctively, also already preoccupied when I turned up for 'work'. It was my lay medievalist – enthusiastic about the roots of civic identity – who'd been keenest to explore the legend of Lefi, and how urban settlements established, protected and promoted their communal personality, typically by conspicuously performing their diversity in participatory expressions of their real or imagined history. Whatever made the individuals and the groups they represented distinctive, there was a common concern for the wellbeing of the community that they shared.

It was my poet – whose work celebrates the language and symbols that help us make sense of our relationships with each other and the time and space we share – who was never more content than when writing the kind of confident celebratory claims for community endeavour that have been foregrounded throughout the study presented in this book.

Whatever work I did in any role I performed, if I was doing anything consistently it was 'working with words'. The irony was not lost on anyone that only a trusted villager of Seething could speak so confidently on its behalf in conversations with authorities, but without enjoying the villagers' far more flexible relationship with traditions of 'fact' that I'd long been celebrating. I couldn't have been more myself, at peace with my purpose, than when I felt confidently able to declare at the inquiry hearing:

> Words are very important to us. We'd ask that everyone listen very carefully because that's how we've chosen them. ... If recent history indicates anything, we might expect others to play with words, sometimes placing them in others' mouths.

All these things mattered, to me and those around me. And the words served a purpose, no less than the merrymaking they were often used in.

Some ran through the community like a stick of rock. It just happened to be in my role at the inquiry hearing that I declared:

> Like any respectful friends, we want to protect those things we care about against unwelcome advances. We want to prevent irreversible damage to their potential, and encourage them to make the most of their opportunities, ultimately helping them make a generous contribution to the future of the community.

As I was coming to care so very much more about so very many things, often at the expense of my own wellbeing, I drew a great deal of succour from the time I'd been spending with the anthropologist in our midst. His more than scant interest in all manifestations of those he met has led to authoritative insights about the productivity of communities and the potential contribution of their labour to wellbeing and resilience, as outlined in his study.

We talked together of liberating people's brilliance through participation, permission and play with a purpose; of heritage sites with vivid mosaics of historical significance and ecological value; of material planning considerations and metropolitan open land; of poetic practice, and of ethnographic moments, affordance, the emic and etic.

I came to understand how unusual it was, but crucial to his practice in this instance and at this time, that he immersed. In journeying towards what is now *Citizenship, Democracy and Belonging in Suburban Britain: Making the local*, it is now obvious that if it was to deliver anything in terms of insight and impact, the ethnography couldn't, as tradition dictates, be dispassionately *on* Seethingers, but only *with* Seethingers.

I'd laboured long and hard to make all the things I was involved with work, because I felt they all mattered. I'm not sure I'd realised quite how much I'd needed witnessing, until these moments of immersion I shared with our ethnographer helped me feel seen, heard and understood. I felt cared about and cared for. Because I mattered too. The moments on which we mused sing so clearly from the pages here.

I think the ethnographic moment signified by the Adaptable Suburbs Project's rebuffing of Seething informants' data reveals much of what is momentous about this study of making the local, marking as it does a hiatus in the paradigm of anthropological preoccupation and practice, at a time of paradigm shift in what makes 'localism' truly productive. In marking a rare moment permitting us to see and do things so very differently, all those that stand to benefit from communities that work effectively have a collective responsibility not to squander the opportunity it offers, to act more imaginatively across the customary boundaries of profession and practice in coalition for the common good.

What it teaches about the kind of 'community that works' we heard about at the outset is that its resilience and sustainability are conditional. What shouts aloud from all the surveys, statistics and commentary is that if you invest in, enable and trust those who live locally anywhere, you can contribute to the building of a resilient, healthy, sustainable community with a similarly distinctive energy, creativity and generosity of spirit that neither weather nor social or economic challenge can dampen.

But no one should underestimate the value of the labour involved from everyone in making it work, and communities rightly expect a reasonable return for their investment of effort. If local and national authorities, institutions and services are to enjoy the continued goodwill of the communities they serve and reap the social, economic and reputational benefits that derive from them, they will need to invest time, trust and resources in those community endeavours. Communities should see a fair dividend that reflects their share of the labour that makes it work.

The creativity, energy and commitment of communities to see constructive change – that's identified in community surveying and here in this book – can be liberated to help deliver the collective ambitions for the wellbeing and prosperity of places that such communities share with government and other public services. But those public sector organisations should learn from what's being revealed about the need for policies, processes and plans that involve, enable and encourage communities, not direct or inadvertently deter them. Communities need to be helped, not hindered. Things of obvious interest and potential value to the community should be devised *with* them, not done *to* them.

The hope is that this text joins other emerging insights to help build understanding, regard and respect from academics, policy makers and practitioners – equipping them with at least some of what they need to make more informed decisions about the kind of advocacy, support and interventions that will be required to help.

Ten years on, and I'd become well in body, mind and heart, living hugely vividly, free from medication, celebrating community and friendships I'd not imagined possible when I first saw that poster, and enjoying making work with words, creatively and commercially.

For much of my journey I have many of the ethnographic moments reflected in this book to thank. They helped give me the permission I didn't really need to be what I am for – in the service of things, no longer a servant to them. I'd laboured in a variety of ways within the community and on its behalf, for the meaningful return of a kind I'd not anticipated – a collective rather than the solely personal wellbeing I sensed I'd need if I was going to make any kind of difference.

What has become clear from the privilege of time spent as an informant and interlocutor on the ethnographic journey so engagingly and persuasively rendered here is that while I'd embarked in Surbiton hoping to be more 'locally productive', my endeavouring as both 'Seethinger' and 'local' meant I contentedly became, instead, more 'productively local'.

It's what Lefi would have wanted.

Index

abandonment 4, 182
academia 19, 24–5, 37, 134
activism 2, 25, 44, 124, 167, 173, 176, 193
adaptable suburbs 2, 7, 51, 140, 205
aesthetics 38, 74, 113, 130, 160
   of diagrams 86, 97
   of power 92
   of play 125–6
affect (theory) 2, 127, 138
affective (force) 128, 138, 151, 167, 175, 177, 184
affluence 37, 69, 112, 188, 192
affordance 105, 205
Agamben (Giorgio) 19, 34, 36–7, 168, 184–7
agential realism 77–8
alterity 29, 31, 41–3, 66
Anand (Nikhil) 181–2
anarchist 141
Antigone 43, 129
antiquarians 63–4
anxieties 23, 69, 174, 188
Appadurai (Arjun) 39, 42, 139
archaeology 63–4, 80
archi-textural 138
Arendt (Hannah) 184
Aristotle 67, 80
artefacts 30, 64, 167
assemblages 67, 181
atmosphere 65, 96, 115, 138, 151
Austin (J.L.) 122–3
auto-ethnography 34, 54, 66, 140
avant-garde 142
axial (line) 85, 87–9

Barad (Karan) 32, 40, 77–9, 97
Bazalgette (Joseph) 179
beating the bounds 141, 143–8, 152, 155
belonging 16, 61, 128, 150, 183, 197
Benjamin (Walter) 142, 181
Benton (the bat) 171–2
biolegitimacy 183–4
biopolitics 84, 179, 182, 184–7, 188
biopower 33, 183–4
bios 69, 102, 129, 192, 198
   maintenance of 184–6
   making of 36–7, 164, 168, 188
Boast (Robin) 162–3
bodies 27, 32, 33, 68, 80, 96, 115, 145, 175
   and buildings 6–7
   and death 43
   and waste 177–9, 181
   dispositions of 127, 188
   experiences of 90
   feelings 128
   policing of 84, 137, 167–8, 186
   that matter 40–1
   that meet 82
boundaries 96, 99, 144–52, 154, 164–5, 206
   around meaning 9, 31
   geographic 88, 90, 93–4, 139
   stone 146
Boyer (Dominic) 33, 89, 96, 125–6, 175
bureaucracy 5, 185
   language of 115, 175
   and governance 33, 52, 84, 178–9, 184
Butler (Judith) 40–1, 43, 70, 123

cake 20, 45, 74, 96, 114
campaigning 1, 3, 124, 188, 191, 203
carnivalesque 120, 124
Cartesian 88
cartography 56, 82, 84, 88, 145
categories 30, 41, 78–9, 124
   of identity 26
   of information 56, 59, 86
cave (of Lefi) 10–11
ceremonies 36, 145, 155
Certeau (Michel de) 137, 142
Chalfin (Brenda) 182, 186–7, 189
cheese 8–9, 11, 135–6, 195
CIC (Community Interest Company) 51, 103, 108, 115, 117, 172, 192
citizen science 85
Clapson (Mark) 104, 107
Claremont Gardens 127, 138
Clifford (James) 23–4, 162–3
colonialism 23, 26–7, 150, 162
commensurate 56, 64, 67–8, 70, 86, 89, 98, 193
communitas 162
commuter 112–13, 200–1
   town 12, 61, 103, 107, 128
convention (Wagnarian) 38, 42, 63, 122–3
corporeality 90, 99, 146, 151, 167, 174–5, 177, 194
Coulthard (Glen Sean) 26–7
Coupaye (Ludovic) 44
curation
   anthropology as 24–5, 134
   of place 194, 137
   of knowledge 75
   as method 157–8, 162–6
cycling 59, 61, 85, 142

dance 127, 145, 153–5, 165
Daubenton Bat 109, 171
Deeton (Thamas) 10–11, 61, 195
demos 17, 27, 33, 34, 184
dérive 142
Derrida (Jacques) 34–5
design 51–2, 55, 57, 58, 74, 80–1, 86, 93, 159
detour 123, 129, 136, 142
Dhanani (Ashley) 82–3, 85, 87
diagram 79, 86, 93–5, 97–8, 202
diaries 120, 138–9
dwellings 17, 26, 139–40
dystopia 12, 103–5, 129, 187, 194

ecology
  local 161, 183, 205
  material 18, 32, 40
  site of 1, 169, 171, 180
  threat to 117
economic activity 53, 90–2
embodied 4, 17, 88, 145, 185
  experiences 127, 175–6, 194
  citizenship 34, 37, 129, 180
emic 9, 12, 39, 205
emotion 2, 95, 127–30, 174–6, 188
  and affect 167
  relationships 16, 21, 181, 185
empiricism 18, 20, 40, 43–4, 70, 78, 121
enthusiasts 2, 37, 140, 162
epidemiology 109, 168–9, 173, 178–80
ethical substance 2, 4, 15, 17, 28, 32, 62, 68, 96, 193
ethnographer 3, 158, 161, 163, 204, 205
exhibition 159–64

Facebook 96, 114, 131, 141, 196
failure 66–9, 81, 89, 95, 107, 113, 129
  of democracy 35, 50
  semiotic 41, 123
  technical 23, 58
Fassin (Didier) 183
Faubion (James) 2, 28, 191
fear 2, 10, 167, 174
  for local area 103, 110, 170
fetishes 33, 43
fisheries 108, 148, 161
free market 6
folk 19, 65, 142, 144, 153, 162, 200
Foucault (Michel) 2, 4, 82, 84, 95, 184
  Foucauldian (theory) 90, 167, 178–9, 182, 187
FUS (Free University of Seething) 59, 134, 136, 142–3, 154, 158–63

Galison (Peter) 94–5, 148
Ganderson (Lefi) 9–10, 60, 105, 154, 194–5, 201
Gell (Alfred) 38–9, 43–4, 121–2
gender 40–1
Gershon (Ilana) 33, 84, 130, 164, 187, 192
gifts 30, 96
goat (boy) 3, 10, 60, 194–5, 198
governmentality 33, 84, 187
Grosz (Elizabeth) 176–7
guinea pigs (of Seething) 118

Habermas (Jürgen) 34, 54, 69
habit 7, 92, 163, 192
  of place 113, 127, 139, 140
hack 159
Halberstam (Judith/Jack) 41, 123, 129
hau 30, 38–9
Hegel (Georg Wilhelm Freidrich) 39, 43
hegemony 34, 43, 57, 70, 98
Hillier (Bill) 52, 71, 80–2, 100
Holbraad (Martin) 28–31
home 37, 103, 105
  anthropology at home 24
  for bats 171
  for Lefi 10, 127
  for Thamas 196
Homo sacer 36
humour 12, 40–1, 121–5, 129, 130

icon 60, 97–8, 121–2, 129
incommensurable 31, 70, 193
  social projects 15–6, 34, 48, 51, 66–7
  knowledge 58
index/indexical (semiotics) 39, 43–45, 102, 121–3, 150
  qualities 40, 129
individualism 49, 103, 117, 192
infrastructure 8, 16–17, 128, 171, 178–82, 180–1, 185–8
  of certainty 40
  transport 106–7, 110
interviews 120, 146, 202
  walking 137–40, 195–6
  map-drawing 146, 170
intra-action 40, 78
invention (Wagnerian) 41–2, 115, 122
  of facts 21, 129
involution 43, 44

Jeevendrampillai (David) 57, 67, 123
joke 18, 25, 88, 104, 116, 143
  linguistics of 41, 96, 123
  politics of 125, 130

Lambert-Beatty (Carrie) 9, 12, 63, 192
Laporte (Dominique) 178, 181–2

material culture 19, 37–8, 43, 76, 121, 159, 160, 163
material ecologies 18, 32
Monty Python 104, 131

Navaro-Yashin (Yael) 127–8
neighbourhood 7, 49–50, 143, 185, 201
neoliberalism 7, 12, 84, 191–2
Nielsen (Morten) 42, 125

observation 15, 18, 76–8, 97
obviate (Wagnerian) 35, 62–3, 95, 121–2, 129, 164
onto-epistemological 97
ontology 29–30, 70, 194
ordnance survey 82, 88
overidentification 125–6, 130

parafacts 155
parafiction 9, 12, 18, 63, 67, 142–3, 192

parody 104, 115, 126
participatory 53, 58, 85, 162, 204
  democracy 55, 67
  development 72–3
patterns 52, 80, 130, 141, 163
Peirce (Charles Sanders) 38–9, 98
perambulation 144–6, 148–9
performance 12, 70, 123, 171, 184–6
phenomenological
  90–1, 115, 140, 167, 188
planning
  application 5, 17, 21, 170–2
  committee 1, 16
  meeting 16, 58, 171–2, 175, 180, 193
  policy 4, 17, 53, 74, 81
  process 183–4, 203
Pooley (Thomas) 110–12
Povinelli (Elizabeth) 4, 23, 26, 45, 69

queering 41, 123

Rabinow (Paul) 52, 178–9, 182
railings 108, 138–9, 169–70, 173
Rancière (Jacques) 33, 63, 126
realign 40, 42–4, 120–2
realism 77
rematerialisation 38
resilience 7, 12, 17, 51, 86, 164, 191–2, 203, 205–6
  community 17, 32, 37, 102–3, 186
rhythm 127, 130, 138–40, 153
riots 197
ritual 36, 121, 125, 144–5, 147

sardine festival 21, 102, 106, 112, 117, 121–3, 127
satire 12, 124–5, 130
Seething
  community 15, 51, 128, 157, 192
  event 9, 12, 105, 122, 147, 196
  fact/facts 13, 62–3, 67, 98, 120, 125, 142, 153, 163
  festival 201, 106, 174
  freshwater sardines 21, 60, 102, 112, 117–19, 121, 124, 154, 160–1
  jewellery 160

legends of 9, 132, 194
  myths 2, 113, 134
self-organisation 25, 37, 192
semiotic(s) 29, 38, 98, 157, 164
  analysis 21, 121
  anthropology 46
  excess 40–3
  ideology 41
  manoeuvres 120–2
  transformation 62–3
sewers 177, 179, 181
sign/signified/signifier 38–41, 77–9, 121–3, 205
Snow (John) 155, 168–70, 180
sovereign 34, 36–7, 68, 184, 187
state
  citizen 5, 17, 41, 179
  governance 74, 176, 182
  infrastructure 179, 182
storytelling 13, 63
structuralist 39, 52, 80
subjectification 182, 187
subject position 5, 7, 70, 124, 183, 197
suburban high streets 3, 81, 108
suburbia 102–5, 129
Surrey 108, 148–50

technologies 65–6, 157
  democratic/participatory 55–7, 84–5, 181–2
territory 56–7, 82, 84, 144, 146, 149
Thamas Deeton 10–11, 61, 195

undemocratic 58
utopia 35, 104–5
utterance (Austianian theory) 122–3

visualisation 76, 86, 94, 96, 98
volunteers 51, 117–18, 169, 171, 202–3

Wagner (Roy) 29, 41–2, 62–3, 121–2
walking interviews 120, 137–40, 195–6
  tours 14, 21, 136, 140, 169–70
waste 179–81

zoë 36–7, 69, 129, 164, 168, 184–6, 188

Lightning Source UK Ltd.
Milton Keynes UK
UKHW020141231021
392662UK00012B/96